PLAGUES
IN THE
NATION

PLAGUES
IN THE
NATION

HOW EPIDEMICS SHAPED AMERICA

POLLY J. PRICE

BEACON PRESS
BOSTON

BEACON PRESS
Boston, Massachusetts
www.beacon.org

Beacon Press books
are published under the auspices of
the Unitarian Universalist Association of Congregations.

25 24 23 22   8 7 6 5 4 3 2 1

This book is printed on acid-free paper that meets the uncoated paper
ANSI/NISO specifications for permanence as revised in 1992.

Text design and composition by Kim Arney

Library of Congress Cataloging-in-Publication Data
Name: Price, Polly J., author.
Title: Plagues in the nation : how epidemics
shaped America / Polly J. Price.
Description: Boston : Beacon Press, [2022] | Includes
bibliographical references and index. |
Summary: "Sheds light on the US government's response to epidemics
through history-with larger conclusions about COVID-19 and reforms
needed before the next plague"—Provided by publisher.
Identifiers: LCCN 2021056250 | ISBN 9780807043493 (hardcover) |
ISBN 9780807043509 (ebook)
Subjects: LCSH: Epidemics—United States—History. | Plague—United
States—History. | COVID-19 (Disease) —United States.
Classification: LCC RA650.5 P75 2022 | DDC 614.4—dc23/eng/20211220
LC record available at https://lccn.loc.gov/2021056250

Claude Bryon Price
November 8, 1914–August 2, 1972

Maggie Lucille Smith Price
February 6, 1913–January 29, 1999

George Washington Hawkins
January 3, 1916–August 7, 1980

Alma Marie Pierson Hawkins
October 8, 1920–January 11, 2004

CONTENTS

"Death Rising from the Iron Scow and Scattering Pestilence Among the People," Harper's Weekly, October 2, 1858.

PREFACE

In early January 2020, the Chinese government sealed off Wuhan, larger in population than New York City, from the rest of China and the world. Fearing the potential spread of a mysterious illness that had already taken seventeen lives and made more than six hundred other people ill, officials shut down public transportation and blocked highways.[1] In the weeks to follow, the measures became more drastic still. The government extended the quarantine-style lockdown to include more than fifty million people living elsewhere in China. Officials ordered door-to-door checks in Wuhan to round up the infected for isolation, confining residents and visitors alike in an attempt to stop the spread of a new coronavirus that Americans would come to know as COVID-19.

As Americans viewed China's heavy-handed response, national news media asked whether the US government could take similar authoritarian measures, and over the next year I commented on legal matters ranging from lockdowns to face masks to vaccination mandates. Journalists wanted to know why state governors could impose wildly varying health measures—or none at all. I knew the weak points in America's ability to respond to epidemics—that the key issues were not really about COVID itself. I knew we could expect conflict and turmoil, even if I could not have foreseen just how poorly the US would fare compared to many other nations. I also served as an expert adviser to both the National Governors Association and the Uniform Law Commission, the nation's oldest state governmental association, on legal issues related to the nation's COVID-19 response.

Yet despite my years of study and thinking about the ways our legal system governed epidemic emergencies in the past, I confess to many, many deer-in-the-headlights moments.

I had seen the fault lines before. During the 2014 Ebola crisis, the US Centers for Disease Control and Prevention (CDC), just up the street from my office at Emory University, were on the front lines in West Africa and in the political hot seat for preventing the Ebola virus from spreading to the United States. Emory University Hospital treated the first American health workers evacuated from West Africa, over protests and bomb threats by some members of the public. Fear intensified after an Ebola victim died in Dallas and two nurses there developed the disease. Fortunately, there was no further spread of Ebola in the country.

But the response of government officials at all levels exposed the fault lines in our ability to control a future, fast-moving epidemic. An understandable but unwarranted public panic led to actions by political leaders that undermined confidence in the government's ability to protect us from deadly contagion. Several governors squabbled publicly with the federal government about who was in charge, about whether to close borders, and about who should be quarantined.

I knew the underlying reasons for what Americans were seeing in 2014, and again with COVID-19, because I have studied and written about America's response to past epidemics for many years. History teaches us that effective disease control is a matter not just of containing (or better yet, killing) pathogens but also of implementing effective laws and governance. We rely on democratically chosen governments to fund research, distribute vaccines, pursue cures, and take other protective measures to control contagions. Our laws and legal system have sometimes aided the efforts of scientists to stop an outbreak and sometimes have proved a hindrance. But epidemics also create conflicts among citizens, sometimes exceedingly bitter ones, as yellow fever did in the late nineteenth century. Ultimately our political system and laws must address those.

• • •

We expect government to keep us safe from epidemics. But the United States has a spotty record of doing so, and this book helps explain why. Epidemic control in the US is unique and controversial because of our deep culture of individual rights and constitutional values. Epidemic control is also made more difficult because the US has one of the most decentralized and fragmented public health systems in the world.

Drawing from our past, I provide a legal history of epidemics that the United States has experienced—including smallpox, yellow fever, the "Spanish" influenza, polio, HIV/AIDS, Ebola, and, now, COVID-19. Choosing 1776 as a starting point to recount America's past epidemics as I do—rather than, say, 1492 or 1607 or 1620—admittedly ignores more than two centuries of colonial government as well as centuries of customary measures to prevent the spread of diseases whose causes were little understood. But the establishment of a new nation on the shores of North America created a set of circumstances that would shape a "law of epidemics" in distinctive ways. The constitution of a federal government that also vested great authority in the individual (and very different) states that made up the nation led to the unusual history that unfolds in this book.

Laws concerning epidemics did not change much in America's first century, after the colonists formed themselves first into independent states and then a nation. As it happens, we still operate with some of the same laws and governing structures that were put in place then to contain disease outbreaks. Those laws still work in many circumstances, as they did when small communities and rural living were the norm, travel was slow and cumbersome, and medical science had few of the tools that we now take for granted. But as the nation expanded and opened up to greater commerce and faster means of transportation after the Civil War, epidemics had a profound effect on the country and reshaped the government institutions and laws that helped meet those emergencies.

Most people do not think of government and legal issues when they think of epidemic disease, but health emergencies like the COVID-19 pandemic present a crisis not only for doctors and public health officials but also for lawyers and politicians. Medical experts may advise burdensome measures to halt the progress of a pandemic, but the lines of authority among local, state, tribal, and federal officials are often unclear and contested, as the COVID-19 pandemic demonstrated. Public health becomes "political," as constituents demand governmental response—or demand that it not respond in a particular way. These fault lines have been with us for a long time.

From America's earliest epidemics, political leaders faced strikingly similar challenges and made strikingly similar decisions. In the years since, we have lacked the political will to strengthen the nation's public health defense system. We have inherited and retained inadequate laws, have underfunded public health agencies, and—most to the point—continue to respond to pandemic threats in the United States not as one nation, but as fifty-five smaller nations—the states, territories, and commonwealths that politically subdivide the country. America's public health defense is further divided among nearly three thousand state and local public health departments. We rely on them to protect us from outbreaks of contagious disease in our communities. But jurisdictional boundaries are jealously guarded, in part because of a philosophical preference toward local control and in part to preserve limited budgets. With this setup, it is difficult, if not impossible, to have an effective national strategy against a pandemic.

This is not a book about healthcare reform or delivery of private healthcare services. Health providers play a critical role in any public health emergency, of course, but this book is not about them. It is about how the United States can mount a better defense to the next pandemic. Understanding how we have come to where we are can help us recognize potential pitfalls and barriers along the way and address them. My hope is to prevent us from stumbling into yet another poor response—one that might be predictable, given our long experience with epidemics.

While this is primarily a work of history, that history suggests several ways we can improve our government's ability to fight epidemics. Our best chance depends on effective governance, trust in our scientific institutions, and changes to outmoded laws that still regulate our public health system. We must not waste the opportunity to repair what we can of our legal infrastructure and institutions to make government more responsive, with less conflict. We have struggled with such lessons before, with similar opportunities to reform our laws. But as history also shows, good laws are not enough if elected officials ignore them or are not up to the task.

As awful as the rapid global spread of COVID-19 has been, the world is lucky that it was not far worse—a hypothetical "flubola," for example, combining Ebola's terrible, swift onset of symptoms and high mortality with the easy airborne spread of a flu virus or the common cold. Scientists still expect "the big one" in our lifetime—or even multiple pandemics occurring at the same time. America has faced many serious outbreaks of contagious disease throughout its history and will do so again. COVID-19 provided us with just one more installment from which to learn, and an opportunity to improve our response next time.

Before plunging into the story, a note on terminology may be helpful. Specialists will note that I misuse the term "quarantine" at times when "isolation" is the correct medical and legal terminology. This is because Americans historically have understood "quarantine" to include both. For the record, the US Centers for Disease Control and Prevention distinguish the terms this way:

Isolation separates sick people with a contagious disease from people who are not sick.

Quarantine separates and restricts the movement of people who were exposed to a contagious disease to see if they become sick.[2]

For that matter, I also tend to use the term "epidemic" when "pandemic" might be more accurate. "Pandemic" is defined by the World Health Organization as "an epidemic occurring worldwide, or over a very wide area, crossing international boundaries and usually affecting a large number of people."[3] But even that definition is elusive. The *New York Times* made this point in 2009 in an article about H1N1 influenza titled, "Is This a Pandemic? Define 'Pandemic.'" The article quoted Dr. David M. Morens, an epidemiologist at the National Institute of Allergy and Infectious Diseases: "There is a lot of misinformation in the medical literature, and it is really quite hard to figure out what is and what is not a pandemic."[4]

"Epidemic," on the other hand, is defined by *Merriam-Webster* as "an outbreak of disease that spreads quickly and affects many individuals at the same time."[5] According to the CDC, "*Epidemic* refers to an increase, often sudden, in the number of cases of a disease above what is normally expected in that population in that area." Helpfully, the CDC notes, "*Outbreak* carries the same definition of epidemic, but is often used for a more limited geographic area."[6]

"Epidemic" is the more commonly used term by the participants in the historical events I describe. I'm referring specifically to contagious disease transmitted person to person, or transmitted by other vectors that depend on infected persons to keep the contagion spreading through a community, not other common uses of the term like the "opioid epidemic," the "youth epidemic of e-cigarette use,"[7] or the "emerging epidemic of obesity."[8]

That is explanation for my very loose use of the term "epidemic" as well as the choice of disease outbreaks I recount in this book. On any given day, most Americans are concerned about an outbreak immediately threatening their community, whether it counts as an epidemic or not.

One last worry about my use of "epidemic" over "pandemic." I'm writing about the United States and its historical experience with a specific purpose in mind. The diseases I have chosen from America's past were frightening enough to demand government officials to help protect us from them. Of course, all humankind share susceptibility to diseases, and global pandemics from ancient times have afflicted (and changed) the world. The US must engage in global public health because an outbreak anywhere can end up here. It is in our interest to do so, and we risk losing sight of this.

I am grateful to the Carnegie Corporation of New York for naming me an Andrew Carnegie Fellow in 2017. Among the opportunities the fellowship afforded me was the chance to work with public health departments in the border region between the United States and Mexico, where I gained valuable firsthand insight into challenges that public health officials face in overcoming jurisdictional boundaries. The fellowship also gave me room to work on two timely articles that appeared just prior to COVID. An observation I made in one of those received wide attention as the pandemic took hold: "Any intervention by the federal government over the objections of a state or territory can be highly politically charged. Environmental, scientific, and medical recommendations can be hijacked for political purposes at any level of government. Perhaps the most pressing problem is a crisis of trust in governmental institutions."[9]

This book tells stories that explain some of that crisis of trust. It also, however, offers grounds for hope that we, the people, have the wisdom we need to overcome the plagues in our nation, present and future.

Street scene in Jersey City, New Jersey, depicting compulsory vaccination during a smallpox scare, 1881.

1

AMERICA'S FIRST PLAGUES

Pestilence, like war, disrupts society, and silences the law.
—TENNESSEE SUPREME COURT, 1880[1]

In 1883, Father John McGoldrick braved a visit to the Minnea̯po-
lis Small Pox Quarantine Hospital, more commonly known as the
"pesthouse." Father McGoldrick reported the overcrowded conditions in horrifying detail:

> The condition of the people there has been almost too terri-
> ble for description, and simply from the criminal neglect of their
> fellow-creatures. People have a superstitious dread of the small-pox.
> The fear which seizes them seems to deprive them of the power of
> intelligent action. The health officers have done their part as well
> as they could, under the circumstances, and their greatest fault
> appears to have been in not keeping the public stirred up on this
> all-important subject. So when the present epidemic broke out, they
> were entirely without proper means of handling it.[2]

Those who died in the pesthouse were buried in the adjacent pot-
ter's field. This was a slightly better fate than what befell the residents
of Sharon, Connecticut, more than a century earlier, when thirty of
them perished from smallpox. In 1777, residents of the town banished
victims to makeshift pesthouses in the woods, where most of them

1

would die.[3] More than two centuries later, state archaeologist Nicholas Bellantoni put it succinctly: "Back then people had no understanding of how diseases are transmitted. They just knew that if you came into contact with the afflicted you would get the pox, too. So they buried the victims who died then and there in the woods, and often burned the pesthouses down when the disease had run its course."[4]

Not eradicated until the late twentieth century, smallpox plagued human communities for thousands of years. An individual infected with smallpox would experience high fever and a distinctive, progressive skin rash with pustules that often left deep pockmarks in the skin, especially the face. The sufferer could be left blind from the disease, if the patient survived at all; the mortality rate for smallpox was extremely high. Hence the great public alarm at the mere rumor of a case.

Colonial Americans, especially the indigenous peoples, were well acquainted with smallpox—smallpox contributed to the catastrophic decline of the native population.[5] William Bradford, governor of Plymouth Colony, described an outbreak among the Indians of the upper Connecticut River in 1633. Of the one thousand who contracted the disease, at least 950 died, and "many of them did rot above ground for want of burial."[6] Centuries later, in the winter of 1900, the community of Jonesville, in Hinds County, Mississippi, was struck by smallpox in its "most virulent and loathsome form," the *Atlanta Constitution* reported.[7] Entire families perished from a disease whose onset was so fast, "the only thing the city officials could think to do was to order a public appropriation for coffins." These outbreaks served to reinforce the reputation of smallpox as "the most terrible of all the ministers of death."[8]

. . .

From the founding of the British colonies in North America to the dawn of the twentieth century, Americans faced terrifying epidemics and deadly contagions they barely understood. Infectious diseases were the leading cause of death. Scarlet fever, measles, and other maladies struck infants and children especially hard. Smallpox, cholera, and yellow fever could sweep through a region with no warning and did so regularly. Survival required combining inherited "wisdom" with impromptu adaptations to the American environment. Because of the size of the country, the weakness of its communication and transportation infrastructure, and the localized nature of disease outbreaks, Americans looked to their local leaders, or at most to their state governments, rather than to the national government. This tendency not only was a response to the circumstances of the day but also reflected early Americans' unwillingness to invest the new federal government with the means to interfere with their liberties.

Germs had traveled the world for centuries before American independence, and they arrived in the young nation's seaports from both exotic and more prosaic places. Quarantine of ships had been practiced for centuries in Europe and the Mediterranean region. But even the strictest maritime quarantine could not prevent epidemics of smallpox, cholera, yellow fever, and other dread diseases. Every community, however remote, guarded against contagions that inevitably worked their way inland and across borders.

But these communities had few defenses. While Americans may not have understood how most diseases were transmitted, they understood the importance of separating those who were sick from those who were well. Once sickness appeared in a town, the sufferers had to be removed—either confined to their home by armed guards or sent outside the town to a pesthouse or lazaretto. The victim's belongings and even their living space would be burned. Towns would guard their borders and turn away strangers. If sickness spread despite these measures, huge numbers would flee the area—as Congress famously did during a yellow fever epidemic that struck Philadelphia in 1793.

What defenses the people did have set the power of government against the individual, taking away liberty and property to protect the community as a whole. Colonial Americans and the new state governments that followed American independence generally adopted English law and practices as they understood them. They conferred on community government an absolute authority to exclude or exile someone suspected of any of the scourges of the time. Town leaders, justices of the peace, and other government officials had nearly unlimited power to stop an epidemic, threatened or real.[9]

Such measures stood in stark contrast to the purposes the framers of the Constitution put forth in creating a new nation, a battle cry for individual freedoms and liberty from arbitrary government that echoed throughout the new nation. The Declaration of Independence asserted "unalienable Rights" of a free people to "life, liberty, and the pursuit of happiness."[10] The first state constitutions listed a plethora of individual rights that no government could interfere with—liberty foremost among them. The federal Constitution, at first lacking such guarantees, gained the Bill of Rights later, but even this set of protections was limited. The protection of private property held the exalted position as "the guardian of every other right."[11]

Yet in response to the regular visitation of contagious disease, Americans would create an entirely separate law, a "law of epidemics," giving elected officials immense power to react quickly, and often drastically, in ways no one would stand for in "normal" times. At least in America's first century, courts were reluctant to intervene. When the danger of an epidemic arose, judges viewed measures to protect public health as questions for legislatures and elected officials to resolve. The prevailing judicial attitude did not question a local government's right to impose a quarantine, frequently citing the ancient maxim *Salus populi suprema lex*—"the health of the people should be the supreme law."[12] As a Tennessee judge noted more than a century ago, "Pestilence, like war, disrupts society, and silences the law."[13]

This sweeping governmental power came from the people themselves, in laws they enacted in their town councils and state legislatures. This "law" of epidemics would evolve gradually in the twentieth century as other plagues arrived. But one thing did not change, even with the great strides in medicine to come. Epidemics in America presented problems of government. Elected officials were obliged to respond to the demands of their constituents—all the while measuring the limits of the community's willingness to pay taxes for their own defense.

• • •

Most colonial cities, especially those on the coast where shipping frequently brought contagious disease, had a health officer responsible for the town's pesthouse and with authority to quarantine ships. Before the American Civil War, most larger towns either established local boards of health or employed a health officer. Laymen served in these roles in smaller towns and villages without a medical doctor.

Local threats required local action. To meet the threat of an epidemic and calm public panic, town officials had to act quickly. In 1899,

Nancy Prichard, a widow living in Morganton, North Carolina, experienced that town's smallpox panic in the worst possible way. Based on a rumor that Nancy had smallpox, two men claiming to act under orders of the Morganton board of commissioners seized her and her family and forcibly transported them to the town's pesthouse. Mrs. Prichard and her children were forced to stay there for weeks. None of them had smallpox, and as Mrs. Prichard maintained throughout her imprisonment, she did not believe she had even been exposed to it. Even worse, the two men, R. T. Claywell and Robert Ross, set fire to Mrs. Prichard's house and other structures on her lot, destroying her home, clothing, household furniture, and other personal property.[14]

As in most other towns throughout the nation, local law authorized these actions. A municipal ordinance permitted the board of commissioners to "take such means as they may deem effectual to prevent the entrance into the town or the spreading therein of any contagious or infectious diseases." Those means included removing "any person in the town believed to be infected with contagious disease" to "some place within or without the town limits." Authorities could destroy property "believed to be tainted or infected with any contagious or infectious disease." In case those actions were not enough, town officials could "take all other reasonable steps to preserve the public health."[15]

Elected officials often took extreme measures because their constituents demanded it. After Capt. Robert H. Blandford, a union ticket agent, died of smallpox in 1905, residents of Wynnton, Georgia, demanded that armed quarantine guards be placed outside his home. A meeting of "concerned citizens" demanded the guards after Mrs. Blandford took in a young married couple as boarders following her husband's death. The young couple contracted smallpox and were taken to the pest house. A local newspaper reported that "all the bedding, carpets and, in fact, every article in the rooms where the cases developed will be burned."[16]

Pestilence victims were also driven away from populated areas by terrified and enraged citizens. One tragic case involved a wagon driver in Georgia who appeared to be suffering from smallpox. Local residents refused to let him continue his journey home, forcing him into an abandoned barn. He died there, without any aid. The local citizens then burned down the barn with his body in it.[17]

One could even be shot for attempting to escape a quarantine—with no legal percussions for the shooter. In 1895, a quarantine officer named Horace Turner shot and killed Caleb Norman at Walls, Mississippi, after Norman escaped from a smallpox quarantine camp. Norman had been run out of Arkansas, then driven away from Cow Island, eighteen miles south of Memphis. Mississippi authorities refused to let him into that state, but he could not return to Cow Island or Arkansas.[18] A newspaper reported that Norman had "attempted to run the gantlet and was shot and killed."[19]

No wonder people tried to hide their illnesses from the authorities, helped by family members or friends who refused to report them. Failing to report or hiding an illness was a crime in most places, as was helping someone evade quarantine. Montgomery, Alabama, on the other hand, also made it a crime to circulate false reports of "any contagious or infectious disease" existing in the city, absent an "honest effort to ascertain the facts."[20] (The ordinance is still on the books.)

• • •

The appearance of smallpox or other feared contagions was a calamity for any town. Not only did it cause neighbor to turn against neighbor, but outlying areas might shut down travel and commerce. Reports of outbreaks elsewhere were hard to verify, but few officials took the chance that they weren't true. In March 1858, the commissioners of Salisbury, North Carolina, declared that smallpox existed at Gold Hill in Rowan County, and they prohibited anyone from Gold Hill from entering the corporate limits of Salisbury under a penalty of fifty dollars for each offense. Charles T. Powe, a practicing physician residing in Salisbury, stopped at Gold Hill to treat a smallpox patient before continuing his journey to Wadesborough. When he returned to Salisbury a week later, town officials took Dr. Powe to court to enforce the fifty-dollar fine.[21]

The Supreme Court of North Carolina rejected the town's lawsuit through a technical parsing of the ordinance. The court believed such bans to be reasonable precautions and the steep fines warranted. But the court absolved Dr. Powe on the ground that the town's officials were poor lawmakers. The ordinance they wrote applied only to a "person from Gold Hill," signifying residence there, as the court interpreted the language. If the ordinance intended to ban a person *coming from* Gold Hill, it made no reference to coming immediately or directly from it after the ordinance went into effect. Dr. Powe—who was "from" Salisbury—had only journeyed through Gold Hill. "The ordinance," the court wrote, "was probably drawn in haste, under the panic inspired by the vicinity of a dangerous contagious disease."[22]

The "dangerous contagious disease" in this instance was smallpox, not one of the many other diseases that annually were the leading causes of death—tuberculosis, pneumonia, and childhood scourges like measles, scarlet fever, dysentery, and whooping cough. But few places in America escaped another pestilence even scarier: cholera. According to historian Charles E. Rosenberg, cholera was "the classic epidemic disease of the nineteenth century, as plague had been of the fourteenth."[23] Like smallpox, cholera could spread like wildfire through a community. The symptoms of cholera were spectacular. Victims suffered a sudden onset of acute vomiting and diarrhea. Dehydration turned the victim's face blue. The most frightening part was that a person could feel well in the morning but be dead within hours. "To see individuals well in the morning and buried before night, retiring apparently well and dead in the morning is something which is appalling to the boldest heart," an Albany resident wrote in 1832.[24]

The worst cholera epidemics in America occurred before the Civil War. The 1832 epidemic killed more than 3,500 people in New York City alone, one out of every 70 residents. The epidemic spread from there, following railroads, canals, steamboats, and the US army in its Indian wars and removal of Cherokee and other Native Americans from the Southeast, decimating the indigenous population along the way. Quarantines did not stop it. Five thousand died in New Orleans. Almost no part of the nation escaped, even remote areas with few settlers.[25]

Cholera is not a virus like smallpox but a bacterial disease transmitted through the human digestive tract. At the time, cholera was blamed on miasmas, filthy living conditions, and, most of all, on poor Blacks and Irish immigrants.[26] After the British physician John Snow proved that cholera spread through a London water pump tainted by sewage in 1854, it eventually became possible to prevent rapid spread of disease through better municipal sanitation measures.[27] But until

American physicians and municipal leaders could be convinced of this, the appearance of cholera evoked the same public panic as did small-pox and other pestilences of the time. Sufferers were isolated in their homes or sent to the pesthouse. Port cities put in place strict quarantine measures, but interior parts of the nation could only dread the inevitable inward march of the disease.

Minorities and marginalized groups fared poorly in any epidemic, but especially with cholera. Cholera was viewed as a disease of poverty that became associated with immigrants, Blacks, and Native Americans in ways that smallpox never quite did. In 1832, the case rate for free Blacks in the North was twice that for whites. The death toll that year among slaves in the South is unknown, but when cholera again hit America in 1849, at least ten thousand slaves died.[28] Yet cholera was no respecter of station: President James K. Polk died of cholera in 1849 and was hastily buried in a Nashville cemetery set aside for cholera victims. He had left office just three months earlier.[29]

Whether the sickness was smallpox, cholera, or another contagion, wealth and social status might keep victims from ending up in the pesthouse. Those in the upper classes could procure a private doctor who would not report them. Property owners might be permitted to remain in their homes with a large "quarantine" sign posted on the door. These signs threatened criminal penalties for any resident who left the building and for anyone who tried to enter. The poor and marginalized, especially tenement dwellers in larger cities, went to a pesthouse, imprisoned with fellow sufferers in often ghastly conditions. Worst of all, you might be run out of town and left to fend for yourself, never mind that one town solved its problem at the expense of another.

For families of means, fear of the pesthouse was not the only incentive to hide from town authorities. Residents also feared isolation of their families and injury to their businesses—strong reasons to hide the fact of exposure or actual sickness as long as possible, all the while potentially spreading disease throughout the community. This was especially true of smallpox; fugitives from the pestilence unknowingly spread it during its asymptomatic incubation period.[30] With cholera, city officials would avoid announcing its arrival as long as possible to minimize its impact on the business community.[31]

. . .

As grim as the situation might be when an epidemic hit, town leaders provided what care they could for those who were ill, as they did as a matter of course for orphans, the elderly, and the destitute. Colonists had adopted the English "poor law," which made each township responsible for housing and feeding impoverished residents. Continuing the practice after independence, towns up and down the East Coast employed an "overseer of the poor." More populated areas established almshouses, as Baltimore County did for the county's indigent, elderly, and infirm. The Baltimore County Almshouse opened in 1874, replacing one of two almshouses run by the city of Baltimore dating back to 1819. The county built a small pesthouse nearby to quarantine residents with contagious diseases.[32]

In New Hampshire, as one example, early state law made it the duty of each township's overseers of the poor to afford relief

> to all persons found within their town who are poor and stand in need of relief. . . . It matters little what may be the duties or obligations of others, whether towns or individuals. If the person is found poor and standing in need of relief, it is to be furnished to him, and it is to be continued until the need of it ceases. Such is the safe and benevolent general rule pointed out under our statute.[33]

Accordingly, the New Hampshire Supreme Court wrote in 1839, "The whole provision for the relief and maintenance of the poor is thus left entirely to the official responsibility and duty of the overseers of the poor."[34]

Until his death in 1828, William Larned served for thirty-five years as the overseer of the poor in Providence, Rhode Island. Historian Gabriel Loiacono has commented that overseers like Larned "held enormous power over the lives of the poor."[35] Larned could banish people from the town, question and keep a close watch on new arrivals, and record the expense to taxpayers for the social welfare of the disadvantaged in their midst. In 1800, Larned's receipts showed distribution of aid in amounts up to fifty dollars to a "long list" of residents after an unspecified contagious disease swept through Providence.[36]

Local communities bore the expense of combatting smallpox, which included building pesthouses, hiring doctors and nurses, and paying guards to ensure the isolation of the quarantined. The money usually came from a tax on the town's residents.[37] In smaller towns, there was no perennial need for a dedicated pesthouse or contagious-disease hospital. Instead, town leaders made do with empty property, hastily constructed structures outside of town limits, or even commandeered property as a temporary pesthouse. State governments rarely offered financial assistance to towns scourged by epidemic. In Georgia, for example, county officials could levy extra taxes to pay debts incurred for preventing the spread of smallpox, including maintenance of a pesthouse, medical attendants, food for the inmates, and quarantine guards. But no money came from state coffers.[38]

If people needing medical care or the almshouse were recent newcomers to the area, the town of their origin could be made to reimburse any expenditures. Court records before the Civil War are replete with lawsuits making just such claims. Augustus Sanborn, a resident of Tuftonborough, New Hampshire, fell ill at his father's house in Moultonborough, fifteen miles from his home. Because his illness appeared to be smallpox, the selectmen of Moultonborough declared the father's home a pesthouse and quarantined those living there. The officials employed a physician and a nurse and sent supplies to the house. Moultonborough town officials then sued their counterparts in Tuftonborough for reimbursement of these expenses, and they won.[39]

Another example comes from Maine. Amos W. Wormwood lived with his wife and nine children in Alfred, Maine. In 1839, Amos contracted smallpox in Kennebunk a short time after his arrival on a boat from Boston, where he worked as a laborer. His wife and four of the children were with him in Kennebunk, and all of them suffered from smallpox for six weeks but ultimately recovered. Kennebunk's overseers of the poor notified the overseers of Alfred about the Wormwood family's condition and requested the overseers of Alfred to "order their removal or otherwise provide for them." Alfred officials denied that they owed anything. The Maine Supreme Court, however, ordered the Alfred overseers to pay expenses "for nurses, attendance, and other assistance and necessaries."[40]

In the nineteenth century, almshouses in America's cities were the closest thing to a hospital that any American would know. As Charles Rosenberg has described them, almshouses functioned mostly as municipal hospitals at a time when few hospitals existed, even in the larger American cities.[41] The first public hospital was founded in Philadelphia in 1752, followed by New York Hospital in the 1790s and Massachusetts General Hospital, in Boston, in 1821. By the Civil War, private groups had established some two dozen hospitals. Municipal governments operated the rest, primarily treating the destitute.[42]

In the South, the enslaved population before the Civil War could not be beneficiaries of town poor laws, but their status as "property" made the appearance of smallpox and cholera among them a monetary concern. Some slave owners employed physicians by contract to maintain a degree of health in slave quarters. Not uncommonly, courts would void the sale of slaves if they were discovered to be ill—the buyer having been sold a defective bill of goods. In 1834, for example, J. B. Ory, a slave dealer in Louisiana, sold three slaves—a woman named Madeleine, a woman named Eulalie (a "good washer and ironer and trusty house servant"), and Eulalie's child Marie Louise.[43] Madeleine died from cholera three days after the sale.

Such circumstances occurred so frequently that many southern states included an implied warranty in their slave codes. Under Louisiana slave law, for example, any disease appearing within three days immediately following the sale was grounds for rescission of the contract, because the illness was presumed to have existed at the time of the sale. In the case of Madeleine, the seller, Ory, argued that poor medical care had led to her death. Because she had shown no symptoms at the time of sale, cholera would have been "easily curable." But the Louisiana Supreme Court disagreed: "It has been contended in argument, in this case, that cholera, the malady of which this slave died, is not an incurable disease in its first stages. The court is of a different opinion; it considers a malady incurable . . . when it baffles the efforts of regular medical aid, and death ensues, notwithstanding this aid is promptly administered." The buyer got his money back. He was also awarded fifty-three dollars, the cost he incurred for medical attendance and funeral charges for Madeleine.[44]

. . .

Almshouses and hospitals held no cures for victims of contagious disease. But at least Americans could hope to escape one of the worst contagions through vaccination. The first smallpox inoculation was introduced in America as early as 1716 by Onesimus, a slave of the Puritan minister Cotton Mather. The procedure, known as "variolation," transferred fluid from the smallpox lesions of an infected person into an incision on an uninfected person. The recipient would experience less severe symptoms of smallpox, but the procedure was said to provide immunity for life.[45]

Variolation carried a very real risk of death, however; estimates are that the process killed one in every fifty who were inoculated.[46] Johnathan Edwards, the great theologian and philosopher, died from the technique.[47] Because recipients of variolation would often develop a milder form of smallpox, they would be contagious to others for several weeks after inoculation. Physicians required inoculated patients to quarantine until their symptoms disappeared—anywhere from three to six weeks.

The nation's second president, John Adams, underwent smallpox inoculation in Boston in 1764, when he was twenty-eight years old. Adams, his younger brother, and four others confined themselves to one room for three weeks, under the care of Boston physicians. In letters to his future wife, Abigail, Adams described the send-off by his neighbors in Braintree: "My brother and I have the Wishes, the good Wishes of all the good People who come to the House. They admire our Fortitude, and wish us well thro, even some, who would heartily rejoice to hear that both of Us were dead of the small Pox."[48] Adams left Braintree "fully satisfied that no durable evil" could result from "the modern Way of Inoculation," a far preferable alternative to running the risk of having smallpox "in the natural Way."[49] He urged Abigail to "Smoke all the letters from me, very faithfully," before she or members of her family read them.[50] Two weeks after receiving the inoculation, Adams wrote Abigail that he had fared relatively well and had less than a dozen pustules. "But others in the same House have not been so happy—pretty high fevers, and severe Pains" for three of his companions.[51]

Despite the risk inherent in inoculation, many believed the horrors of smallpox to be far worse. As a young man, Benjamin Franklin opposed inoculation, in part because he despised Puritan ministers like Mather.[52] But then tragedy struck:

> In 1736 I lost one of my Sons a fine boy of 4 years old, by the Small Pox taken in the common way. I long regretted bitterly & still regret that I had not given it to him by Inoculation. This I mention for the Sake of Parents, who omit that Operation on the Supposition that they should never forgive themselves if a Child died under it; my Example showing that the Regret may be the same either way, and that therefore the safer should be chosen.[53]

A little more than fifty years later, an English physician, Edward Jenner, created a vastly improved smallpox inoculation. Cowpox from cattle could be substituted for live smallpox in the inoculation and achieve the same effect. This "vaccination," unlike variolation, did not require contact with live smallpox. Jenner published his findings in 1798; vaccination gradually replaced variolation as the inoculation of choice in nineteenth-century America.[54]

Most physicians, at least those with a degree of education, strongly supported vaccination. In 1828, the Philadelphia Medical Society published a report on a recent occurrence of smallpox there, intent on proving the efficacy of smallpox vaccination to doubters.[55] A New Hampshire physician used the example of the small town of Holland, Vermont. It seems a young man from New York, who thought he merely had the chickenpox, visited neighbors, attended a Christmas Eve gathering, a school meeting, and other social activities. He started a smallpox outbreak that infected thirty-nine people in the small town, eight of whom died. None of the eight had been vaccinated during a previous campaign in the town. The physician published a report, wanting it known that "Had these persons been protected by vaccination they would most probably have been living today."[56]

Similarly, the Board of Health of Charleston published a detailed review of distinguished medical authorities in Europe to urge more widespread use of vaccination following a smallpox epidemic in 1829. The smallpox vaccine, they wrote, "has been regarded as one of the greatest blessings conferred upon the human race." Charleston doctors, though, agreed unanimously that "the careless manner in which persons are vaccinated by those who are not physicians ought to be considered a great evil, and a source calculated to lessen confidence in a valuable preventive of small-pox."[57]

But untrustworthy vaccine sources diminished public confidence. Anyone could sell a vaccine, and peddlers traveled the country with their wares. Physicians did not believe smallpox vaccination conferred lifetime immunity, so they recommended revaccination whenever an outbreak occurred. As a result, a Wild West of vaccine suppliers stepped in to fill the need. As the nineteenth century progressed, one physician lamented that "the market is flooded by irresponsible producers."[58] Provenance and efficacy, let alone safety, had to be taken on trust. For this reason, town ordinances often prohibited the introduction of small-pox vaccination through unofficial channels. The New Hampshire legislature permitted any town to appoint a vaccination agent who "may vaccinate all persons at the expense of the town," receiving "a suitable compensation . . . to be paid by the selectmen." The best solution, a physician urged in 1881, was for state governments to obtain vaccine to ensure quality, then sell it to towns "at so low a rate as to destroy any competition."[59] Until then, the New Hampshire state government protected towns against dubious vaccine suppliers by prohibiting the peddling of vaccines, subject to a fine of $150, half to be paid to any person bringing suit, and the other half to the town where the offense was committed.[60]

Milton, Massachusetts, is said to have been the first city in the US to provide free vaccinations to all of its residents, in 1809. The following year, the Massachusetts legislature required every municipality in the state to make smallpox vaccines available.[61] Other states purchased vaccine to distribute to their citizens free of charge, or permitted local governments to do so. But some governors opposed inoculation because it brought live virus into the state, threatening a wider outbreak. In Georgia, for example, forward-looking physicians in the port city of Savannah offered variolation to help the city deal with a smallpox outbreak in 1800. By offering inoculation, however, the physicians violated state law and enraged the governor of Georgia, James Jackson. Under a 1793 state law that prohibited introducing or spreading "malignant and contagious disorders in this state," Governor Jackson punished Savannah by ordering a quarantine around the city for over two months, with no one permitted to enter or leave, lest smallpox travel to the state's interior. Governor Jackson lifted the travel ban around Savannah only after a report from a "confidential officer" (Savannah's elected leaders could not be trusted to supply reliable information) that there was no longer any danger of smallpox being spread by persons leaving Savannah.[62]

Maintaining a reliable and safe supply of vaccine was no easy matter, and throughout the nineteenth century it was buyer beware. For a short time, the federal government undertook some semblance of quality control.[63] In 1813, President James Madison "unhesitatingly" signed An Act to Encourage Vaccination, Congress's plan to provide reliable smallpox vaccines free to any part of the country. Madison appointed Dr. James Smith to distribute vaccine from his Baltimore laboratory through the US mail at no charge. The experiment lasted nine years, until vaccine sent to North Carolina allegedly caused an outbreak of smallpox in the city of Edgecombe. Congress launched an investigation and repealed the vaccine law in 1822.[64] It was the first foray of the federal government into vaccines. The experiment would not be repeated for another century.

• • •

As confidence in vaccination for smallpox grew in the nineteenth century, local, state, and even federal authorities mandated vaccines and financed them at least partially. Some cities required all of their residents to be vaccinated when smallpox appeared, and legislatures authorized school boards to require vaccination of students. Employers in mills and factories would purchase vaccine for employees, as did slave owners on large plantations.[65]

In Georgia, the state legislature authorized cities and counties in the state to order compulsory vaccination of all residents, "in the event the health officers or the proper authorities think it advisable," to prevent the spread of smallpox.[66] The Atlanta city council, confronting a series of smallpox outbreaks in the 1880s, made vaccination compulsory for anyone over the age of fifteen. The penalty for refusal was a fine of up to $500 or thirty days in jail. A second refusal merited the same penalty. "The practical result," a journalist noted, "is submit to vaccination or stay in jail."[67] The ordinance applied to "any person, black or white," but whites could choose to remain in jail until the threat passed rather than be vaccinated. Black residents who refused were subject to "brute force"—according to an observer, "A stout Negro man . . . had to be held by main strength while the physician vaccinated him."[68] Whether forced vaccination of Blacks still occurred during a deadly outbreak in 1897 is not clear, but Mayor C. A. Collier saw to it that policemen accompanied the hundred physicians who canvassed the entire city "to see that the doctors are protected and to aid in the work of vaccinating."[69]

That same year, the Columbus city council ordered compulsory vaccination of every resident over the age of two, unless they could produce a doctor's certificate that they had been recently vaccinated, were immune, or were in such poor health that vaccination would be dangerous. In September 1897, Columbus officials authorized a "house to house" vaccination. George W. Morris and two other men refused; they were charged in the city recorder's court with violation of a municipal ordinance and ordered to pay a fine.

Morris appealed the fine, taking his case to the Georgia Supreme Court. City officials prevailed. Justice Andrew J. Cobb, writing for the court, declared the "right to enforce vaccination is derived from necessity." The municipal authorities had reasonable grounds for fearing an imminent epidemic of smallpox because it was prevalent in nearby Birmingham, Alabama. For this reason, mandatory vaccination did not violate federal or state constitutional rights.[70]

Justice Cobb believed his court was the first to consider the constitutionality of mandatory vaccination laws, noting that "At the present time a great majority of the United States have such laws." Citizens who opposed vaccination, Cobb explained, should seek a solution through the political process, not the courts:

> With the wisdom or policy of vaccination, the courts have nothing to do. The legislature has seen fit to adopt the opinion of those scientists who insist that it is efficacious, and this is conclusive upon us. Under our system of government, the remedy of the people, in that class of cases where the courts are not authorized to interfere, is in the ballot box.[71]

Cobb added that judges have no authority to declare a law void "merely because it does not measure up to their ideas of abstract justice." The "natural right" to life, liberty, and the pursuit of happiness "is not an absolute right." The individual must "sacrifice his particular interest or desires, if the sacrifice is a necessary one, in order that organized society as a whole shall be benefited." Danger to public health, Cobb wrote, "has always been regarded as a sufficient ground for the exercise of police power in restraint of a person's liberty."[72] The Georgia court's decision came just seven years before the United States Supreme Court would consider the same question, in a case known as *Jacobson v. Massachusetts*. Boston and surrounding cities suffered a series of smallpox outbreaks from 1901 to 1903.[73] When the Cambridge Board of Health saw a dramatic increase in cases, it ordered all residents to be vaccinated or pay a five-dollar fine. Henning Jacobson refused, claiming that he had had an adverse reaction to an earlier vaccination. He was fined, and over the next two years appealed his case all the way to the US Supreme Court.[74]

With two justices dissenting, the Supreme Court affirmed the right of city officials to enforce a smallpox vaccination law in an emergency. Writing for the court, Justice John Harlan noted that the court decades earlier had "distinctly recognized the authority of a state to enact quarantine laws and health laws of every description." Principles of "self-defense" and "paramount necessity," Harlan wrote, give a community "the right to protect itself against an epidemic of disease which threatens the safety of its members." It was appropriate for the legislature to lodge the authority "to determine for all what ought to be done in such an emergency," and "surely it was appropriate for the legislature to refer that question, in the first instance, to a board of health composed of persons residing in the locality affected."[75]

The Massachusetts Anti-Compulsory Vaccination Society backed Henning Jacobson's four-year odyssey through the judicial system to the nation's highest court. In 1902, a jury convicted Jacobson for refusing to comply with the vaccination order, and the following year the Massachusetts Supreme Judicial Court affirmed the jury's verdict. Chief justice Marcus Perrin Knowlton portrayed the penalty for refusal—five dollars—as relatively trivial: "If a person should deem it important that vaccination should not be performed in his case, and the authorities should think otherwise, *it is not in their power to vaccinate him by force.*" The "worst that could happen to him," Knowlton wrote, "would be payment of the penalty of $5."[76] The Georgia Supreme Court had said nothing about vaccination by force in 1898, even though news accounts reported Blacks had been forcibly vaccinated. Penalties for whites, on paper at least, were not trivial either. The $500 fine in Atlanta likely was never collected, but the prospect of consecutive thirty-day jail terms supplied all the compulsion needed.[77]

But the US Supreme Court had only the Cambridge health order before it, with its relatively light penalties—not the draconian measures in Atlanta and elsewhere in the nation. In that context, *Jacobson v. Massachusetts* affirmed the basic power of government to safeguard the public's health in an epidemic. Constitutional doctrine changed profoundly over the ensuing century, yet *Jacobson* remained the preeminent authority, the final word for judicial review, for the epidemics to follow. The US Supreme Court would not revisit it again until a novel coronavirus, COVID-19, upended American life in 2020.

• • •

From the founding period through the close of the nineteenth century, the nation's defense against epidemic threats depended entirely on the elected leaders and financial resources of each town or city. Whether facing the threat of smallpox, typhoid, cholera, or yellow fever, these local communities responded in strikingly similar ways— with quarantine camps, the pest house, and the expulsion of outsiders. Panicked citizens demanded that government leaders take action, but sometimes they took matters into their own hands, while voiceless victims of ill-treatment could only accept their fate. Courts of law did not interfere. When judges played any role at all, it was usually to enforce penalties assessed by health officers—either a fine or jail time for anyone who ignored a health officer's order. Only in the twentieth century would judges begin to address the appropriate balance between protecting the public's health and safeguarding individual rights and liberties. In the twentieth century, too, the federal government would assume a greater role in protecting the nation from pandemic threats.

But when COVID-19 circled the globe, we saw distressingly similar problems of law and governance as earlier Americans had experienced. By 2020, the public health system and "law of epidemics" had grown from an accumulation of two centuries of legislation. What did we learn, or not learn, from the many epidemics that would follow cholera and smallpox? The next lessons came from the shotgun quarantine.

"Shotgun Quarantine in Florida—A Patrol Near the St. John's River Turning Back Yellow Fever Fugitives," 1888.

2

YELLOW FEVER AND
THE SHOTGUN QUARANTINE

*There can be no question as to the suffering in the State
of Mississippi. Half the towns and cities have quarantined
themselves against the living world. Around villages are
cordons of armed men, ready to shoot down the first
invader. Traffic has been extinguished. How much longer
will Southern States continue in this madness?*

—*THE WASHINGTON POST* (1898)[1]

B ishop Francis Xavier Gartland waded through scores of yellow
fever sufferers, washing desperate faces, offering what spiritual
solace he could. It was a hideous scene in Savannah, Georgia, that
summer of 1854. From house to house and in emergency makeshift
hospitals, patients bled from the mouth and nose, suffered from delir-
ium caused by high fever, and, before dying, vomited copious amounts
of black bile. Savannah's elite had already fled the city to escape the
pestilence.[2] Of the population who remained in Savannah that summer, more than a thousand were reported to have died, a number
grossly undercounted because the deaths of slaves and free persons of
color were not recorded.

Bishop Edward Barron, a close friend of Gartland's, came from
Charleston to help. To add to the apocalyptic misery everywhere evident, a hurricane swept through the city on September 8, ripping the

roof off of Bishop Gartland's house. Bishop Barron died from yellow fever a few days later. Engraved on Barron's tomb is the verse, "I most gladly will spend and will be spent myself for your souls." The "genteelly robust" Bishop Gartland himself nearly made it through to the end, but he died of yellow fever on September 20 at the age of forty-nine.[3] We know little about the dozens of nuns who also died from yellow fever, not even where many of them are buried. Likely they are interred with hundreds of others in unmarked mass graves in Savannah's historic Colonial Park Cemetery, anonymous in the haste to dispose of the overwhelming number of bodies amid a dearth of coffins.

Savannah had suffered horribly from yellow fever before, especially in 1820, when town leaders ordered the observance of "days of humiliation and prayer." As the crisis worsened, Mayor Thomas Charlton advised all citizens of Savannah who could do so to flee. More than half of the population did, evading quarantine lines thrown up by surrounding towns. Of those who stayed, more than six hundred died.[4]

Today, tourists in Savannah can see *Dreadful Pestilence,* a play about the 1820 epidemic presented annually at the Davenport House, a federal-style brick building that is one of the oldest in the city. Its builder, Isaiah Davenport, lived in the house until his death from yellow fever in 1827. The play tells the story of Dr. William Coffee Daniell, health officer of the city and the only survivor of the four physicians appointed to handle the crisis. Cast member Jeff Freeman characterized the play as "a study in how people handle a crisis, one of questioning, searching for answers, blaming, exasperation, and loss."[5]

Throughout the South, museums, historical markers, and yellow fever–themed tours engage the curious. In Holly Springs, Mississippi, the Yellow Fever Martyrs Church and Museum commemorates six nuns and a Catholic priest who died during the epidemic of 1878. Built in 1841 as Christ Episcopal Church, the wooden structure consists of one large room, a porch, a bell tower, and a slave gallery. When the congregation outgrew the building, the Catholic bishop of Mississippi purchased it. Father Antonio Oberti was serving as priest when the epidemic began late that summer. The first victim was the town's mayor, A. W. Goodrich. Over the next six weeks, 300 people died. All who could leave the town did—an estimated 2,000 of the

town's population of 3,500. Father Oberti and the Sisters of Beth-
lehem Academy stayed, nursing yellow fever sufferers at the nearby
courthouse, which had been transformed into a makeshift hospital.
In early September, Father Oberti died of yellow fever at the age of
thirty-one. One after another, the nuns all died in subsequent days,
until only Sister Laurentia Harrison was left. She died on October 12.
The town's remaining doctor died, too.[6]

The Yellow Fever Martyrs Church is now a museum, where visitors can view a depiction of what the courthouse must have looked
like as an emergency hospital, complete with a mannequin nun attending mannequin patients on straw beds. Along one wall is a series of
painted images showing the progression of yellow fever in a victim. In
the first image, an immaculately dressed, smiling young man is in the
prime of health. In the second, he lies prone in bed, frightened, with a
sickly pallor. By the third, his skin has turned pale yellow and blood
seeps from his nose. The last picture shows blood from the victim's
face smeared on his shirt, the pillow, and sheets, interspersed with
black vomit. His eyes are vacant.[7]

Holly Springs was just one of many communities along the Mississippi River valley decimated by the 1878 epidemic. In late August,
surviving residents in Grenada sent a plea for help to Governor John
Stone: "Our sheriff and city marshal and deputies are dead or gone.
Our mayor is dead . . . our population is reduced to the sick, the doctors, nurses, and undertakers—our people generally have fled the city."[8]

• • •

There is little wonder why yellow fever was contemplated with such
fear. It is a viral hemorrhagic disease, a hideous, acute illness with an
especially high mortality rate. Alarming symptoms appear in quick
succession. As the disease progresses, the skin turns yellow from jaun-
dice. Black vomit signals that death is near, all within a week of the
first onset of symptoms.[9]

Following the American Revolution, points to the north were hit
hard by yellow fever (particularly Philadelphia, in 1793), but after the
Civil War yellow fever had become primarily a southern phenomenon.[10]
Yellow fever touched some portion of the South every year, from
the big commercial cities of New Orleans and Memphis to smaller

towns in Florida, Georgia, Alabama, the Carolinas, Missouri, Arkansas, Texas, and Virginia. Starting in late spring, residents in the South feared yellow fever's appearance through the end of the "season," generally the first frost. The Texas governor, for example, issued annual proclamations authorizing quarantine effective April 1 of each year.[11]

Major yellow fever epidemics in the southern US occurred throughout the nineteenth century but were especially severe in 1878, 1897, and 1905. All told, yellow fever is believed to have killed more than 200,000 Americans during this period. The 1878 epidemic alone is estimated to have stricken 120,000 people, resulting in at least 20,000 deaths and an economic loss of around a $100 million—the equivalent to $3.3 billion today.[12]

Even though malaria and other diseases caused more deaths in the southern region, yellow fever was fast moving and more terrifying. The disease seemed contagious in the same way smallpox was believed to be—able to spread from person to person as well as through contaminated objects. In the early twentieth century, scientists learned that yellow fever is spread by the *Aedes aegypti* mosquito, an insect that can also transmit dengue fever, West Nile virus, and Zika. Scientists developed an effective vaccine, which went into use in 1938. But until then, no one knew for certain how the disease was spread or how to prevent it. Yellow fever was such a prominent annual risk that life insurance companies included a standard clause voiding the policy if the insured traveled below the "yellow fever line," a geographic demarcation running from just south of Washington, DC, to St. Louis, Missouri, and El Paso, Texas, that state's westernmost point. Beneficiaries of policyholders who died of yellow fever forfeited any claim unless the insured had had the foresight to pay a "yellow fever" supplement.[13]

• • •

Long experience had shown that even one case of yellow fever could quickly infect a town, and, if left unchecked, the disease would spread from there quickly by railroads, steam ships, and stagecoaches. The appearance (or rumor) of a single case of yellow fever anywhere set in motion defensive quarantine measures throughout the South, as armed guards patrolled entire communities that banded together with the hope of keeping the contagion out. The best bet was to escape north, where yellow fever seemed unable to spread. Thousands of people fled in particularly bad epidemic years, fully aware that they might end up stranded as quarantine lines were thrown up and transportation in the region shut down. Quarantine lines trapped residents in pestilential cities and caught up those trying to escape, even those who had not been present anywhere near the rumored location of yellow fever. People in affected regions were often too frightened of strangers in their midst to help.

This was the era of the "shotgun quarantine." A writer for the *Chicago Daily Tribune* employed the phrase in an article about his recent travels in the South:

> We asked a dweller in one of these villages if the yellow fever would come again with Midsummer. "No, sir," he answered: "not if shotguns can keep it out of this town." They have adopted the theory that yellow fever is spread solely by contact. They therefore propose to prevent all intercourse between neighborhoods—to station patrols, armed with shotguns, on all their highways, and to entirely prevent all traveling.[14]

Whether this writer coined the phrase or heard it elsewhere, soon other newspapers discussed the "shotgun quarantine," and it quickly became the customary terminology used to label any town or state's declaration of a quarantine against entry from places infected, or rumored to be infected, with yellow fever.[15]

News articles about the shotgun quarantine captivated the nation. Major US newspapers featured headlines such as "Terrified South Ties Up Traffic," "Frightened People Are Refused a Refuge," and "Many Towns without Medicines and Short of Food."[16] According to one reporter from the *Washington Post*, "City is barricaded against city, town against town, and village against village," creating scenes of "chaos, hardship, and frenzied fear."[17] Articles depicted scenes barely imaginable to the rest of the nation. The *Washington Post*, describing the "madness" of the shotgun quarantine in the epigraph to this chapter, also told its readers, "Hundreds if not thousands of laborers have been thrown out of employment."[18]

Formal declarations of quarantine gave official imprimatur to enlist citizens or militias to aid sheriffs in guarding the line or in preventing trains from entering or stopping.[19] Local officials had unilateral power to determine the need for a quarantine and its duration, and to fine or imprison anyone who failed to obey. In most states, this authority was made explicit by legislation granting county and municipal health officials the power to declare quarantines. Government officials scrupulously noted the legality of their actions, bristling at the equation of the shotgun quarantine with mob rule. In reality, it was likely difficult to distinguish measured decision making from the political persuasion of the local population to compel governments to act.

Shotgun quarantines could be put in place quickly, relying on deputized volunteers where militias or law enforcement officers were lacking. In one episode, as described in the *Washington Post,* "there was never a more rigid quarantine established than that with which Meridian, Mississippi, sought to protect herself from the invasion of yellow fever." At the first appearance of yellow fever in neighboring Louisiana, Meridian declared a quarantine against any infected place. When the fever began to spread, "the city shut herself up tight, placing a military guard in the outskirts and forbidding any person to come across the line."[20]

The worst stories are of those forced to remain in areas where the disease was rampant. In the deadly epidemic of 1878, around half the population of Memphis (some forty-seven thousand at the time) managed to escape quarantine lines, fleeing to more northerly regions where the disease was not present. The *Washington Post* described how Arkansas enforced its quarantine when Memphis residents attempted to flee the city: the state ordered "the arrest and imprisonment of all Memphians caught in the act of crossing" the Mississippi River, with the whole Mississippi riverfront "closely watched by armed police."[21] For those unable to leave Memphis—about fourteen thousand Blacks and six thousand poor whites—the death rate was high: more than five thousand died.[22] Understandably, those residents viewed the armed cordons imposed by their neighbors to be a death sentence.

These were lawless scenes, pitting residents of one town against another, and one state against another, in a futile attempt to stop yellow fever's spread. The US Senate, searching fruitlessly for a way to help, considered the appearance of the shotgun quarantine year after year to be "a stigma upon our institutions and civilization."[23]

. . .

During the epidemic of 1878, Holly Springs, Mississippi, had been one of the few places open for refuge. Town officials had at first welcomed refugees from Memphis, believing the elevation and relatively dry environs would keep the epidemic at bay. But the tragic results of those erroneous beliefs meant that Holly Springs would not make that mistake again. In the future, a rumor of yellow fever anywhere in Mississippi, Alabama, Louisiana, or Tennessee set in motion a strict quarantine to protect the town. No one—merchants, travelers, even returning residents—could enter the city limits of Holly Springs without the written permission of the town's appointed health officer.

That vigilance led to an act of cruelty the residents of Holly Springs would come to regret. In September 1905, brothers Archie and Ralph Roane, ages eighteen and twenty-two, were on their way home to their parents in Oxford, Mississippi, by way of Holly Springs. They had been out west, in New Mexico, seeking treatment for tuberculosis. Both boys were exhausted and visibly ill when they reached Memphis, where they purchased train tickets to their home in Oxford. They were to change trains in Holly Springs for the final leg of a long journey.

The timing of their journey couldn't have been worse. In 1905, yellow fever had once again reached epidemic proportion in several states, including the entire Mississippi valley from New Orleans to Memphis. To travel anywhere in the region, rail passengers had to produce a health certificate attesting either that they had not been in any infected territory or had already suffered a case of yellow fever and thus were immune to the disease. Some residents obtained or forged physicians' notes to this effect. For everyone else, they somehow had to prove that they had not traveled through an area rumored to have even a single case of yellow fever.

Some state boards of health issued "official" immunity cards to aid their state's citizens. Florida, for example, issued a "Yellow Fever Immunity Card," certifying that the carrier had "experienced an attack of Yellow Fever" at a specific location and year, signed by an attending physician and countersigned by the "State Health Officer of

Florida."[24] Obtaining a card depended upon the credibility of the individual and the cooperation of a doctor. Scams abounded, including "contemptible petty robbery of the ignorant" by way of certificate and other fees.[25] Dozens of cardholders were turned back on suspicion of fraudulent papers, as local authorities grew to mistrust the authenticity of the cards. Town health officers and local sheriffs apparently believed most people would lie about where they had been and whether they had had yellow fever in the past. No official state certificate, especially one from another state, would allay that suspicion.

If the value of state-issued travel cards was in doubt, there was little doubt about a local health officer's authority to refuse them. For a time during the 1905 yellow fever epidemic, residents of Natchez, Mississippi, could come and go from that town so long as they had a county permit or a state-issued health certificate. But the health officer of Adams County, Dr. W. H. Aikman, suddenly put an end to that. In early October, Aikman ordered that "all permits or passes, verbal or otherwise of every kind and description, to enter the county from the city of Natchez, issued heretofore to immunes or any other persons are hereby revoked." Any guard who permitted "any person to pass the quarantine guard lines on any such passes" would be terminated and fined. The order would stay in place "until further notice."[26]

Fortunately for Archie and Ralph Roane, as they made their way home to Oxford, they not only had certificates proving they had been out west, nowhere near any place with yellow fever, but also had permission from the city government of Holly Springs to change trains there. The boys showed their permits to the ticket agent in Memphis and were allowed to board the train to Holly Springs, where they planned to change trains for Oxford. But a few miles into the journey a quarantine officer from Holly Springs ordered the conductor to stop the train and told the boys to get off.

Weak and ill from tuberculosis, the boys had to make their way back to Memphis on foot. Had the quarantine officer even glanced at the papers the boys held, he would have seen they both had permission to change trains at Holly Spring, a necessity their father had taken great care to arrange before the boys began their journey.

The quarantine officer, whose name is lost to history, in all likelihood was a hired citizen deputized by the health officer of Holly

Springs to enforce his orders, as in so many other towns throughout the state.[27] The boys looked sick, and to an untrained eye they might as well have had yellow fever as anything else. But it was not tuberculosis that got them tossed from the train. Instead, it was simply the fact that they had passed through Memphis, where yellow fever was present, and had planned to get off the train at Holly Springs.

Ralph and Archie found their way back to Memphis, where a hotel owner took pity on them. They eventually made it to Oxford by taking a train through Grenada, Mississippi, some 150 miles out of their way, to avoid Holly Springs. The Roane brothers were reunited with their parents at last, but Archie died of tuberculosis two days later. Ralph died a few weeks after that, both deaths attributed to their ordeal.[28]

What recourse did the average US citizen have against such treatment? In most situations, not much—except that William A. Roane, Archie and Ralph's father, was no average citizen. He had been a conspicuous figure in public affairs in Mississippi for more than a quarter of a century. He was the grandson of Governor Archibald Roane, the second governor of Tennessee, and had served in the Mississippi Senate before being elected a judge in 1893. For two decades, Judge Roane presided over felonies and civil cases in a jurisdiction that covered seven counties, including Holly Springs. According to a Mississippi newspaper, Roane was "one of the best beloved citizens in the commonwealth" and a well-respected jurist whose rulings "were seldom reversed by the Supreme Court."[29]

This is why the lawsuit he brought on his sons' behalf stood any chance of success. Soon after Ralph died, the grieving father hired attorneys to take on the Saint Louis and San Francisco Railroad Company, whose employees had stopped the train for Archie and Ralph to be put off before they could reach Holly Springs. The real wrongdoer, of course, was the Holly Springs quarantine officer. Whoever he was (the court records don't give his name), the law protected his actions. As a matter of law, any petty tyrant "clothed with the authority" of a local quarantine officer could order railroad employees to stop trains and eject passengers, because any town could enforce whatever quarantine it saw fit to impose—just like the quarantine the Roane brothers faced when their train left Memphis bound for Holly Springs.

One could try to sue the railway company who let it happen, but such suits were rarely successful. Over the years, courts throughout the country dismissed these kinds of claims on the ground that the railroad companies were merely obeying the dictates of a government official. In Holly Springs, the jurors were angry about what had happened to the Roane brothers, and no doubt embarrassed that a city employee—one of their own—had refused to look at the health certificates Judge Roane had gone to such trouble to secure. Roane had even alerted the mayor of Holly Springs to be sure his sons would be permitted to change trains there. The jury awarded $7,500 in damages against the railroad.

But would the jury's verdict be upheld on appeal? Settled case law suggested not. The Mississippi Supreme Court ultimately reached a compromise of sorts. It reduced the jury's verdict by $5,000, to $2,500. This was still a significant sum for the day, equivalent to $75,000 in today's currency.[30]

It took nearly three years for the lawsuit to wind its way through the courts. Any solace or vindication Judge Roane felt wouldn't last long. The year after the ruling by the Mississippi Supreme Court was a terrible one for Judge Roane personally. His wife died in January. A few months later, his son Temple died from tuberculosis while in Fort Bayard, New Mexico, the same place Archie and Ralph returned from shortly before they died. Judge Roane had lost his wife and three sons in the space of four years.[31]

• • •

State governors set their own quarantine rules, too, shutting down travel at state lines. During the 1905 epidemic, Governor James K. Vardaman of Mississippi convened the state's Board of Health in Jackson to declare a quarantine banning all travelers coming from Louisiana.[32] Governor Vardaman had accused Louisiana officials of covering up cases of yellow fever there. "Epidemics are usually resultant of placing commercial interests above the public health," Governor Vardaman said. "And in the effort to suppress the truth, the disease gets a foothold and the whole community is infected with it."[33]

Mississippi would lift its quarantine against Louisiana by the end of October, but towns throughout Mississippi declared their own quarantines against outsiders, as Holly Springs did, without regard to any direction of the state health board. The same was true in other states. Brunswick, Georgia, is a typical example. Each fall, the city council passed a resolution authorizing the mayor "to quarantine against any places he believed to have yellow fever and at any time he deemed proper."[34] Even returning residents were barred from their homes. As one newspaper reported, when the state board of health declared Mississippi "wide open" at the end of October, that did not mean that towns, cities, or counties had to follow suit. Nor did they, until they believed that the threat of yellow fever was at an end.[35]

Like other states throughout the South, Alabama believed it could protect itself from yellow fever only by preventing travelers from entering the state. One man from Atlanta tried to get to Faunsdale, Alabama, to reach his wife, who had become sick while visiting her sister. He was compelled to leave a train thirty miles from his destination. Attempting to reach Faunsdale on foot, he found himself "escorted" out of three towns by armed guards. In the end, he was forced to walk twenty miles under guard to a railroad station, where he boarded a train back to Atlanta, without seeing his wife or knowing whether she was still alive. There is no record he ever saw her again.[36]

Occasionally, city leaders fought back against statewide orders. Following the first reports of yellow fever in the fall of 1905, the Georgia Board of Health telegraphed the mayors of towns containing all fifteen railroad centers in the state to quarantine travelers coming from "all infected points" and declared a statewide quarantine. To enforce the quarantine, state health officers boarded trains at state lines and ordered passenger doors locked until the train had passed completely through the state.

Atlanta, by far the state's largest city and largest rail hub, refused to cooperate on the grounds that preventing travel was unnecessary, inhumane, and counterproductive. James G. Woodward, Atlanta's mayor, invited refugees to come, even telegraphing the mayor of Pensacola and other hard-hit Florida cities. Experience had proved to city leaders that Atlanta's climate made it relatively safe, inhospitable to yellow fever. The convergence of rail lines made Atlanta's rail terminals the first haven of refuge open to persons leaving southeastern coastal areas. An estimated five thousand people fled to the city during the 1905 outbreak alone.

But in September of that year, they arrived in railcars that were locked by order of the state health board, not to be opened until the trains had passed beyond state lines. More than once, city authorities under Mayor Woodward's direction forced open the doors of passenger coaches at Atlanta's Union Station to allow passengers to disembark. On one occasion, city officers arrested two state health board inspectors for refusing to unlock the doors of a Pullman car from New Orleans. As the medical board advising the mayor had predicted, Atlanta experienced no surge in cases of yellow fever as a result of his decision.

The American Medical Association would have advised Mayor Woodward the same way. Quarantines like those ordered by the Georgia health board were not only ineffectual but harsh. The AMA also condemned the shotgun quarantine because of "its brutality of administration in so many places":

> With all its rigors and entailed human suffering, the shotgun quarantine always fails of its object to arrest every incomer[.] There is ever a loophole—a careless or avaricious or potatious guard, or a byway that escapes watch. The traveler of the better class, going openly, cannot miss detention or deportation, but the criminal and the tramp, and at times the local celebrity of powerful connections, can always find an open door. Town after town in the infected area is demonstrating these truths.[37]

• • •

An earlier quarantine war—this one between Louisiana and Texas— got the attention of the United States Supreme Court. In 1898, Texas sealed its borders with Louisiana following reports of yellow fever in New Orleans. (It was not the first time Texas had done this.) The Louisiana governor claimed that the strict Texas quarantine was not a public health measure at all, but was designed to benefit the port of Galveston and other cities in Texas at the expense of the commerce of New Orleans.[38] The Texas quarantine, according to Louisiana, was an embargo on all interstate commerce between the states and merely a pretext for economic gain.[39] This, Louisiana argued, violated the federal Constitution's Commerce Clause.

Louisiana took its grievance to the US Supreme Court. Would the nation's highest court settle the dispute, not just for Louisiana and Texas but for the entire country? Legal scholars had mulled over similar problems many times before. In 1891, a writer in the *American Law Review* explained:

> It is well settled . . . that the power to establish quarantine regulations rests with the States and has not been surrendered to the Federal government. The source of this power lies in the general right of a State to provide for the health of its people, and although the power when exercised may, in a greater or less degree, affect commerce, yet quarantine laws are not enacted for that purpose, but solely for preserving the public health.[40]

For over a century, the Supreme Court had encouraged states to look out for themselves when it came to protecting residents from contagious disease, even to the point of stopping people from crossing the state's boundary.[41]

The case was closely watched throughout the nation. In the end, though, the Supreme Court dismissed the suit on technical grounds. Justice John Harlan, however, in a separate concurring opinion, suggested that the courts might scrutinize state-line quarantines closely in the future. "This Court has often declared that the States have the power to protect the health of their people," Harlan wrote, but that power could not be used as a cover to interfere with interstate commerce "beyond the necessity for its exercise." Given the failure of Congress to pass national quarantine legislation, Harlan thought the federal courts must "guard vigilantly" in situations like this.[42] Precisely how they would do so was left unanswered. Judges were in no position to decide when, where, or whether a state-line quarantine was really needed.

Just fifteen years earlier, the Supreme Court had upheld stringent quarantine rules imposed by the Louisiana Board of Health in a case brought by an out-of-state shipping company.[43] But in announcing that decision, the justices let Congress know that they preferred a national solution and encouraged Congress to enact a quarantine law. The federal government could preempt state and local quarantines if it chose to. As Justice Samuel Freeman Miller, a lawyer and a physician, explained, "Whenever Congress shall undertake to provide for the commercial cities of the United States a general system of quarantine, or shall confide the execution of the details of such a system to a National Board of Health, all State laws on the subject will be abrogated, at least so far as the two are inconsistent." But until Congress acted, Justice Miller said, "the laws of the State on the subject are valid."[44] The very next year, yellow fever swept through the South again. The nation saw once more that state and local governments could impose wildly inconsistent quarantine rules and restrict the movement of large numbers of people.

Congress had attempted to address the problem before. In 1879, they created a National Board of Health with authority to provide money to state and local health boards "and to assume quarantine powers when states did not appear competent or willing to do so."[45] Most states, after all, had boards of health—why shouldn't the United States have one as well, to coordinate the fight against epidemics? The board was to give "special attention . . . to the subject of quarantine, both maritime and inland, and especially as to regulations which should be established between State or local systems of quarantine and a national quarantine system." Congress recognized the need for quarantine rules to prevent transmission "into one State from another," laying an interstate commerce basis for federal authority over inland quarantine.[46]

The National Board of Health, the nation's first public health agency, lasted less than five years.[47] Congress failed to renew it. The National Board never had much authority anyway, and it could not compete with the jealously guarded jurisdiction of state and local health boards.[48] The National Board had been a compromise in any event. Proponents of a stronger quarantine measure known as the "Yellow Fever Bill" justified the federal government's inland intervention under its constitutional right to regulate commerce and to protect the country.[49] Opponents of the bill argued that it was unconstitutional and violated states' rights.[50] Before its demise, the National Board insisted that the federal government address the problem in some more effective way: "To no other great nation of the earth is yellow fever so calamitous as to the United States of America."[51]

. . .

The disruption to commerce from shotgun quarantines, perhaps more than the plight of refugees, provoked business leaders and the politicians they lobbied to pursue legislative solutions. The North was well aware of the commercial harm caused by shotgun quarantines in the South. To warn its business readers, the *Wall Street Journal* reported local quarantines as they were imposed in the South.[52]

Beyond the immediate deaths and displacement of refugees, travel and commercial transportation shut down throughout the region for extended periods, causing widespread business losses and unemployment. Under such circumstances it was difficult for people to plan even ordinary commercial transactions, with the result that some businesses, large and small, closed their doors permanently. During the worst panics most banks closed. Courthouses were shut, too. Unscrupulous persons took advantage of the chaos in any number of creative ways, not all of which could be remedied by the courts once they reopened.

Unsurprisingly, business interests outside the afflicted areas backed efforts to put the federal government in charge. At various points, chambers of commerce, hoteliers, railroad officials, and the League of American Municipalities lobbied Congress for relief.[53] But these same groups also had an incentive to suppress reports of yellow fever in their cities, for fear of economic losses that would result from quarantines imposed against them. Health officials frequently accused each other of bowing to political pressure by failing to report legitimate cases of yellow fever.[54]

With little enthusiasm to renew the experiment with a National Board of Health, Congress tried a different approach in 1890 with legislation popularly known as the Epidemic Diseases Act.[55] The full title of the legislation revealed the specific aim: "to prevent the introduction of contagious diseases from one State to another."[56] Under this legislation, the federal government could intervene whenever any of a handful of specified diseases threatened to spread from one state into any other. How, exactly, the government could take action was not specified. The president could authorize the secretary of the Department of the Treasury to make rules and employ inspectors "as may be necessary" to prevent the spread of disease within the US.[57] The act's language was broad enough to permit the federal government to intervene inland, including by abrogating state quarantines if it wished.[58]

The Epidemic Diseases Act proved essentially useless. Two subsequent yellow fever epidemics—in 1897 and 1905—showed that the federal government was still powerless to prevent cities and states from enforcing quarantines against each other. The Marine Hospital Service, an obscure federal agency in charge of the few ports owned by the national government, had neither the resources nor the will to face down state health boards intent on declaring quarantine at the least rumor of yellow fever in another state. They nonetheless established train inspections at state lines and tried to quell false rumors by visiting suspected towns. In theory, the federal government could transcend parochial interests, but as a practical matter, it could only provide expert advice, and then only if asked.

While Congress dithered, "quarantine conventions" of political leaders, scientists, and business executives tried to solve the interstate quarantine problem through regional cooperation. Reported in depth in the national press, a National Quarantine Convention took place in Memphis in 1898, at the invitation of merchants there. The group passed resolutions urging national control of quarantine. But Senator George Vest of Missouri told the delegates he did not think Congress could fix the problem. The primary impediment, he said, were state boards of health. They "are determined to retain their jurisdiction as it now exists, and this is absolutely inconsistent with the idea of such a national quarantine as will secure rapid and efficient opposition to Yellow Fever."[59]

The *Atlanta Constitution* favored a national quarantine law "broad enough in its provisions to meet every emergency." With federal control, "We should hear no more of shotgun quarantines, and there would be no basis for irritation or ill feeling between states, or between communities in different states."[60] Yet federal officials stood powerless, even as state governors, doctors, and local business leaders begged for help.

After yet another devastating outbreak of yellow fever in 1905, regional leaders tried again. Meeting in Chattanooga in 1905, nine governors, two US senators, and eighteen US representatives attended the Southern Quarantine and Immigration Convention, which sought national control of interstate quarantine.[61] Over some objection on grounds of states' rights—including by Governor James K. Vardaman of Mississippi, who warned the convention "against taking any steps which will trample upon the autonomy of our States"—the delegates attained remarkable unanimity on the need for congressional action. They concluded that Congress alone could solve the problems posed by the shotgun quarantine. Some form of national control over interstate quarantine, in the words of the *Atlanta Constitution*, would "wipe out the state line foolishness in the contingency of a dangerous epidemic, placing the responsibility for quarantining and the care of the pestilence victims upon the broad shoulders of Uncle Sam."[62]

Political leaders from southern states had come to the view that only the federal government could provide an effective solution, and they called for federal intervention. This was odd. Southern states after the Civil War rarely cooperated with the federal government, let alone asked for assistance. Their adherence to states' rights was the most extreme in the country. But on this one thing they could agree.

Regional cooperation had failed. A US Senate committee reported that during the 1897 yellow fever epidemic, "hundreds of lives were lost by reason of defects in existing law." The committee favored legislation bolstering federal authority during an epidemic because "the evils of the present system have become intolerable." The commerce of the entire South was paralyzed, and "the rights of citizens disregarded by lawless methods," with train passengers "forcibly taken from the cars and carried to improvised fever camps, where they were exposed to hardship and contagion."[63] Senators were not willing to remedy those defects in law, even though most of them recognized that state lines made every epidemic emergency far worse than it had to be.

Two sessions of Congress—in 1898 and 1906—considered whether to amend or replace the 1890 Epidemic Diseases Act, but they did neither. The federal government needed the ability to impose or lift inland quarantines to restore the semblance of order in the face of an epidemic. But many in Congress did not believe the US Constitution allowed the federal government to prevent a state or local government from imposing a quarantine that it believed necessary to protect itself.

Could the federal government deprive a state or local government of this right? Presidents William McKinley, Theodore Roosevelt, and William Howard Taft all believed the federal government had the authority to override a state or local quarantine and should use it.

As Congress debated the problem of the shotgun quarantine, Representative T. M. Mahon of Pennsylvania related a story from the epidemic of 1897:

> A man traveling there, perfectly well, was pulled off at the State line, at the mouth of the shotgun, and not allowed to go into another State, and not allowed to go back. Will you tell me the United States, under the powers of the Constitution regulating interstate commerce, does not have power to interfere on behalf of that citizen and say that no such treatment shall be accorded him?

Mahon insisted to the contrary that anyone going from state to state should be "as fully protected under the interstate-commerce clause of the Constitution as a barrel of flour."[64]

• • •

Repeated epidemics throughout the nineteenth century made painfully clear that the United States government could not prevent the shotgun quarantine or quell the panic that brought it on. It took no stretch of the imagination to picture similar scenes in the rest of the country, given the right circumstance of a scary, fast-moving disease and a panicked local population. Anyone who thought about the problem at all realized that state lines and the independent political control of local communities could make any epidemic emergency worse.

For over four decades, the shotgun quarantine challenged the capacity and will of the federal government to manage epidemics. Congress explored the constitutional question of its authority but never figured out how, practically, the federal government could help. Congress did nothing to stem the chaotic scenes of panic in the face of a little understood disease.

Debates in Congress over control of state and local quarantine tested Commerce Clause and federalism principles that held state lines to be the limiting point of action for the federal government. Yet there was widespread agreement that only the federal government could prevent the chaos and suffering when "mob law seem[ed] likely to rule."[65] Just as *Jacobson v. Massachusetts* would remain the primary authority for judges in future epidemics, the ineffectual resolution to the shotgun quarantine would continue to limit the federal government's role in preventing spread of disease within the nation.[66]

But in the meantime, yellow fever was considered a southern problem. The rest of the nation was confident that it need not fear that disease or the semi-lawlessness of the shotgun quarantines that accompanied it. If yellow fever raised little concern or sympathy outside the South, Americans sat up in alarm with the arrival of bubonic plague in San Francisco in 1900.

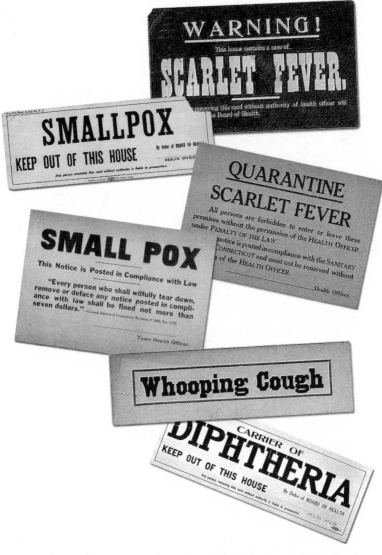

Quarantine warning signs, some printed in San Francisco,
others in unidentified locales, ca. 1900.

3

BLACK DEATH ON THE WEST COAST

*The rate at which the bubonic plague is increasing
in California is causing alarm. The time has come
for the general Government to act in the matter and
take steps to remove the menace to the health of the
whole country.*

—THE NEW YORK TIMES (1902)[1]

N ewspaper accounts of the South's travails in the late nineteenth century frequently referred to yellow fever with the shorthand term
"plague."[2] The same had been true for more than a century for visi-
tations of smallpox and cholera—they were "plagues." In the Great
Influenza to come, headlines such as "State Plague Is Unchanged"[3]
capture the essence of how Americans equated epidemics with terminology of the Middle Ages.

But on March 6, 1900, the real plague—the Black Death—arrived
in San Francisco. A lodger at the Globe Hotel—a rundown boardinghouse for newly arrived immigrants—had died after a mysterious, horrifying illness, with swollen lymph glands the size of baseballs around
his groin and armpits.[4] The pathologist on duty, Frank P. Wilson, was
only one year out of medical school. As Dr. Wilson began an autopsy,
his alarm quickly grew to the point that he called for his superior,
the senior health officer, Dr. A. P. O'Brien, and the city bacteriologist,
Wilfred Kellogg, to come in. What they saw suggested "an infectious
disease that makes even the most brave and experienced physician

shudder."[5] The cause of death was bubonic plague, from the bacterium *Y. pestis,* one of the deadliest pathogens on earth. It is thought to have been responsible for between one hundred million and two hundred million deaths throughout history.[6] In just five years, between 1347 and 1351, more than one-third of Europe's population died from the medieval strain of the plague.[7]

The bacteria causing bubonic plague thrives in the burrows of wild rodents, such as ground squirrels and rats. Bites from infected fleas transmit it to humans.[8] Most likely, plague-infested black rats from Hawaii arrived on the cargo steamship *Australia* on January 2, 1900. The rats quickly nestled into adjacent settlements inhabited by Chinese laborers. Over one hundred people died that year, but San Francisco would see more plague deaths during the next decade.[9]

Rats boarding a ship in one port and disembarking in another could happen anywhere at any time. But if an American city could not control its rat problem, bubonic plague threatened the entire nation. Headlines from newspapers across the nation raised the alarm. The *New York Times* warned of the "terrible menace to the country" because of the "carelessness of the health authorities" in San Francisco.[10] Two years from the first outbreak, plague in San Francisco was "more than ever dangerous" to the United States "because of our rapid means of transit" and the habit of Americans to travel: "It is but three days from San Francisco to New Orleans or Chicago, and in this time a traveler could carry the germs of the disease in his clothes or baggage from one city to the other." With good basis, the *New York Times* accused the business community of using its political influence "to keep the health authorities from publishing the facts in regard to the cases that have occurred," thus aiding the spread of the disease. The federal government must act at once, opined the editors, "to remove the menace to the health of the whole country."[11] The Epidemic Diseases Act of 1890, meant to allow the federal government to address yellow fever, would get its first real test.

• • •

While health authorities awaited confirmation of the first case of bubonic plague, Dr. O'Brien, as the city's senior health officer, advocated cordoning off the entire Chinese quarter. The police stretched ropes of braided hemp around a six-by-two-block area, and Chinese residents were ordered to remain inside the line.[12] Officials in San Francisco felt justified in erecting their "cordon sanitaire," as Dr. O'Brien explained. The city blockaded Chinatown "because the general clamor had become too great to ignore."[13]

Two months later, in May 1900, the hemp ropes were replaced by a cordon of barbed wire, causing riots to break out in the quarter. Chinatown had become, in essence, a prisoner-of-war camp. While Chinese residents protested their curtailed liberties, unfair treatment, and inability to earn a living, Mayor James Phelan responded by blasting the entire community in no uncertain terms: "They are fortunate," Phelan said, "with the unclean habits of their coolies and their filthy hovels, to remain within the corporate limits of any American city. In an economic sense their presence has been, and is, a great injury to the working classes, and in a sanitary sense they are a constant menace to the public health."[14] More deaths followed. While politicians and merchants, fearing devastating economic consequences, denied the plague's existence, the Chinese themselves began to conceal their dead, hoping that the quarantine would soon be lifted.[15]

A similar quarantine of white citizens by health officials would never have been tolerated. That Asians would be singled out to blame for bubonic plague is no surprise. Many whites believed that the Chinese harbored diseases in their bodies due to weak constitutions and living conditions in the Chinese quarter.[16] The Chinese were easy scapegoats, already subject to disturbing acts of violence at the hands of whites.[17]

When bubonic plague first appeared in 1900, San Francisco, a city of over 340,000, was home to 14,000 Chinese.[18] Chinese immigration had been encouraged as a source of cheap labor in the United States from the 1840s through the 1870s. Chinese labor contributed greatly to building the western portion of the transcontinental railway, completed in 1869. But unemployment and economic depression drove resentment against immigrants, especially the Chinese, leading to hate crimes in California and elsewhere. In 1886, US troops were ordered to Seattle to quell rioting by white laborers against the Chinese in that city, after the governor of Washington Territory had declared martial law.[19] The *North American Review* wrote that a war of races seemed imminent.[20] In California, the Workingman's Party and other labor groups pursued all sorts of legislation designed to make life harder for the Chinese so that they would essentially "self deport."[21]

Western states pressured Congress to act. In 1876, both the Republican and Democratic National platforms "took strong ground" against the Chinese, and they did so again in 1880.[22] In 1882, Congress passed the Chinese Exclusion Act, the first legislation to exclude would-be immigrants by race. The law banned new Chinese laborers, but merchants, teachers, and others of the professional class could still enter freely. The ban against Chinese laborers would remain in place until 1943.[23]

• • •

On the afternoon of June 15, 1900, just two weeks after health officials sealed off and posted guards around Chinatown, federal judge William Morrow shocked the city's leadership when he told them they must stop. By the time the plague came to the shores of San Francisco, courts throughout the nation had shown reluctance for a century about second-guessing the decisions of local elected officials in an epidemic, and they would largely continue to do so for a century afterward. But in a case brought by a local Chinese merchant, Jew Ho, for the first time ever a federal court struck down a quarantine order by local officials. Attorneys for Jew Ho argued that the quarantined district was, geographically, grossly overbroad because it was drawn around the entire Chinese quarter. Moreover, city officials applied that quarantine solely to persons of Asian descent, gerrymandering the quarantine around white businesses but strictly prohibiting Chinese from leaving. Judge Morrow said that this state of affairs violated the US Constitution for two reasons. First, the health measure was "unreasonable, unjust, and oppressive, and therefore contrary to the laws limiting the police powers of the state." Second, it was discriminatory "in its character" and was thus "contrary to the provisions of the fourteenth amendment of the constitution of the United States."[24]

In an unusual move, Judge Morrow read aloud the court's opinion in his courtroom because he did not want to delay the urgent news, as typesetting for official publication certainly would do. Morrow's reading that day would have taken some time, as the judicial opinion was nearly ten thousand words long. The federal Constitution, Morrow said, prohibited health officials from "discriminating against any class of persons in favor of another," even for health orders. This was "precisely the point" that the US Supreme Court had said must be avoided: "the administration of a law 'with an evil eye and an unequal hand.'"[25]

It was the first acknowledgment by a federal court that the power of states to protect the health of their citizens might be used to perpetuate racial discrimination. Such actions were both racially motivated and ill-suited to stop the epidemic. Health officers could maintain a quarantine "around such places as it may have reason to believe are infected by contagious or infectious diseases," but "the general quarantine of the whole district must not be continued." Judge Morrow's ruling put health officials on notice regarding continuing efforts to battle the plague in San Francisco over the next eight years.

Only five years later, though, the US Supreme Court would decide *Jacobson v. Massachusetts,* the smallpox vaccination case from Boston described in the first chapter. In the midst of an outbreak, local authorities could mandate vaccination on penalty of a fine for refusal because "a community has the right to protect itself against an epidemic of disease which threatens the safety of its members."[26] Authorities in Boston required everyone to be vaccinated, not just one ethnic group. The Supreme Court in *Jacobson* counseled judges to afford a wide latitude to the judgment of health experts, so long as such measures were neutral, generally applicable, and justified by a medical necessity. In 1900, *Jew Ho v. Williamson* turned out to be one of the most significant cases establishing constitutional protection when health officials target racial groups or minorities. It would be a long, long time before a federal court would again strike down a health measure ordered during an epidemic.

· · ·

Although the national press paid scant attention to Judge Morrow's ruling, fear mounted in other states that San Francisco officials were covering up the true extent of the plague outbreak. When health officials around the country demanded a strict quarantine of all people or goods that originated in or passed through San Francisco,[27] the mayor,

James Phelan, and the governor of California, Henry Tifft Gage, were anxious to assure a worried nation that the situation was under control and that commerce to and from their state was safe. When they made limited headway with these efforts, they turned instead on the health officials in their midst. They even proposed that it "be made a felony to broadcast the presence of plague."[28]

Well before then, health officials from two dozen states gathered for the first of several self-styled "Plague Conferences" to address the threat to the nation. Meeting in Washington, DC, in January 1903, the group published this resolution:

> The present danger to California and to the United States lies primarily in the persistence, during nearly three years, of plague infection in that part of San Francisco known as Chinatown; but the gravity of this circumstance is greatly increased by the gross neglect of official duty by the State board of health of California and the obstructive influence of the recent governor of California, [and] by the failure of the city government of San Francisco to support its city board of health.[29]

The resolution further demanded that the "city and State health authorities act in harmony with the Public Health and Marine-Hospital Service to carry out any sanitary regulations which that Service may deem necessary." Otherwise, at the group's next meeting in April, they would call for a national quarantine against the entire state of California, preventing both passengers and cargo from leaving the state.[30]

The Public Health and Marine Hospital Service was a federal health agency just beginning to play a role in fighting the nation's epidemics. First established by Congress in 1798 as the Marine Hospital Service, this small agency, lodged in the Treasury Department, was charged with the relief of destitute sailors and the establishment of hospitals for them. It had grown significantly in size and budget since the Civil War. In 1912, it became the United States Public Health Service, dropping the "Marine Hospital" name.[31] During yellow fever outbreaks in the South, the Marine Hospital Service could do little more than establish refugee camps for those attempting to flee epidemic areas. But its officers, all medical doctors assigned throughout the South, continuously reported what statistics they could gather on numbers of cases and deaths. The annual reports of the service's surgeon general were the only way Congress and the president could know what was going on in the rest of the country.

Surgeon General Walter Wyman appointed Assistant Surgeon Dr. Joseph James Kinyoun to be Wyman's "one man in supreme control" of the situation in San Francisco.[32] The forty-year-old Kinyoun was already a long-time officer with the Marine Hospital Service and its top scientist. Arguably, he was also its most significant legacy. In 1887, Kinyoun founded a one-person federal "hygienic laboratory" in a small room on Staten Island, New York, for clinical research in the new field of microbiology and germ theory.[33] Kinyoun's small establishment would grow to be renamed the National Institutes of Health (NIH) in 1930.

Perhaps it was because the US Marine Hospital Service had finally moved in to wrest control from local authorities, but California's elected officials reacted with a vengeance.[34] Kinyoun further enraged Governor Gage when he sent a bulletin warning other states that plague could be carried from California by passengers and freight. Governor Gage told reporters that Kinyoun had created the plague himself by mishandling lab specimens.[35]

Henry Gage served only one term as governor of California, losing reelection in 1902 to George C. Pardee. Gage had consistently contradicted news reports about the plague's spread, and under his leadership several states enacted quarantines against California, with more states likely to follow.[36] To head off threats from even more states to shut off all commerce, Governor Pardee at once offered a more conciliatory stance than Governor Gage.

Two national "plague conferences" had already met when Surgeon General Wyman convened the first annual conference of health authorities of each state and territory in the nation. Delegates from twenty-three states met on June 3, 1903, at the Willard Hotel in Washington, DC. Seven other state boards of health sent telegrams expressing regret they could not attend. The first order of business was the reading of a letter from Governor Pardee of California. "In view of recent events," he wrote, "I desire to add a brief statement which will show what is the attitude of the State health authorities toward the matters" discussed at the first plague conference in January. All of the relevant health authorities in California were now rowing in the same direction: "Nothing which was advised as expedient by the head of the Public Health and Marine-Hospital Service has been left undone." In closing, Pardee stressed, "there is no disposition to cover up or conceal anything. On the contrary, if any cases of plague should appear the fact shall be freely and fully acknowledged."[37] The secretary of California's state board of health, Dr. N. K. Foster, added: "It is impossible to control disease within State lines. It is in the interests of the United States that harmony must prevail."[38]

Reassured, the delegates expressed confidence in "the earnest efforts and ability of the governor and State board of health of the State of California, acting in harmony with the Bureau of Public Health and Marine-Hospital Service, to thoroughly eradicate bubonic plague heretofore existing in the city of San Francisco." So long as "the present effective work is continued, there is no need for quarantine restrictions of travel or traffic to or from that State."[39] Even the state health officer from Texas, Dr. George R. Tabor, agreed. Because "Texas was not at all satisfied with the situation with reference to the plague in California," Dr. Tabor went personally to investigate. "We had been getting false reports," Tabor told the other delegates.[40] Among those false reports might have been some from the *San Francisco Call,* whose March 8 headline read, "Plague Fake Is Part of a Plot to Plunder."[41] The morning of his arrival in Los Angeles later that month, Dr. Tabor saw that the *San Francisco Call* again claimed that plague did not exist there, and "was nothing but chicken cholera."[42]

• • •

Plague in San Francisco finally gave the nation the beginnings of a true epidemic-fighting branch of the federal government. News reports sufficiently frightened constituents elsewhere that Congress voted money to the cause. With the headline "U.S. to Fight Plague," the *New York Tribune* reported that the federal government would assume costs of fighting the bubonic plague. "The burden of fighting the bubonic plague has become too heavy for San Francisco to bear unaided," and Surgeon General Wyman assured city officials that the Treasury Department could cover some costs, primarily for inspection and rodent extermination, until Congress convened to appropriate funds.[43] But not only San Francisco was at risk: a "rigid quarantine" had been extended up and down the West Coast, from Seattle to Los Angeles. "It is the expectation of the members of the California delegation that when the gravity of the situation is submitted to Congress ample funds to combat the disease will be immediately supplied." They were not disappointed.

It wasn't just money that helped, necessary as that was for rodent control and sanitation. Twenty years after Congress had enacted the 1890 Epidemic Diseases Act, Surgeon General Wyman invoked it to impose draconian measures on San Francisco's Chinese quarter. Convinced that local authorities needed his direction, in May 1900 Wyman issued the first "Interstate Quarantine Regulations" under the Epidemic Diseases Act "to prevent the spread of plague in the United States."[44] The regulations prohibited common carriers from accepting any person suffering from plague "or any article infected therewith," and specified that bodies of plague victims could not be transported without the consent of health authorities; they should be cremated instead.

But like their counterparts in San Francisco, federal authorities, too, suspected all Chinese of harboring plague and reserved the harshest treatment for them. The first set of rules devised under the Epidemic Diseases Act reflected a pervasive bigotry. "During the existence of plague at any point in the United States," the Treasury Department ordered, the surgeon general of the Marine Hospital Service could bar "Asiatics or other races particularly liable to the disease" from transportation by any common carrier—by rail, steamship, streetcar, or carriage. Wyman put Joseph Kinyoun in charge of enforcing the order. Any member "of the Chinese race" would need Kinyoun's permission to leave the city.[45]

Wyman also instructed Kinyoun by telegram to deny any travel certificate unless the applicant submitted to an experimental inoculation against plague known as Haffkine Prophylactic, developed three years earlier by the Swiss bacteriologist Waldemar Haffkine for use in a bubonic plague epidemic in India.[46]

Businessman Wong Wai wanted to travel outside of San Francisco but refused to submit to the vaccine, and Kinyoun would not give him a travel pass. As Jew Ho later that month challenged the quarantine of Chinatown, Wong Wai also went to federal court, as his lawyers said, "on behalf of 25,000 persons of the Chinese race" residing in San Francisco county.[47]

Once again, the case came before Judge William Morrow, joined this time by Thomas Porter Hawley and John Jefferson DeHaven. Dr. Kinyoun defended his actions on the ground that the 1890 Epidemic Diseases Act authorized federal travel restrictions, and he had been specifically ordered by Wyman to condition travel passes on submission to inoculation. But Judge Morrow would have none of it. The fatal flaw was the application of Kinyoun's restrictions to only one racial group. As Judge Morrow explained, the travel ban was "not enforced against other residents of said city and county than those of the Mongolian race." This deprived Chinese residents of their rights under the federal Constitution.[48]

Elaborating further, Morrow wrote:

> They are not based upon any established distinction in the conditions that are supposed to attend this plague, or the persons exposed to its contagion, but they are boldly directed against the Asiatic or Mongolian race as a class, without regard to the previous condition, habits, exposure to disease, or residence of the individual; and the only justification offered for this discrimination was a suggestion made by counsel for the defendants in the course of argument, that this particular race is more liable to the plague than any other. No evidence has, however, been offered to support this claim, and it is not known to be a fact. This explanation must therefore be dismissed as unsatisfactory.[49]

Put plainly, federal officials could not enforce the travel restrictions because they were "directed against the Asiatic race exclusively, and by name." There was no effort to establish whether any particular person might have been exposed to plague, or even where that person resided. Asians were denied the privilege of traveling from one place to another "upon conditions not enforced against any other class of people."[50] To make matters worse, Judge Morrow wrote, even Surgeon General Wyman recognized the danger of inoculating someone who might already have been exposed to plague, for "if by chance he is already infected, the Haffkine injection may produce fatal results."[51]

But Morrow recognized the need for emergency measures if under-taken in an evenhanded way. "The conditions of a great city frequently present unexpected emergencies affecting the public health, comfort, and convenience," Morrow wrote. Health officers under such circum-stances "should be clothed with sufficient authority to deal with the conditions in a prompt and effective manner." Appropriate measures, if uniformly applied and "reasonably adapted to the purpose of pro-tecting the health and preserving the welfare of the inhabitants of a city," are "constantly upheld by the courts as valid acts of legislation, however inconvenient they may prove to be, and a wide discretion has also been sanctioned in their execution."[52]

The court's ruling on May 28 put a halt, at least temporarily, to the travel restrictions and, thus, federal control under the Epidemic Diseases Act. But neither Wyman nor Kinyoun would be deterred. Surgeon General Wyman ordered the armed barricade of Chinatown and planned to send more than a thousand residents of the Chinese quarter to detention camps.[53]

By early 1904, plague had ended in San Francisco. One hundred twenty-one cases of bubonic plague had been diagnosed, 113 of them resulting in death. Of those who died, 107 were Chinese, 4 were Japa-nese, and only 2 were white.[54] Sanitation efforts had ended the imme-diate threat, but two years later, the 1906 San Francisco earthquake and fire scattered rats to other parts of the city, leading to outbreaks in 1907 and 1908.[55] Whether this outbreak originated from the *Aus-tralia* or from later-arriving rats on government transports from the Philippines, as the *New York Times* alleged, is unknown.[56] The 1906 earthquake devastated the Chinatown neighborhood. By the end of the decade, the largest Chinese population in the United States—four-teen thousand in 1900—had fallen to just over ten thousand.[57]

• • •

Twenty-four years later, in 1924, and 350 miles to the south, almost the same play would be staged again: an immigrant quarter, blamed and persecuted for an outbreak of the plague; a tight-lipped local gov-ernment unwilling to hurt its city's commercial prospects; national newspapers seeking to expose the medical facts; and the need for the federal government to step in and override local and state health authorities to safeguard the health of the nation. This time, however, another form of plague had arrived: pneumonic plague, a severe lung infection caused by the same bacterium as bubonic plague.

The similarities between Los Angeles in 1924 and San Francisco in 1900 began almost immediately. On October 3, 1924, a health officer, Dr. Giles Porter, was called to the heart of the Mexican quarter in the city. There, Francisca Lajun, the daughter of a railroad worker, seemed to be battling a mysterious infection. Porter reported, "This child was not considered to be in a serious condition." Yet two days later, Luciana Samarano, a family friend who had been nursing Francisca, sent for an ambulance to take Francisca to Los Angeles General Hospital. She died on the way, of a cause officially listed as "double pneumonia."[58]

A week later, Francisca's father, Jesus, fell ill with the same mysterious condition and died, followed by Luciana Samarano who owned a local boardinghouse on Clara Street. With terrifying speed, thirty-three people who attended Luciana's wake or lodged at her boardinghouse contracted the plague. Thirty-one of them died. Luciana Samarano's home became known as "the death house."[59]

The cases were originally attributed to "epidemic meningitis." But a hospital pathologist, Dr. George Maner, suggested that the disease was plague. The city's health commissioner, Dr. Luther Powers, at first refused to believe that plague was at large in the Mexican quarter.[60]

But something was. Powers sent quarantine officers to the district, telling them that the Spanish flu had returned. Armed guards surrounded the neighborhood, roping off eight city blocks surrounding Clara Street. Although no one had mentioned the plague aloud, the superintendent of the Los Angeles General Hospital sent a telegram to state and federal officials inquiring about the availability of plague serum and vaccine. One of those telegrams was intercepted by Benjamin Brown, a US Public Health Service officer stationed in Los Angeles. When Brown asked whether the hospital was housing plague patients, he was met with fervent denials. Not satisfied with that answer, Brown wired the US surgeon general, Hugh S. Cumming. Cumming ordered James Perry, a Public Health Service physician from San Francisco who had been through the plague outbreaks there from 1900 to 1908, to investigate. But when Perry arrived, he found that journalists were already asking the same questions.[61]

"Police Cordons around Los Angeles Mexican Quarter," screamed a headline in the *Boston Daily Globe* on November 3, 1924.[62] "Pneumonic Plague Is Feared After 13 Die in Los Angeles," wrote the *Washington Post* on its front page, and in smaller type, "U.S. Public Health Service to Help in Stamping Out Dread Disease."[63] The mortality rate of the disease, the *Globe* reported, "approaches 100 percent."[64]

Elected leaders in Los Angeles went to extreme measures to cover up the presence of the pneumonic plague, the extent of the outbreak that was raging in the city, and even the timeline of their own knowledge—sort of a cover-up of the cover-up. Los Angeles's tourism industry and real-estate market were on the line, not to mention bad press for the port of Los Angeles in its competition with other West Coast cities for commercial traffic. Suspicion of plague anywhere near the port would force the hand of the surgeon general to close the harbor and impose a strict ten-day maritime quarantine.[65] The city was aided in its battle by the local press. Newspaper editors continued to portray the outbreak to be merely a "malignant form of pneumonia."[66] In the words of historian William Deverell, "Plague was not the sort of thing expected in the proud city of tomorrow."[67]

• • •

Rats congregate in urban areas that are neglected by local officials because the residents there are poor. In Los Angeles, the Mexican quarter was such an area. The authorities began door-to-door inspections, forcibly evacuating to the county hospital anyone whose exposure to the plague was even dimly suspected. Reminiscent of the response of health officials in San Francisco, police cordoned the area under strict quarantine. The *Austin Statesman* called it a "shotgun quarantine," the "infected zone" guarded day and night by seventy-five police officers working in three shifts. Food and other necessities, provided by local charities, had to be sent in through the police line.[68] Residents, of course, were trapped with the very rats responsible for the outbreak. A Catholic priest who administered aid in the quarantine zone died from plague, as did an ambulance driver, Emmet McLauthin.[69]

Nora Sterry, principal of the Macy Street School, asked Mayor G. E. Coyer for permission to cross the quarantine line to "look after her children." When the mayor approved, Sterry's first act was to raise the US flag at the school, which had been closed since the outbreak. She did so, the *Baltimore Sun* reported, "as a message of cheer and hope to the now isolated people among whom she has labored for more than 12 years."[70]

Compared to twenty-four years earlier in San Francisco, the federal government's response this time was faster. Congress promptly voted funds requested by the surgeon general, adding to an ongoing federal plague control program in western states to eliminate ground squirrels thought to have carried plague from Oakland to Los Angeles. The US Public Health Service (by now renamed to omit Marine Hospital Service) was on the scene quickly. Rupert Blue, a former US surgeon general, was called out of retirement to take charge as a sort of "plague czar." Blue had been involved in the 1900–1908 San Francisco plague outbreaks as Dr. Kinyoun's replacement. At that time, Blue had encountered the same obfuscation from urban and business leaders as Kinyoun, although he had been able to handle these objections with more diplomacy while he launched a war on rats and poor sanitation. Demolishing houses, baiting rat holes with arsenic, and hunting down and killing over two million rats had alleviated that outbreak. Blue now led the same assault on the rats of Los Angeles.[71]

The Los Angeles plague outbreak went away quietly; there were no more deaths from pneumonic plague after November. In all, there had been thirty-nine cases of plague with thirty-three deaths. The Public Health Service continued to find plague-infected rats through that month, however.[72] It would intensify a rodent monitoring and eradication effort that had been underway since the appearance of bubonic plague in San Francisco.

Pneumonic plague returned to the big screen in 1950, in the film noir *Panic in the Streets*. US Public Health Service officer Clinton Reed (played by Richard Widmark) discovers that an unidentified man has died of pneumonic plague in New Orleans. Impressive in the uniform of the Public Health Service, Reed warns city officials they have only forty-eight hours to find other plague carriers to prevent an epidemic. When municipal leaders challenge Reed's authority, he responds, "I'm Dr. Reed of the United States Public Health Service, and one of the jobs of my department is to keep plague out of this country."[73] Together with a police captain (played by Paul Douglas), Reed locates two associates of the victim and averts an outbreak. Of course, it hadn't worked like that in either Los Angeles or San Francisco. Like Kinyoun before him, even Rupert Blue, a former surgeon general, could only advise local authorities what to do and assist them with rodent eradication and surveillance if Congress thought the expenditure worth it. Fortunately, Congress did.

A plague outbreak in New Orleans may have been an unlikely scenario for the film, but not for Los Angeles in 1924, or for other areas of the United States today. Plague bacteria circulate among wild rodent populations, including chipmunks, prairie dogs, mice, voles, and, especially, western squirrels.[74] The United States averages seven cases of human plague each year, mostly the bubonic form, in rural areas in the West.[75] Fortunately, prompt treatment with antibiotics can prevent serious illness and death.

· · ·

By the end of the California plagues, jurisdictional fights and a blame game between local and federal health officials over who could best control the plague seemed to have been settled in favor of federal authorities. Bubonic plague in San Francisco had made it abundantly clear that failure to control an outbreak at the local level threatened the entire nation. The presence of plague in California had upended the idea that the stark federal-state division of authority—with most responsibility jealously guarded at the local level—could, in fact, protect the nation. But the nation's escape from the plague with a relatively low death toll may have been simply a matter of luck. When bubonic plague first appeared on American shores in 1900, it had already struck British India, Egypt, Japan, South Africa, France, Great Britain, and Australia.[76] San Francisco's experience was part of a plague pandemic originating in Canton and Hong Kong in 1894. It would continue to circulate the globe for the next five decades. By the time the plague pandemic ended, in 1959, it had caused over fifteen million deaths, the majority in India.[77]

Rupert Blue, meanwhile, had leveraged his experience fighting plague in San Francisco to become, in 1912, the Surgeon General of the Public Health Service, appointed by President William Howard Taft when Blue was just forty-four years old. Sending congratulations, editors of the *California State Journal of Medicine* noted that Blue had been "publicly and privately deluged with the thanks of California, and particularly San Francisco, for his monumentally efficient labors in his sanitation work out here."[78] In just a few years, though, San Francisco and the rest of the nation would forget how terrible bubonic plague had seemed. In 1918, the great influenza pandemic arrived, with Rupert Blue in charge of the federal government's response.

St. Louis Red Cross motor corps, St. Louis, Missouri, October 1918.

4

THE 1918 GREAT INFLUENZA

No public health law is worth the paper it is written on unless the people really want to obey it and really want to see it enforced. The psychology of Americans is such that if you try to bully them into doing a thing they will turn right around and go the other way as fast as they can, but if you explain a matter and show them they are getting a square deal you can get what you are going after.

—DR. WILLIAM C. RUCKER, 1916[1]

On the eve of the devastating pandemic that Americans would come to know as the Spanish influenza, the medical profession could congratulate itself on remarkable scientific advancements that promised a new ability to combat contagious disease. When the American Academy of Medicine met in Detroit in 1916, Dr. William Colby Rucker of the US Public Health Service reminded the gathering that there had been no yellow fever outbreaks since 1905, that bubonic plague had been stamped out on the West Coast, and that a cholera epidemic in Europe in 1910 had been kept out of the United States.[2] Army researchers led by Dr. Walter Reed had identified mosquitoes as carriers of yellow fever in 1901. With this discovery, the United States launched a massive mosquito eradication campaign to avoid yellow fever while building the Panama Canal, completed in 1914; the disease had stymied an earlier French attempt to build the canal. A vaccine for typhoid used by the US military became widely available to the public, while a vaccine for cholera showed promise. Antitoxin for diphtheria, produced in Philadelphia and by the New York City Health Department, contributed to a decline in deaths from the disease.[3] In short, the worst epidemics of the past century now seemed possible to prevent, thanks to effective new methods of disease control.[4]

What had shifted, though, was not just faith in scientific advancement but also a remarkable confidence in the role of government to protect the health of the nation. This explains why, in 1916, two years before the pandemic hit, law and legislation preoccupied seemingly everyone in the US medical establishment. Medical subjects were notably absent from the Academy of Medicine's annual meeting in 1916, for example, displaced by the theme "Medical Problems of Legislation." The nineteen papers presented in Detroit all assessed some aspect of law and were later published in a volume running to 242 pages.[5] At the beginning of that year, Rupert Blue, surgeon general of the US Public Health Service and the newly elected president of the American Medical Association, issued a densely packed 248-page compendium of "all judicial cases relating directly to the public health" from courts throughout the nation—all from the previous eighteen months alone.[6] Dr. E. G. Williams of Virginia, president of the conference of state and territorial health officials, opened that group's 1916 annual meeting in Washington, DC, with an address identifying law as one of "the most powerful weapons" to prevent disease and raise the standard of health in America.[7] Health officers heard and discussed presentations on "Model State, District, and County Health Laws," and "Recent Advances in Sanitary Laws," among other law-related themes.

The distinctive focus on law that year showed that many of America's health officers, medical doctors, and researchers believed law to be an important means to keep America safe from epidemic outbreaks. For the Academy of Medicine, the "extensive and extending" boundary between legislation and medicine now included new state laws regulating medical practice. Dr. Florus Fremont Lawrence of Columbus, Ohio, for example, spoke about "Legislative Protection of the People from the Evils of Patent Medicines and Medical Fakers."[8] The great majority of presenters, however, addressed what the conference organizers termed "the regulations grouped together under public health laws."[9] Legislation in this category reflected a greatly expanded role for state and local public health departments, running the gamut from laws to improve sewerage systems to food safety laws, including regulations governing milk and dairy products (which could be contaminated both from diseased cows and by improper handling).

"Public health law" was a relatively new term for the explosion of state and local regulations since the turn of the century. Until James A. Tobey's 1926 treatise, *Public Health Law: A Manual of Law for Sanitarians*, there were only collections of judicial decisions like the Public Health Service's 1916 compilation.[10] The "sanitarians" for whom Tobey's book was intended had been prime movers in the adoption of sanitary codes throughout the country, especially standards for municipal water supplies to prevent diseases like typhoid and cholera.[11] Dr. Williams, in his address to the state health officers, referred to this kind of law as a tool to control "excrement-borne diseases," which, if strictly enforced, would rapidly cause typhoid fever to disappear.[12]

In 1916, the leading proponent of the sanitary movement was New York's state commissioner of health, Dr. Hermann Biggs. Internationally, Biggs was America's best-known medical researcher, and he had recently coauthored the book *An Ideal Health Department*.[13] At the Academy of Medicine, Biggs held out New York's sanitary code as a model for other states because it applied uniform standards statewide. New York City's superb health department, which Biggs used to run, had long had the authority to enact sanitary regulations on its own. But with this new legislation, which Biggs helped to write, towns throughout New York could now be brought into conformity. The state law, Biggs claimed, was especially helpful in smaller towns, where the health officers were usually also practicing physicians; the law gave them "great moral support," especially when local elected officials opposed sanitary inspection laws.[14] Surgeon General Blue, like Herman Biggs, believed that all states should set public health standards and should enforce them, an opinion he shared with Congress in 1916: The lack of such regulations would lead to "a condition favorable to the spread of disease."[15]

The National Medical Association (NMA), representing the nation's Black doctors (whom the American Medical Association excluded from membership), also noticed legal developments in 1916. The NMA's well-regarded academic journal took note of what it termed a "momentous decision" from the US Supreme Court in January of that year, delivering a serious blow "to nostrums and quack medicines."[16] A unanimous court affirmed the federal confiscation of a shipment of medicines from a Chicago drug company to Omaha, Nebraska, which the company had advertised to be a cure for tuberculosis. It was not merely a difference of medical opinion, wrote Justice Charles Evans Hughes. Congress was equally entitled to condemn interstate transportation of "swindling preparations accompanied by false and fraudulent statements, as well as a lottery ticket."[17]

The year 1916 was also pivotal for the nation's health in other ways. The Rockefeller Foundation endowed the nation's first school of public health at Johns Hopkins University. (It would open two years later, during the 1918 influenza epidemic.) Both the Rockefeller and Carnegie foundations increased funding for American medical research, convinced that curing disease was the best way to prevent the epidemic outbreaks of the prior century.[18] The year 1916 was also the last time the nation's surgeon general would advocate publicly for compulsory health insurance, as Rupert Blue did in his inaugural president's address to the American Medical Association. There were "unmistakable signs," Blue said, "that health insurance will constitute the next great step in social legislation."[19] Public financing of the costs of medical care would draw attention to public health measures to prevent disease, he said. That same year, Blue told Congress the nation needed a true national health program to combat contagious disease, and he believed the Public Health Service should be expanded to serve that role.[20]

In the calm before two coming storms—America's entry into World War I and the worst influenza pandemic of the twentieth century—public health and medical experts in 1916 focused on law as a way to prevent dangerous disease outbreaks. Legislatures had been busy producing the law. But when the influenza pandemic raced through America two years later, confidence in both law and science proved to have been misplaced.

In 1916, William Rucker tried to warn the Academy of Medicine (and anyone who would listen) that existing law could not help prevent or allay an epidemic catastrophe, for two reasons: First, Rucker gave a prescient warning of the limited federal role. There would be little help from the federal government "in time of grave epidemic," because states were in charge of all health matters within their borders, and states alone could not prevent the interstate spread of disease. As a practical matter, Rucker said, states could not be expected "to control every situation or to grapple with every problem which arises within their borders." Although the states could call upon the US Public Health Service for help to "eradicate the disease before it can spread to other states," the service had too few personnel if several states all needed help at the same time, assuming a state called for help in time to do anything about it in even one location.[21]

The second reason had to do with attempts to standardize public health laws for every community. Rucker's most prophetic remarks in this regard came in the discussion that followed his presentation. Few were interested in the interstate quarantine question but instead wanted to explore the ideas Herman Biggs had raised. Dr. William H. Price of Detroit noted that a code of health regulations is useful only if it has the support of the community and the average citizen because there will always be a minority of citizens who "from opposition, indifference, or an exaggerated sense of personal liberty" will not be "guided by the judgment of the majority."[22]

Rucker agreed, revealing his somewhat irascible nature: "No public health law is worth the paper it is written on unless the people really want to obey it and really want to see it enforced. We have stuff on our statute books that is worse than useless, and which would never hold in court," he added, and continued:

> The psychology of Americans is such that if you try to bully them into doing a thing they will turn right around and go the other way as fast as they can. . . . The general public in this country is nobody's fool, and people can tell when you are trying to fool them. If, on the other hand, they know you are telling them simply what ought to be done and are asking for their help, then health regulations will be shown to be worthwhile.[23]

Events would soon prove the truth of this observation. But Dr. Edward Jackson identified a more significant problem health officials would face—the conflict between state and local authorities. Local boards of health had plenty of authority, he said, but that meant in an epidemic emergency that each city or county could decide its own safety measures, or none at all, with no state government authority to direct them. Rucker had been concerned about national authority to help prevent interstate transmission of disease, but Jackson pointed out that most states had little control over their own communities. That was why, Jackson said, contagious disease "is all the time passing beyond state lines."[24]

Rucker and Jackson were both right. Because every city, town, and county could decide for itself the emergency rules that would govern its citizens, every American experienced the influenza pandemic differently. But all Americans would share the fear, chaos, and death to come.

• • •

The first cases of a new strain of influenza were reported at a military base in Kansas in June 1918, mostly unnoticed by the civilian home population. By the time it arrived in Europe in August, it was clear that this was no ordinary influenza, unlike the flu outbreaks Americans had experienced in 1888 and 1893. In Europe, ravaged by World War I, influenza exploded and began its virulent and deadly march around the world. The epidemic spread in the traditional manner of influenza—from person to person via droplets coughed or sneezed into the air, or by touching objects on which the germs had landed. The malady often came on suddenly. A headache was typically the first sign, followed quickly by a fever that usually lasted from three to five days. Death could occur within days or could come later from complications of pneumonia. That it came to be known as the Spanish flu had nothing to do with its geographic origin. Military leaders prohibited public reports of the severity of illnesses and death, but in neutral Spain, newspapers were free to report on the epidemic, giving the (false) impression that Spain was particularly hard hit—hence the name "Spanish flu." Scientists estimate that it killed at least fifty million people worldwide, including about 675,000 in the United States.[25]

Before the pandemic's second wave came to America that fall, President Woodrow Wilson had become aware of the terrible devastation it had caused in both military and civilian populations in France, Germany, and Great Britain and that it would almost certainly overtake the US in a matter of weeks. But Wilson never mentioned the influenza pandemic in public—not once. That would have distracted from the patriotism and loyalty still needed at home to sustain the war effort.[26]

In early September, Massachusetts became the first state to be hit, and it was hit hard indeed. Despite the efforts of state health officials to slow the spread of the virus by closing schools, preventing public gatherings, and even banning funerals, hospitals were quickly overrun and deaths mounted. Governor Calvin Coolidge asked for federal help on September 26. Not coincidentally, the US Senate held its first hearing on the issue two days later. Surgeon General Rupert Blue, in the crisp blue military uniform of the US Public Health Service, was there to ask Congress to help.

"Where do you expect to get the doctors?" Senator John Wingate Weeks of Massachusetts asked this most pressing question, the elephant in the room. Spanish influenza had struck all of New England, but especially Boston. The Senate Appropriations Committee convened that Saturday afternoon in September to ask how the surgeon general intended to spend federal money.[27] Just the day before, the House of Representatives had voted for one million dollars to be made immediately available to the Public Health Service. Senator Weeks expected most of it to be used for emergency medical aid, to bring doctors and nurses from other parts of the country to New England, where tens of thousands were sick, hospitals overrun, and physicians, nurses, and hospital attendants scarce. The same was true for Pennsylvania and North Carolina. And those were only the most recent states appealing for medical staff.

The immediate concern for Senator Weeks was his home state of Massachusetts. He was, after all, the Senate sponsor of the appropriation bill, and the hearing was politically important, especially to him.[28] Not only did members of Congress have to be seen doing something to let constituents at home know of their concern, but he himself was up for reelection in less than two months. (He would lose that election.) But others on the committee wanted to know how to prevent the flu from spreading—how to protect the parts of the country that had yet to experience the flu in epidemic form.

Where, indeed, would Rupert Blue find doctors? A great many of the nation's trained doctors were then serving in the military, about 30,000 of the 150,000 practicing physicians in the United States.[29]

World War I still raged across Europe. The army and navy told Congress it was impossible to spare any of their doctors, given the thousands of sick soldiers at US bases. "That will be our most difficult task," Blue replied. The Public Health Service had fewer than one hundred trained physicians it could deploy. It had no stockpile of medical supplies and no experience in the logistics of nationwide distribution, even if it had supplies. Blue thought he might be able to find as many as three or four hundred doctors, a "Volunteer Medical Service Corps" that could be moved to the most desperate areas of the country, with salaries paid by the federal government. The Public Health Service would also set up emergency hospitals wherever they were needed. The Red Cross would provide as many nurses as it could. In fact, it had already mobilized hundreds of nurses, largely recruited in the Midwest.[30] Red Cross nurses were often the only help influenza sufferers would ever receive.

It was a foregone conclusion that the Senate would approve the Joint Resolution to Aid in Combating the Disease Known as Spanish Influenza, Congress's answer to what the federal government could do to help. Money, after all, looks like action. A million dollars was a relatively small sum, both in hindsight and as a percentage of the federal government's non-war spending that year. The navy's medical representative at the hearing, J. R. Phelps, quickly insisted that one million dollars would not be enough: "It is a very serious situation. I should think a million dollars would not go far if this thing develops as it has in eastern Massachusetts and in Connecticut." Blue added, "We expect that the disease will spread all over the country in a very short time."[31] Senator Wesley Jones of Washington asked whether Blue had any additional emergency funds he could use. Blue replied that the Public Health Service had an emergency fund called the "epidemic fund," but it could only be used for a limited set of diseases: cholera, typhus fever, yellow fever, smallpox, and bubonic plague. "I do not understand that," Jones said. Blue explained that the limitation had been set by Congress, in the 1890 Epidemic Diseases Act. The federal government could act without invitation of state authorities only for those specified diseases, Blue said.[32]

Senator Lee Overman from North Carolina asked Blue whether the money "is to be used to stop the spread of influenza, or just to treat the people who have it?" Blue replied, "It is to be used to isolate those who are ill, in hospitals, as near as possible." The pandemic could not be stopped, but it might be slowed, and in the meantime the government could provide humanitarian aid. "You cannot stop the spread of an infection of this kind unless you impose a quarantine that would stop traffic of all kinds," he added. Given the impracticability, indeed futility, of attempting to stop the flu by quarantine, Blue told the senator the best use of the money would be for two things. First, it would be used to isolate those who are ill, isolating them in hospitals if possible. The Public Health Service could build temporary hospitals, and it could serve as a central clearing house to find nurses and doctors willing to go to the most affected areas. Second, Blue proposed "educational measures" to explain what people could do to avoid the flu and to "advise them so that they will not expose others to the disease."[33]

Senator Robert L. Owen of Oklahoma readily agreed about the need for public instruction, telling Blue: "You are not going to begin to have enough doctors and nurses for all of them, because these cases will arise by thousands, and suddenly."[34] Owen was right, of course. There was little the Public Health Service could offer other than to build emergency hospitals and try to coordinate the distribution of doctors, nurses, and supplies from richer states to poorer ones, with no leverage to make that happen. But what the surgeon general could do was lead a national messaging campaign—and no other government official was in a better position to do that.

• • •

The influenza spread across American in three waves over two years—a saving grace that it did not hit every state at the same time. On the other hand, Americans had to be warned that it was coming. Large cities, especially, had to prepare for the inevitable. A national messaging campaign was sorely needed.

Surgeon General Blue had already begun that campaign a few weeks before he testified before the Senate committee. Three days after Boston reported an outbreak on September 11, Blue telegraphed a bulletin to the Associated Press for distribution by newspapers throughout the nation. "The disease is characterized by sudden onset," Blue wrote. "People are stricken on the street, while at work in factories, shipyards, offices, or elsewhere." He then described the symptoms, urging anyone experiencing them to "go to their homes at once, get to bed without delay, and immediately call a physician." Patients should remain in bed until the fever was gone to avoid serious complications, such as bronchial pneumonia. Anyone attending the patient should wear a gauze mask.

While there was "no such thing as an effective quarantine in the case of pandemic influenza," Blue said, the outbreak might be controlled "by intelligent action on the part of the public." The public should "avoid crowded assemblages, street cars, and the like," and should recognize the "danger of promiscuous coughing and spitting." It was also fair to assume, Blue said, that this type of influenza "might spread through a school as easily and rapidly as measles."[35] Blue regularly updated state and local health authorities and urged bans on public gatherings anywhere the flu was present. He stressed the need to avoid crowds, as "all evidence points to human contact as being the means of spread." The Public Health Service eventually published six million bulletins, in addition to posters and newspaper articles distributed to ten thousand newspapers.[36]

Although some state health officials were optimistic that a vaccine could be devised, in the interim they could only repeat the surgeon general's advice: isolate the sick, wear masks if around a sick person, keep away from crowds, wash hands frequently, and especially cover one's mouth and nose when sneezing or coughing. But medical experts could not agree on the measures local governments should take to prevent the spread of the flu. Meeting in Chicago in December 1918, the American Public Health Association failed to agree on the best measures to stop the epidemic's spread. The association's president, Dr. Charles Hastings, told the *New York Times,* "We cannot expect to draw up a definite program for combating influenza epidemics when we see so wide a divergence of opinion among medical authorities as has been shown here."[37]

Health officers from the Southeast, including Dr. S. W. Welch of Montgomery, Alabama, argued for strict quarantine of towns that had not yet encountered the flu. (This region of the country was familiar with such quarantines from yellow fever epidemics, as recently as 1905.) Most others argued that such quarantines would not work and were impracticable, especially in more populated areas. They argued instead about business and school closures, limits on public gatherings, and the mandatory use of face masks where flu was already present. Doctors from Charleston, Richmond, and Baltimore, among other cities, believed that prohibiting public gatherings of any sort was efficacious once a single case appeared. Health officers of some of the larger cities opposed these measures. Dr. J. W. Inches, health commissioner of Detroit, spoke against closing schools, theaters, and stores. He also ridiculed mandatory wearing of face masks as simply not feasible measures in larger cities. The lack of consensus hardly mattered in one respect—each locality would make its own decision, as it had in epidemic emergencies in the past. As Dr. Welch put it, "After all, it is a question of applying to your own community the most practical remedies for the conditions encountered there."[38]

But others were not satisfied. "We came here to find the means of prevention, and the public expects it of us," said Kansas City Health Commissioner E. H. Bullard. But "our experiences have not yet shown us the successful way to combat the disease." Kansas City had closed businesses and schools and prevented public gatherings for several weeks, but the cases had increased nonetheless. When another round of flu hit the city in November, Kansas City imposed what it called a "general quarantine" again. This time the number of flu cases declined—but that was not solid proof that the quarantine action had helped. "We must take back to our communities some reasonably definite results," Bullard pleaded.[39]

Meanwhile, city and county officials made their own decisions about when to close schools, stop travel, and prevent public gatherings. In modern terminology, this variety of restrictions on daily life constituted "social distancing" measures. The greatest hardship for families and individuals was economic: restaurants, bars, and other businesses were ordered to close. Such measures took away livelihoods and caused widespread unemployment with no recourse to a social safety net; this was, of course, before the advent of the country's major welfare programs during the New Deal. Local welfare barely existed, and private charities, often the only option, were overwhelmed, just like everybody else. Prohibitions on church services and funerals pained people emotionally and spiritually.

Examples abound of the variation in decision-making abilities among local leaders. St. Louis, with a population of 687,000,[40] took the surgeon general's advice to close schools, churches, and places of entertainment and to cancel public events. Philadelphia, with a population of 1.7 million,[41] did not. The result was a dramatic difference in death rates between the two cities. In Philadelphia, health officials suggested to the mayor that a parade in support of the sale of war bonds should be canceled in light of the epidemic, but the mayor refused. Huge crowds showed up, and flu cases spiked afterward. By contrast, St. Louis more quickly and promptly shut down public gatherings and had one-eighth as many flu-related fatalities.[42]

The laws giving state and local health officers power to meet emergencies, lauded by health officials in 1916, quickly became irrelevant. A local health officer might have the authority, on paper at least, to direct a community's response, but elected county and city officials could overrule those measures. In Atlanta, for example, the city's board of health in October recommended that all schools, theaters, movie houses, churches, and other public gatherings be closed for two months. The city council agreed with the recommendations and put them into effect. But two weeks later, Atlanta mayor Asa Candler, founder of the Coca-Cola company, vetoed the restrictions because of fear of its impact on the local economy.[43]

In fact, both large cities and small communities acted on the principle that emergency measures were strictly local decisions, even if there was disagreement about who had the authority to order them. For example, the residents of Lenoir, North Carolina, voted on the question of whether to close the town's school when influenza struck in January 1919. Although there was "considerable agitation in the town, both pro and con, as to opening the school," those in favor of temporarily closing the school prevailed by a vote of 150 to 70. The school board complied with the majority's wishes, and the North Carolina Supreme Court upheld that decision against a lawsuit brought by residents who wanted the school opened.[44]

Conflicts arose most readily when state health boards tried to direct the response of towns or overruled the wishes of local communities. A prime example came from New Jersey. Citing "the greatest emergency the state had ever confronted," on October 7 state health director Dr.

Jacob C. Price ordered a statewide shutdown of all places of assembly, including movie theaters, saloons, and churches.[45] Newark's mayor, Charles P. Gillen, strenuously disagreed. Gillen announced that Newark saloons could remain open, arguing that whiskey was a treatment for influenza. But Newark's police commissioner said he would strictly enforce saloon closures, despite the mayor's proclamation. After Dr. Price telegraphed Gillen insisting on "strict compliance" with the state's order, Gillen lifted the ban and reopened Newark entirely on October 21, claiming that the epidemic was over. When the *Newark Evening News* questioned the legality of the mayor's actions, he threatened to "close the paper immediately under the laws of the state, as a menace to the public health, just as I would close any place of assembly."[46]

Even New Jersey's attorney general was uncertain who had legal authority to enforce the closure order in Newark. On one hand, New Jersey law clearly gave the state health board authority to issue orders to local health boards, but nothing in state law seemed to support a statewide closure order.[47] Gillen even wrote directly to the state's governor, Walter Evans Edge, asking that he fire Dr. Price. "It seems to me that the terribly drastic step taken by Dr. Price should have been taken only after mature deliberation and discussion of all members of the State body and not by one man," Mayor Gillen wrote. "I respectfully ask your excellency to thoroughly investigate this matter, and if you find that Dr. Price issued the order without proper authority of the State Board of Health conferred on him at a regular meeting of that body, I ask that you demand the resignation of Dr. Price."[48] The worst of the fall wave in New Jersey ended by mid-November, not long after Gillen's letter. Dr. Price retained his job. Gillen served only one term as mayor.[49]

When the state legislature reconvened the following spring, the Newark controversy featured again, as the state's lawmakers sought to clarify the powers of the state's health department. A proposed law would have given the state health department authority to compel communities to obey its orders during an epidemic. The measure easily passed the Senate but fell short in the General Assembly, leaving the question unresolved for another century.[50]

In some cities, elected leaders either abandoned their responsibilities altogether or appointed unelected emergency committees of private citizens to make day-to-day decisions. Some governors also appointed emergency committees, bypassing designated health officers. In a few communities, citizens likewise circumvented their elected leaders in electoral referendums on questions such as whether schools should open or close. On the whole, it is fair to say that the confidence shown in law and government in 1916 was misplaced. The response of the nation to the 1918 flu did not work at all in the way Herman Biggs might have hoped.

• • •

Because the Spanish flu did not affect all parts of the country equally or at the same time, various regions sought ways to defend themselves, ranging from mask orders to the closing of establishments or some combination of these measures. While many of these efforts undoubtedly helped prevent further spread of the flu, elected officials sometimes took drastic steps with faulty information about how the flu was spread.[51] Some believed that eating particular foods caused the disease. Others, like officials at the University of Minnesota, believed that "germs lurked in the dust," and they ordered streets to be swept and refuse burned. That was insufficient for the health officer of Saint Paul, who threatened to use police, if necessary, when university officials refused to postpone the fall semester.[52]

Perhaps the worst confusion involved claims by laboratories, drug companies, medical researchers, and health officials that vaccines could prevent the flu. There were dozens of competitors offering so-called vaccines to the public, none of which had any effect at all.[53] Chicago offered vaccines developed at the Mayo Clinic, and San Francisco received a shipment of vaccines from Boston. As historian John Barry wrote, some desperate physicians even tried the relatively new typhoid vaccines, and many physicians administered quinine, a malaria drug, "with no better reasoning than desperation."[54]

Scientists could not find an effective vaccine because they fundamentally misunderstood what caused influenza. The prevailing theory was that it was a bacterium. It would take nearly two more decades before researchers determined it was a virus, and the first effective influenza vaccine would not be available for civilian use until 1946. Not only was there no cure, but without a vaccine there was also no way to prevent the spread of flu except through measures intended to limit public gatherings and promote the wearing of face coverings.

Despite all of this, a resigned and terrified population mostly complied with orders from elected officials, at least during the worst months of the fall wave. (Those ordered into complete isolation were too sick to be outside of home anyway.) For the safety of their parishioners, many church leaders grudgingly acquiesced with restrictive orders, including the Archdiocese of Chicago, which suspended services, confirmations, and other ceremonies.[55] Perhaps Americans turned against each other less in 1918 than they did during the COVID pandemic a century later because the war effort (and the propaganda that accompanied it) had provided some degree of unity against a common enemy. Even then, there was substantial dissent to America's participation in the war and the unprecedented suppression of that dissent. The armistice on November 11 brought only limited relief to deep rifts in American society. Americans had already turned against each other on issues of race. Race riots and indiscriminate killing of Blacks intensified after the war's end, including in Chicago in 1919, where a week-long killing spree resulted in thirty-eight deaths. Chicago's was the most severe of more than two dozen race riots throughout the nation in 1919's "red summer."[56]

If the average citizen was too exhausted to mount much of a protest to influenza restrictions, that was certainly not true everywhere. But residents sometimes turned to the courts to challenge these measures— not surprisingly, perhaps, given US legal traditions and strong notions of individual liberties among Americans. In response, state and local judges routinely upheld restrictive measures. For example, residents of Globe, Arizona, objected to their local health board's order closing "all theaters, motion picture shows, banks, business houses, pool halls, shooting galleries, lodges, schools, and churches," throwing in for good measure "any other place people are congregated." The Supreme Court of Arizona was unsympathetic to the complaining residents and upheld local authority: "Necessity is the law of time and place, and the emergency calls into life the necessity . . . to exercise the power to protect the public health."[57] The influenza epidemic, like an "act of God" in legal parlance, took precedence over what judges might privately view to be unnecessary measures by government officials.

No judge at any court level seemed willing to set individual liberties against the US Supreme Court's 1905 decision in *Jacobson v. Massachusetts*. The Supreme Court had recognized that local health emergencies required local solutions, and judges should not second-guess those decisions: "Upon the principle of self-defense, of paramount necessity, a community has the right to protect itself against an epidemic of disease which threatens the safety of its members." As the Supreme Court of Illinois would state in 1922:

> There is probably not a Legislature in the country that would have named the deadly Spanish influenza as a contagious and infectious disease prior to the epidemic of that disease that took a greater toll of lives throughout the country than any other epidemic known in this country. In emergencies of this character, it is indispensable to the preservation of public health that some administrative body should be clothed with authority to make adequate rules which have the force of law, and to put these rules and regulations into effect promptly.[58]

Interestingly, most lawsuits challenged which level of government had the authority to make the decision, not whether a particular measure itself violated someone's individual freedom or liberty. The citizens of Globe believed the school board could by law make its own decisions about whether to remain open, but the Arizona Supreme Court ruled instead that the health officer had that authority.[59] In another example, a small town in Idaho ended up defying the apparatus of the state when it sought the kind of quarantine last seen during yellow fever outbreaks in the South. Not even the state's judiciary could force the town of Challis, Idaho, to back down.

In October 1918 residents of Challis, in central Idaho, watched with alarm as the flu made its way toward them from the west and south. The population of about five thousand lived near the Salmon River, relatively secluded by natural topography except for the three highways connecting to other towns not far away. Challis was the center of government for Custer County, established in 1881. It was also the home of Dr. Charles Luther Kirtley, the county's one-man board of health and the town's only physician.

Quarantine lines, like those established during earlier yellow fever epidemics, were extremely rare during the flu epidemic, except for quarantines around military bases imposed by the military itself. But Challis tried. When the city of Boise reported flu cases that October, Challis residents posted guards on all roads and highways leading into their town. No one could enter without first spending four days in quarantine, to make sure they weren't carrying the flu.[60]

When Dr. Kirtley ordered the local sheriff to arrest six men he claimed "had run the quarantine," they sought the help of Judge Frederick Cowen, a district judge whose jurisdiction included Challis. Judge Cowen ordered their release, but process servers could not get through the quarantine lines. Guards also turned back county commissioners and a federal officer, and courthouse business shut down entirely. Even US mail was blocked for over a month.

Alarmed at the situation, Judge Cowen went to Challis in person, taking with him the local US attorney, but they were turned back by a crowd of angry citizens. Judge Cowen called on the sheriff to disperse the crowd so he could pass, but the sheriff refused and insisted that Judge Cowen would either have to turn back or be arrested.[61] As a local newspaper described, "Hundreds of citizens, both men and women, are barricading the roads leading into the Challis section of Custer County, to keep District Judge Cowen from breaking what they allege to be an established quarantine against the flu." Judge Cowen informed the governor that "bloodshed was feared because of the bitterness shown."[62] The state attorney general notified the officials at Challis that they must permit officials of the county, state, and nation to pass back and forth without interference.

Despite all efforts, however, the flu inevitably broke through the Challis quarantine line in mid-November, with more than twenty cases reported within weeks. Dr. Kirtley blamed some "enterprising traveler who forded the river in order to get by the quarantine guards."[63] The citizens of Challis blamed Judge Cowen for making Dr. Kirtley go to his courtroom in Mackey. In Dr. Kirtley's short absence the epidemic spread rapidly, the *Challis Messenger* alleged.[64]

The Idaho Supreme Court finally took up the matter two years later, long after the influenza threat was gone. The chief justice and two of his colleagues believed Challis officials to have been in the wrong.

Two dissenting justices, while conceding that the conduct had been reprehensible, pointed out that it had been a time of emergency. Even if mistaken, the sheriff and Dr. Kirtley believed their quarantine orders took precedence over anything else. As Judge Alfred Budge wrote in his lengthy dissent, the people of Challis "were panic-stricken, even to the extent that they barricaded themselves against officers of the federal and state government."[65]

The story of Challis, Idaho, was unusual because communities elsewhere relied on methods we would today term "social distancing"; rather than cut off commerce entirely, medical authorities encouraged limits on public gatherings. But the residents of Challis demonstrated the natural human reaction to a deadly contagion—the shotgun quarantine so ridiculed in the American South in the previous century.

• • •

While medical experts could not always agree on the steps local governments should take to prevent the spread of the flu, the most widely recommended were restricting public gatherings and the mandatory use of face masks in public, although, as the *New York Times* reported on December 13, 1918, health officials in some of America's larger cities "opposed both these measures and placed great reliance on [the development of a] vaccine."[66]

When local governments ordered residents to wear face masks outside their homes, they often had to make their own; masks were not available for purchase. The Red Cross organized volunteers to make masks and distributed them free throughout the nation. But more were needed. On September 28, 1918, the *Boston Daily Globe* instructed readers how to make a gauze mask; the Boston commissioner of health urged his constituents to "make any kind of a mask, any kind of a covering for the nose and mouth and use it immediately and at all times. Even a handkerchief held in place over the face is better than nothing."[67]

Compulsory face-mask laws were not popular. News reports noted resistance in many towns across the nation. The local health officer might order it; whether the police chief would enforce it was another matter. Tucson, Arizona, even featured what a local reporter called "influenza court," to handle the cases of citizens who had been issued citations for not wearing face masks, or not wearing them properly (including cutting holes in masks to smoke). The police chief declared, "We are going to enforce this ordinance or close up the town entirely." Fines were ten dollars, about half the average weekly wage. Judges would listen to excuses, although they were rarely countenanced. One day in court, twenty-eight people appealed for relief from the ten-dollar fine. None were excused, although some were creative. The judge noted that "when one's mask is in the wash, it is no exemption from wearing it." (Presumably one should stay home on wash day—or have more than one mask.) One resident wanted only "a brief privilege of fresh air"; he hated that the privilege cost him a week's wages. The judge also held that "a pink muffler is not a legal substitute for a mask."[68]

San Francisco's face-mask requirement was generally accepted by its citizens, with one notable exception. Under the alarming headline, "Refuses to Don Influenza Mask; Shot by Officer," a reporter described how the attempted arrest of a man for his refusal to wear a face mask led to a shooting in San Francisco. On October 27, 1918, a special officer for the board of health named Henry D. Miller shot and severely wounded James Wisser, described as "a horseshoer," in front of a downtown drugstore following Wisser's refusal to don an influenza mask. Scores of passersby scurried for cover as shots rang out. According to conflicting accounts, when Miller attempted to arrest Wisser for not wearing a mask, Wisser either pulled a gun on the officer or at least struggled with him before Miller drew his own revolver and fired it, perhaps accidentally or as a warning—it's unclear. In any event, Wisser was wounded and taken to the central emergency hospital for treatment—then placed under arrest for failure to comply with Miller's order.[69]

A study in 2007 asked what pandemic planners could learn from the social-distancing measures imposed during the 1918–19 pandemic. The authors concluded that school closures, public-gathering bans, transportation restrictions, limited closure of businesses, and even face-mask ordinances almost certainly mitigated the consequences of what they termed "the most deadly contagious calamity in human history." The 1918 experience, they wrote, teaches that sustained social-distancing measures are beneficial, and need to be "on" throughout the particular peak of a local experience. Despite the lack of an effective vaccine, US cities that "were able to organize and execute a suite of classic public health interventions before the pandemic swept fully through the city" appeared to do better than those that did not.[70] Judges routinely had upheld the emergency measures identified in the study, recognizing the need to defer to health authorities in the face of the unknown.

• • •

Although the 1918 flu epidemic is often portrayed as indiscriminate in its choice of victims, the burdens of the disease fell quite differently on the rich and poor, and on persons of different races. Any airborne contagion is capable of infecting without discrimination; it only needs human-to-human contact to keep spreading. As historian Patricia J. Fanning pointed out, as late as the 1970s the conventional wisdom remained that the 1918 flu, compared to other epidemic diseases like typhoid, "ignored the differences between rural and urban, patrician and peasant, capitalist and proletarian, and struck them all down in similar proportions."[71] That simply wasn't true. In 1931, the US Public Health Service published a study showing "marked and consistent differences" in influenza's effects among persons of different economic status. The conclusion: "The mortality rate for the very poor was nearly three times that of the well-to-do."[72] The economic losses caused by the pandemic, not merely by mandatory restrictions on businesses, also fell disproportionately on those with the least means, just as rich states fared better than poorer ones.

Racial discrimination played a significant role. African Americans and people of mixed race had little access to doctors and were refused admission to "white" hospitals, especially in the South. Native Americans living on reservations in the continental United States died by the thousands; no one is really sure of the precise number.[73] In theory, the federal government was in charge of health services for Native Americans, but the reality was woeful. In 1919, the US Public Health Service believed 4 percent to 6 percent of Native Americans living in Arizona, Colorado, New Mexico, and Utah died of the flu. Mortality was high in groups who were too sick to care for themselves, which was true of many tribal populations who were the responsibility of the federal Bureau of Indian Affairs.[74] The predicament for natives in Alaska was even more dire. Alaska was a US territory when flu broke out in October 1918. Before the epidemic was over, officials in Alaska estimated that at least 90 percent of flu deaths occurred among the native population. In Nome and its environs, at least 75 percent of the so-called Eskimos died. Governor Thomas Riggs Jr. described the spread of the Spanish flu among the Native Americans plainly: "The natives showed absolutely no resistance."[75]

Prisoners were another overlooked population. Influenza could rip through a county jail or a state prison system in a short time, with guards absent because they themselves were ill. At least one judge decided to do something about it. James W. McCarthy, a district judge in Hudson County, New Jersey, was said to be the first from the judiciary to order all county prisoners with minor offenses set free, a "worthy and humane act" according to local press.[76] Nationwide, I could find no statistics for deaths in jails, either of prisoners or guards.

. . .

The 1918–19 flu epidemic wrought unprecedented devastation across the world and throughout the United States. Hardship, fear, and dejection accompanied the nearly complete shutdown of social life in many US cities. Yet it also brought out a remarkable spirit of charity. For those who lived through the pandemic, the lifting of bans on public gatherings brought great celebration. The *Los Angeles Times* noted the "fiesta spirit" that pervaded that city, bringing to an end the city's "longest funless" season. On December 3, 1918, the paper reported, "From the depression of closed theaters and other places of amusement, closed churches and assembly halls, the city reacted yesterday to the spirit of gladness." People who had been "staying closely at home for weeks" joined the throngs downtown to celebrate, shop, attend a movie. Stores were filled with shoppers, and "long lines of people reached even out into the corridors at the Public Library."[77]

A return to normalcy occurred throughout the nation as public-gathering bans were gradually lifted. People celebrated when the worst was past—not even knowing that the Roaring Twenties were right around the corner. In the upbeat mood of the decade that followed the pandemic, it perhaps seemed unnecessary to reflect on the lessons that the ravaging flu could teach. Among the lessons were some about public health law.

Laws that in 1916 seemed to ensure that health officers could meet any disease emergency had not worked as expected, if they were consulted at all. Worse, it was often not clear to the average citizen who, if anyone, was in charge during an epidemic. Probably no one was more disappointed by this outcome than Dr. Herman Biggs. After all, he had held out New York law as a model for other states. What did Biggs conclude about America's response to the flu catastrophe? Did the model law that Biggs suggested for other states even work for New York?

While many of his colleagues from the 1916 Academy of Medicine conference experienced the influenza pandemic as US military officers, Biggs remained as New York's state commissioner of health for the duration. Biggs was probably the most respected health officer in the nation, at any level of government. Before he was named to the state's top health post, Biggs had made the New York City health department an internationally respected institution. But he had no say in what measures New York City actually implemented to control the flu. That was up to the city's board of health and the mayor. His jurisdiction was the rest of the state. In that role, he advised local health officers on the medical aspects of treating patients and when, or whether, to close schools or limit public gatherings. He engaged in a massive public education campaign, beginning with a public warning to state residents in late September. Biggs spelled out the dangers of this new influenza, especially the dangerous pneumonia that "frequently developed from it." Those who had symptoms "should rest at home in bed until they were fully recovered." Everyone else should avoid poorly ventilated or crowded places.[78]

But as the situation worsened that fall, Biggs was stuck with the dilemma that faced health officers everywhere. The traditional means of containing an epidemic, including the strict use of quarantine, was "not practical in view of the highly contagious character and the widespread extent of the malady and the general susceptibility to it."[79] After the worst had passed, Biggs wrote about what had transpired. "The question naturally arises," he said, "as to how such a pandemic of disease should be possible at the present time."[80] Daily newspapers from October and November had given "full indication of the almost hopeless, helpless attitude of the authorities toward the outbreak." Part of that was a science problem—"Very little has as yet been added to our actual knowledge, although the disease has been prevailing almost continuously either in Spain or France or Great Britain or the United States for nearly a year." Biggs was immensely skeptical of the various vaccines offered to the public because "we have even now no definite information" as to the precise contagion. This lack of knowledge meant the rapidity of the spread of influenza was limited only by the rapidity of transportation. "The disease is carried from place to place by persons, not things," Biggs emphasized. "There is no mystery about its spread, and it is perfectly possible by proper isolation, although it is not usually practicable, to protect a group or a community from the infection."[81]

Biggs did have a specific suggestion to avoid such calamities in the future. America needed a better way to "formulate administrative measures to deal with epidemics."

> There does not exist in any country an institution or an organization which has the resources, the personnel, or the facilities, for immediately taking up the study of such a problem, when it presents itself, or which contemplates within its program of work the investigation of such problems. It is manifestly not for our local or State authorities to undertake such a work and the Federal Government has no facilities for it. Neither the United States Public Health Service, nor the Medical Service of the Army or the Navy is equipped for such a study—and there is no scientific institution prepared for such work.

Biggs foresaw the need for institutions that did not yet exist in the United States but would be created later: the federal Centers for Disease Control and the National Institutes of Health. "There are many public-health problems which ought to be dealt with as research problems," Biggs wrote. But there had been "very little real research devoted to the questions of public health, administration and policy." It was of the utmost urgency to provide for "an institution or an organization which can undertake the study of such world health problems as influenza presents, and which shall be prepared to take up the investigation at once, and anywhere and at any time."[82]

When Herman Biggs died of pneumonia in 1923 at the age of sixty-three, tributes poured in from around the world for his scientific achievements. Historian Howard Markel pointed to an additional quality: Biggs was "the very model of a public health officer" because he was also a talented communicator and politician.[83] Biggs preached the doctrine, "Public health is purchasable." Biggs believed disease to be "largely a removable evil," brought about by harsh economic and social conditions that could be remedied. "No duty of society, acting through its governmental agencies, is paramount to this obligation," he said."[84] The 1918 influenza pandemic proved to be the greatest challenge of his life. One hundred years later, the United States would face nearly identical challenges of governance in response to another new virus—COVID-19.

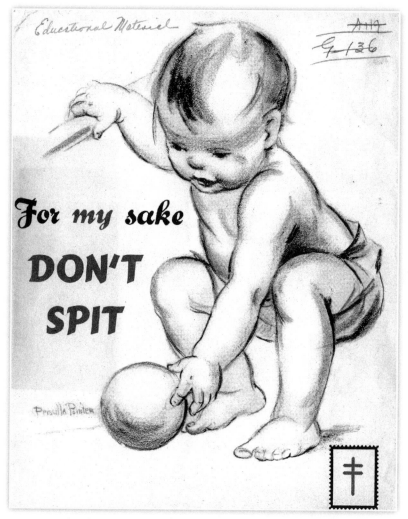

National Tuberculosis Association anti-spitting campaign poster, 1943.

CONFRONTING TUBERCULOSIS

Homeless, friendless, dissolute, destitute, dissipated, and vicious persons suffering with this disease, are those most likely to neglect all the necessary precautions and to be most dangerous to the community. If not cared for in an institution . . . , they disseminate infection in every place which they visit. Such cases must be provided for by the sanitary authorities at any cost and must, when necessary, be forcibly removed to a hospital and there permanently detained.

—DR. HERMAN M. BIGGS (1912)[1]

In the 1920s, viral diseases continued to mystify scientists in Europe as well as America. The highest priority was to determine, definitively, whether influenza was caused by bacteria or by a yet undiscovered virus—an urgent matter indeed, because medical experts feared the imminent return of another influenza pandemic. The 1918 flu, after all, had faded away as mysteriously as it had begun, after a third and final wave in the spring of 1919. In the aftermath, Surgeon General Rupert Blue had gone before Congress to request federal money to study influenza. He would get none. One reason was the opposition of James Phelan, the former San Francisco mayor, now an elected US Senator from California.[2] Phelan's infamous clashes with the US Public Health Service during San Francisco's bubonic plague outbreak obviously still rankled, a grudge evident almost two decades later.

Progress came in the 1930s when scientists isolated an influenza virus, but many more years would pass before that knowledge could be translated into an effective flu vaccine. In the meantime, scientists discovered a second virus that they named Influenza B, underscoring just how much had yet to be learned.[3] In the immediate wake of the 1918 pandemic, the specter of another devastating strain of influenza would haunt the rest of the century.

This uncertainty is why, in 1939, Dr. Wilbur A. Sawyer of the Rockefeller Institute identified "virus diseases" to be of the utmost importance for health officials. They not only needed new methods to identify viral diseases but also had to find practical and effective means to control them. Dr. Sawyer mentioned polio as one example of a virus that health officials did not know how to control, let alone cure. But he emphasized, above all, "the influenza group" of viruses in order to "illustrate how far the unknown still exceeds the known."[4] In 1918, the only way to control the spread of influenza had been to separate the sick from the well and to limit public gatherings as much as possible. Face masks helped, too. Otherwise, health officers had been helpless.

The 1918 influenza pandemic stymied even Dr. Herman Biggs, America's premiere medical scientist and researcher. Biggs died a decade before the etiology of influenza was settled. Like most researchers of the day, Biggs had believed the cause to be bacterial. It was natural for him to think so because throughout his career, he had focused on germ theory and the new strides in bacteriology long underway in Germany. One discovery, in particular, had caught his attention. In 1882, Robert Koch isolated the bacterium that caused tuberculosis, from the sputum of patients. Not only did Koch discover the infectious agent, *Mycobacterium,* but he also established that tuberculosis was a contagious disease.[5] With this new knowledge, Biggs would make the control of tuberculosis in populations his life's work.

For centuries, pulmonary tuberculosis (TB) was believed to be an inherited condition or the fault of a sufferer's weak constitution. Partly this belief was due to the prolonged, asymptomatic period between exposure to the disease and the development of active symptoms. And it did tend to run in families.[6] The discovery that tuberculosis was contagious, able to spread from person to person, was so shocking to American doctors that for decades many would not accept the theory. Herman Biggs, however, was a believer, and he soon became the leading American expert on tuberculosis and its leading advocate to end it. When Biggs preached that "public health is purchasable," he had in mind, above all, tuberculosis—that "greatest remaining disease scourge of the civilized world."[7] Relief from this scourge was purchasable through tax dollars that improved living conditions and sanitation, but for tuberculosis an additional cost would be to individual civil liberties.

Tuberculosis had been one of the most terrible plagues of all. Europe had long known tuberculosis as "consumption," sometimes called "the white plague" because of the paleness of sufferers who slowly wasted away from the illness. Experts estimate that by 1800, tuberculosis had killed one in seven people who had ever lived.[8] Throughout the nineteenth and early twentieth centuries, more Americans died from tuberculosis than from any other cause.[9] But it was not a dramatic killer like smallpox, cholera, or yellow fever. The disease developed slowly, ravaging the lungs and sometimes debilitating victims for years before it killed them.

Although a cure for tuberculosis would have to wait for the discovery of antibiotics in the 1940s, knowing that it was a contagious disease meant that something might be done to prevent it. The beginning of the twentieth century was a key moment for health officials to assert government authority to curb its spread. Stamping out contagious disease in communities had long been the specialty of health officers, who were accustomed to preventing outbreaks of cholera, smallpox, typhoid, and the like. As more of the American medical profession accepted the contagion theory for tuberculosis, health officers added it to their portfolios.

It was not an easy transition. Tuberculosis would remain a priority of local health departments for the rest of the century, even to the present.

• • •

The first effort to control the spread of tuberculosis began with bans on spitting. Because Koch and other scientists isolated the tuberculosis bacteria in saliva, health officials first tried to convince Americans to change their promiscuous habit of spitting in public. Herman Biggs drafted the first anti-spitting ordinance for New York City in 1896. Soon, medical experts urged local governments everywhere to ban spitting in public places, and municipal anti-spitting ordinances sprang up throughout the nation in the years leading up to World War I.[10] Journalists took up the cause as well. Under the provocative title "Spitting and Murdering," a news article in 1904 claimed that "the most important method of distribution of the tuberculosis bacillus is probably promiscuous spitting." Spitting "used to be entirely a matter of manners," the author continued. "It has of late years become also a matter of morals. The man who spits in public places increases the death rate."[11]

Restrictions on individual liberties during an epidemic scare were nothing new in the American experience at the turn of the twentieth century. When smallpox, yellow fever, or measles appeared in a community, local authorities ordered school closures, quarantines, and travel restrictions as urgent but temporary responses to an immediate threat. Spitting bans were something new, though. These were not intended as temporary health measures but were permanent, applicable to all.

Robert J. Newton, secretary of the St. Louis Municipal Commission on Tuberculosis, reported to the *New York Times* in 1910 that "the tuberculosis war is spreading throughout the union." Based on a national survey, Newton estimated that twenty-five million Americans "have been forbidden by law to expectorate in public places." Seven states had anti-spitting laws applicable statewide, including Massachusetts, Maine, New Hampshire, Rhode Island, Pennsylvania, Kansas, and Texas. An additional seventy-four cities enacted municipal ordinances. As to the penalty, "The cheapest place to spit in is Indianapolis," Newton reported, "where people paid an average of 78 cents" in fines. Baltimore, Pittsburgh, Kansas City, and Spokane fined offenders one dollar for each offense. Newton lamented that one-third of cities with populations over thirty thousand did not respond to the survey, making it fair to assume that they had no laws on the subject.[12]

Enforcement was another matter, Newton reported. In sixteen cities, health officers could issue citations to offenders, while in eleven other cities those duties were shared with police officers. According to the survey, a total of 3,421 spitting arrests were made throughout the nation in 1909, "undoubtedly all males," the author opined. "Nine cities," Newton said, "were honest enough to say that no one enforced the law." In Canton, Ohio, the mayor alone had the power to enforce the ordinance, and he made exactly one arrest during 1909. In Cincinnati, prosecutors had difficulty securing witnesses, citing one instance when "women agreed to appear as witnesses, but failed to do so." The health officer in Jacksonville, Florida, offered the excuse, "This being a tourist city, it was deemed inadvisable to enforce the law." In Lincoln, Nebraska, the response was one sentence: "Strangers spit, but town people do not." A health officer of an unidentified city wrote, "I do not believe that the enforcement of a spitting ordinance . . . would materially help in abating the spitting nuisance. You cannot cure the spitting habit by arresting spitters."[13]

The National Tuberculosis Association, an umbrella organization for private charitable organizations, commissioned the survey. The war against tuberculosis, in fact, was a massive public education campaign begun by local organizations such as the Pennsylvania Society for the Prevention of Tuberculosis, organized in 1892, followed by the New York City Tuberculosis Committee (led by Herman Biggs) in 1902 and the Chicago Tuberculosis Institute in 1906. Chambers of commerce and insurance companies joined the campaign. In 1907, the Red Cross began its Christmas seals campaign, a wildly successful endeavor over the next four decades as it gained public endorsements from presidents Calvin Coolidge, Woodrow Wilson, and Franklin Roosevelt. Funds from the sale of Christmas seals were used initially to educate the public about tuberculosis but over time were used to provide free screening services, including expensive mobile X-ray units for local health departments.[14] Historian Frank Snowden reported that by 1920, tuberculosis associations existed in every state in the union.[15] Among other successes of the war on tuberculosis, the common drinking cup used at schools and public fountains in communities everywhere slowly became a thing of the past.

Some thought the war against tuberculosis went too far. Tuberculosis sufferers were publicly shunned and found it difficult to obtain lodgings and employment.[16] The *New York Tribune* published a particularly forceful critique:

> The American people and their officials, animated with zeal not according to knowledge, are in danger of going to senseless and cruel extremes in hunting down consumptives. There is a tendency on the part of people who have grasped the idea of the infectious nature of this disease to become panic-stricken and act as badly as we from time to time see communities doing when they burn down contagious disease hospitals.[17]

The writer continued, "In California and Colorado talk of barring invalids from other states has been heard, and there is danger that the common and natural anxiety to guard against consumption may be indulged with a heartlessness more characteristic of the Middle Ages."[18] Federal immigration officials even got into the act. A new ruling by the commissioner of immigration called for a stricter examination of immigrants at Ellis Island and threatened to deport all noncitizens already in the country who had "tuberculosis of the lungs."[19]

Public scorn of spitters was one thing, but health officials also began to actively hunt down tuberculosis sufferers. The first step was a new reporting requirement imposed on physicians. Beginning in New York City in 1897, physicians were required by law to report to the health department any patient they suspected of having tuberculosis. Understandably, physicians were reluctant to do so, given the potentially dire consequences to their patients, including termination from employment and eviction from their living quarters. The wealthy learned which physicians were willing to conceal cases, and they had other means to hide from health authorities more effectively than their poorer counterparts.[20] Above all, no one wanted to end up forcibly detained for weeks on end, especially not as one of the persons whom Herman Biggs described in 1912 as "homeless, friendless, dissolute, destitute, dissipated, [or] vicious."[21]

• • •

In the early decades of the twentieth century, the control of tuberculosis and other diseases was the responsibility of local governments.

From the 1920s to the 1940s, however, some state governments began to play a more active part against tuberculosis. By 1916, thirty states operated what they termed "sanatoriums," or hospitals exclusively for tuberculosis patients.[22] Because "treatment" required a lengthy stay, the wealthy avoided these public institutions entirely and sought out private establishments, which had both better accommodations and less strict rules. Neither public nor private sanatoriums could actually cure tuberculosis; the institutions run by the state (even those originally founded with private money) came to be seen primarily as a means to isolate sick patients so that they could not infect others.

These new state tuberculosis hospitals followed a long tradition of "seeking the cure" in better climates, preferably dry, warm, and mountainous. By the turn of the century, entrepreneurs in America's Southwest established hundreds of sanatoriums for tuberculosis sufferers, capitalizing on their despair. Some were well run and supervised by a physician; all were distinctly better than the crackpot operation that Dr. John Croghan established deep inside Mammoth Cave in Kentucky in the 1840s. Croghan subjected his patients to conditions that made their symptoms worse, not better.[23]

Well into the 1940s, physicians continued to prescribe warm, dry climates for "rest cures" for those with the disease, and thousands moved to the Southwest in a bid to preserve their health. A veritable tuberculosis industry had long operated there. In 1880, New Mexico alone had more than fifty sanatoriums across the state, and that number grew exponentially as entrepreneurial towns and private physicians got into the act. New Mexico's Bureau of Immigration wasted no time advertising the territory's healing climate. A circular it produced claimed "the lowest death rate from tubercular disease in America." The bureau partnered with railroads to distribute its brochures, including one in 1898, complete with testimonials from physicians, claiming "a ticket to New Mexico . . . costs less than the doctor's visits."[24] The Roane brothers (from chapter 2) were returning home from one such establishment when they were trapped by a yellow fever quarantine at Holly Springs, Mississippi, in 1905.

As the contagious nature of tuberculosis became more widely accepted, not only New Mexico but also Texas and Arizona came to regret the extensive advertising for patients and their governments' laissez-faire attitude toward privately run sanatoriums. The thousands arriving each year were now seen as dangerous to the public, with every case a potential source of disease. In 1915, Ernest Sweet, a US Public Health Service officer, observed that each year "10,000 consumptives who are hopelessly diseased go West to die."[25] The "great belief in the efficacy of climate" was the leading factor, and Sweet blamed their travel on the recommendation of physicians in the East who could do nothing for them. Charity organizations and city and county authorities, too, were at fault. They preferred "to furnish transportation rather than quarters and care, and relief societies have found that it is much cheaper in the end to provide tickets, even to far eastern points, to patients who have no chance of recovery than to care for them during their last days and to provide burial at the end."[26]

The advertising was largely abandoned after the wrong sort—the desperately poor and those unable to work or earn a living—began arriving at train depots. But the "evil effects" of this health tourism, as Dr. Sweet put it, continued for decades. The floodgates were open to anyone who could pay for a train ticket. This created tensions, especially in Texas and New Mexico, as local officials were inundated with "vagrants" from outside who threatened to spread tuberculosis more widely.

Not only was there no magical cure awaiting these patients in the Southwest, but their traveling on trains was an especially bad idea. Dr. Sweet emphasized this point:

> At El Paso a patient, friendless, unattended, and too poor to afford a berth in the sleeper, was being transferred from one train to another by the railroad attendants when he collapsed and died in his chair. A tuberculous invalid en route to San Antonio died in a drawing room of a Pullman when within a few miles of his destination. In the year 1912, on trains running into Albuquerque alone there occurred five deaths from tuberculosis, and since 1904 there has been an average of two a year. These facts are indubitable proof that the advanced cases that travel are still far too numerous.[27]

Sweet wrote that any tuberculosis patient dying within thirty days after arrival ought never to have been sent, and he was appalled that railroad companies allowed obviously ill tuberculosis patients to board at all: "Pullman cars accept for transit all classes, the sick and the well. People who are severely ill do not purchase their own transportation and they are often brought to trains on stretchers, to be loaded into a car by way of a window." To make matters worse, "The ordinary traveler is filthy beyond belief. A day coach at the completion of a 600-mile run is a sorry spectacle. Bread, meat, pickles, and banana skins litter the floor, sputum is everywhere. No remedy for promiscuous spitting, the greatest evil, has yet been found."[28]

By 1940, the situation was even worse, due in no small part to the continuing economic displacement of the Great Depression. Dr. William B. Grayson, the state health officer of Arkansas and president of the national conference of state and territorial health officials, emphasized the costs associated with migrant tuberculosis sufferers. Traditionally, local governments assumed responsibility for medical care of the destitute in their midst in order to contain contagious disease, if not for humanitarian reasons. A problem "that is facing us today is that of the migratory indigent medical care case," Grayson said, especially in western states where "traveling tuberculosis cases have produced a most difficult public health problem." Grayson thought the care of these patients should be "a three-way governmental responsibility"—shared among the federal government, the "state where the patient is at present," and the state "from which the patient came or the state of legal residence."[29] The location where the patient needed medical care might not have the resources to provide it, or local residents might refuse to spend their tax dollars on strangers in their midst—especially ones thought to pose a danger of spreading disease. The cost problem was significant because housing and treating tuberculosis patients to keep them separated from the community meant months or even years, until the patient died.

A century ago, the tradition of "poor laws" permitted one town to recoup expenditures on nonresidents from that person's town of residence.[30] But town poor laws soon would fade into history, especially for the extended, expensive care of tuberculosis patients. The poor laws of the nineteenth century came from simpler times—when populations were smaller and less mobile and before the advent of speedy rail travel could move tuberculosis sufferers across many states in less than a day. Rather than accept the premise that care of indigent patients was a local financial responsibility, Texas and other western states (no doubt copied elsewhere) began to "warn out" consumptives, often putting them on trains to other locations, to shift the migrant problem elsewhere. In 1911, Texas passed legislation in a further attempt to rid itself of the "traveling tuberculosis cases" Grayson had described. A sponsor of the bill noted: "Consumption has wrought more want and woe and misery and suffering to the human race than have all the wars, pestilences and famines in the history of the world, and today it is running riot in the heyday of its destructive course." The bill provided for "tent colonies" to be located in different parts of the state, but these would be limited to state residents only. Even that was not a real solution, a critic noted, because only the destitute would go to the encampments. Patients with means would continue to flock to private sanatoriums for treatment.[31]

. . .

One explanation for the sweeping growth of tuberculosis migrants is that beginning in the 1920s, local health officials took increasingly aggressive measures against anyone suspected of having the disease. These measures included, especially, the detention hospital first advocated by Herman Biggs and later emulated throughout the nation. Patients who were formally committed to one of these institutions could not leave until "cured." Before antibiotics brought any hope of a cure, however, state tuberculosis hospitals acquired the reputation of being places where one was sent to die. Better to take one's chances elsewhere. It is fair to conclude that an unknown but large number of migrants traveled west not just in the hope of a cure but to avoid mandatory detention in a state-run facility.

Tuberculosis was not the only target of newly aggressive measures by health officers in the era between the two world wars. In fact, that period stands out for the extreme use of quarantine by some government officials. Perhaps in reaction to the helplessness health officials felt against pandemic influenza in 1918, the 1920s saw a renewed zeal to control diseases thought to be better understood.

Tuberculosis may have been the more urgent problem after the disappearance of the 1918 flu, but in the years between the two world wars, health officers throughout the nation focused their mission on stamping out venereal disease as well. This would come to have lasting impact on the way health officials would manage TB patients or those suspected of carrying the disease. The process began with a federal mandate to prevent sexually transmitted disease in troops massed for training at US military bases before World War I.[32] Health boards sought to limit the spread of venereal disease not by investigating soldiers but by targeting women with "loose morals." Police officers rounded up women rumored to be prostitutes, or those with a flamboyant lifestyle, and kept them in jail until they submitted to medical testing.

The harassment and imprisonment of lower-class women was part of a decades-long, coordinated push that became known as the "American plan," carried out from the 1910s into the 1950s, to combat sexually transmitted diseases. The story is compellingly told by Scott W. Stern in *The Trials of Nina McCall*.[33] Health officials routinely publicly humiliated women who were believed to suffer from a sexually transmitted disease. Edna Woods of Seattle was one of those caught up in the hunt. In 1918, Woods was arrested as a "disorderly person," a broad legal category mostly used to arrest suspected prostitutes. At the city jail, health department officials forcibly examined Woods and placed her under quarantine in the jail's hospital ward. She demanded to be examined by her own physician, promising to remain quarantined in her home while under her physician's care. Woods's attorney went to court to plead for her release, offering to post a substantial bond to ensure that she would comply with her promise. The judge denied her petition, stating simply that the local health board's decisions would not be questioned by the courts. Woods remained in jail for the duration of her treatment, directed by a doctor not of her own choosing.

In Los Angeles, in 1923, Marie Clemente was arrested by order of the city's health department, to be held in jail until she submitted to an examination to determine whether she had a venereal disease. The order was based entirely on the allegation that Clemente conducted a "house of ill fame." She, like Woods, refused to submit to a jailhouse exam. She would eventually relent, only because the judge hearing the matter approved her continued imprisonment until she did so.[34] There were many more like Woods and Clemente. Kansas, for example, ran a "Quarantine Hospital for Women," where women arrested by local police were sent merely on suspicion of having a venereal disease.[35]

Women were not the only victims of such high-handed treatment of persons with venereal disease. The most infamous abuse of medical authority over venereal disease patients was the Tuskegee syphilis study. Beginning in 1932, the US Public Health Service enlisted six hundred African American men from Macon County, Alabama, to participate in a scientific experiment on syphilis titled the "Tuskegee Study of Untreated Syphilis in the Negro Male." Over the next forty years, this governmental medical experiment allowed hundreds of men with syphilis to go untreated, even though penicillin would cure it, so that scientists could study the effects of the disease.[36] By the time the AP broke the story, seven men had died of syphilis and more than 150 of heart failure that may or may not have been linked to syphilis. Participants who were still alive in 1997 received an apology on behalf of the nation from President Bill Clinton. In stark language, Clinton described a "clearly racist" study orchestrated by the federal government: "That can never be allowed to happen again."[37]

These episodes reveal that by the 1920s, health officers, especially those at the local level, had amassed enormous authority—power over others that could be misused. In many towns, the most powerful government official might well be the health officer, with unchecked authority over one's freedom and livelihood. Would courts intervene if that power were abused?

The answer came in a closely watched case from the Illinois Supreme Court in 1922. While that case was not about tuberculosis, it set the terms for how health officials would handle TB for the rest of the century, long after state quarantine and isolation laws were used for any other disease.

The case involved typhoid, but the victim was not the better-known Typhoid Mary, a cook who spent twenty-six years in quarantine in New York even though she herself never had the disease. The story of Mary Mallon, the first asymptomatic carrier of typhoid to be confined by a quarantine order, is tragic and well known.[38] But history has overlooked a number of Typhoid Marys, including the one who sparked the important court decision that would guide decisions about tuberculosis for decades.

Jennie Barmore, from Chicago, was thought to be, like Mary Mallon, a carrier of typhoid, though she never had any symptoms of the disease. When Chicago health officials ordered Barmore to be quarantined, she lost her boardinghouse business and lived an isolated life for years. Barmore sued for her freedom. The key question in Typhoid Jennie's case was whether health officials could take away the freedom of someone who was not sick. Perhaps surprisingly, no court had addressed that issue before.

According to court records, health officials learned that several people who had previously roomed at Barmore's boardinghouse had been ill with typhoid fever. The officials quarantined Barmore inside her house and placed a large placard outside, warning that "a typhoid carrier" resided in the house. Laboratory tests confirmed "large numbers of typhoid bacilli" in stool samples Barmore was required to provide. Barmore claimed that she had never been sick with typhoid fever, that no member of her family and no boarder at her house had ever been sick with typhoid fever while they lived with her, and that, so far as she knew, no one had contracted the disease from her. She was not allowed to prepare food for anyone except her husband, and no one could enter her home unless they had been immunized against typhoid fever.[39]

Attorneys for Barmore filed a habeas corpus claim against the city, arguing that state law did not permit the quarantine of someone who had no symptoms and was not sick. With only one dissent, the Illinois Supreme Court upheld the right of health authorities to confine Barmore:

> It is not necessary that one be actually sick, as that term is usually applied, in order that the health authorities have the right to restrain his liberties by quarantine regulations. Quarantine is not a cure—it is a preventive. Effective quarantine must therefore be not so much the isolation of the person who is sick or affected with the disease as a prevention of the communications of the disease germs from the sick to the well.[40]

The court seemed untroubled by the serious deprivation of liberty that Barmore would have to endure, through no fault of her own:

"Among all the objects sought to be secured by governmental laws none is more important than the preservation of public health," the court wrote. "Every state has acknowledged power to pass and enforce quarantine, health, and inspection laws to prevent the introduction of disease, pestilence, and unwholesome food, and such laws must be submitted to by individuals for the good of the public." That sacrifice did not mean that constitutional rights did not apply; it meant that constitutional guarantees "were not intended to limit the subjects upon which the police power of a state may lawfully be asserted in this any more than in any other connection."[41] The Illinois court, echoing the US Supreme Court's decision in *Jacobson v. Massachusetts* from 1905, disavowed any significant role for the judiciary:

> Generally speaking, what laws or regulations are necessary to protect public health and secure public comfort is a legislative question, and appropriate measures intended and calculated to accomplish these ends are not subject to judicial review. The exercise of the police power is a matter resting in the discretion of the Legislature or the board or tribunal to which the power is delegated, and the courts will not interfere with the exercise of this power except where the regulations adopted for the protection of the public health are arbitrary, oppressive and unreasonable. The court has nothing to do with the wisdom or expediency of the measures adopted.[42]

The Illinois court acknowledged that a person could not be quarantined "upon mere suspicion" of harboring a contagious disease. Health officials must have "reliable information on which they have reasonable ground to believe that the public health will be endangered by permitting the person to be at large."[43] But no doubt scarred by the recent experience of pandemic influenza, the court concluded, "Where danger of an epidemic actually exists, health and quarantine regulations will *always* be sustained by the courts."[44] Shortly after the court announced its decision, *Public Health Reports* published in their entirety the court's lengthy majority and dissenting opinions, an indication of the intense interest in the legal question.[45]

What did Jennie Barmore's case have to do with tuberculosis? A great deal, as it turned out. The war on tuberculosis happened to coincide with an expansion of the legal authority that health officers could wield. As more and more health officials followed the advice of Herman Biggs, "incorrigible consumptives" were forced into state institutions, isolated from the well to prevent further spread. In the decades following Jennie Barmore's enforced confinement, a number of states—among them, New Jersey, Minnesota, Wisconsin, and Virginia—enacted laws allowing health authorities to forcibly segregate consumptives, essentially locking them up in institutions that already had the reputation of a place where one went to die.[46] Judicial precedents like *Barmore v. Robertson* only cemented that authority. And because most consumptives singled out for compulsory treatment were poor, they rarely had lawyers to plead their case.

In time, the enforcement of these laws became less automatic and draconian for two reasons. First, advances in medicine, especially the discovery of antibiotics in the late 1940s, eventually made harsh quarantine practices like those typified by the *Barmore* case extremely rare. Typhoid, for example, could be cured in a short time, even in asymptomatic carriers like Mary Mallon and Jennie Barmore. Public health practice itself changed significantly in the second half of the twentieth century to emphasize cooperation over coercion, a sea change from the aggressive tactics of the past.[47]

Antibiotics meant that more tuberculosis patients could be cured, or at least would be less of a threat to others with treatment. Yet curing tuberculosis was not simple, even with effective antibiotics. Then, as now, the course of treatment is long, requiring daily doses of medications for as much as a year or more. Inpatient treatment dropped dramatically as physicians learned that tuberculosis is not as easily contagious as airborne viruses like influenza. Tuberculosis generally requires prolonged exposure to another sufferer rather than a passing encounter. And the infectious stage is relatively short, even while treatment is long.

A second reason for the change in methods for containing tuberculosis was that the judicial branch became more receptive to civil rights and liberties involving patient autonomy. In the 1950s, judges began to protect the rights of tuberculosis patients specifically. An example is a 1959 case from Arkansas. Local health officials tried to have W. F. Snow, a World War II veteran, committed to the Arkansas

Tuberculosis Sanatorium, arguing that he had tuberculosis in an active and communicable stage and was unwilling to voluntarily submit to medical treatment. The Arkansas Supreme Court rejected the health department's request because it had put forward no current medical evidence to support its claim—no sputum tests, no current X-ray, no expert medical testimony. There was also no evidence that Snow had failed to isolate himself at home, as ordered. The health department had offered only one report, from more than three years earlier, diagnosing active pulmonary tuberculosis. The court gave health officials another opportunity to prove their case, however, because "a reading of the entire record indicates the probability that appellee is a very sick person who stubbornly refuses to allow treatment and is probably a source of danger to those around him." Justice Robinson dissented, upset that the court had left Snow "free to go his way with wanton disregard of the fact that perhaps he is giving the dreaded disease of tuberculosis to others."[48]

. . .

While the legal approach may have changed and tuberculosis is now preventable and treatable, tuberculosis remains one of the world's top infectious disease killers, taking the lives of approximately four thousand persons every day. One-fourth of the world's population—nearly two billion people—are infected with tuberculosis bacteria, and approximately ten million become ill with the disease each year. Until the COVID-19 pandemic, tuberculosis was the most deadly infectious disease globally.[49] It will likely return to the number-one rank as the pandemic eases, the World Health Organization has warned.

But the worst problem is that tuberculosis has now become resistant to many of the drugs used to treat it. The World Health Organization reports around a half million new drug-resistant cases each year. Fewer than half of patients with extensively drug-resistant tuberculosis will be cured, even with the best medical care. In the United States, tuberculosis rates have steadily declined in the last decades. In 2019, there were around nine thousand new cases reported (a rate of 2.7 per hundred thousand residents), the lowest number on record, and of those, only a hundred or so were resistant to all of the most commonly used tuberculosis drugs. But up to thirteen million people in the US live with latent TB infection.[50] So far, we have been lucky; the low numbers hide the precarious nature of the nation's public health defense.

One challenge is that responsibility for tuberculosis control is divided among 2,684 state, local, and tribal health departments. That infrastructure is politically and legally fragmented, underfunded, and disproportionately strained in many poor communities. Patients with infectious tuberculosis need medication to be regularly administered over many months; local public health workers provide the medication and observe that the patient takes it, requiring as many as five visits a week. If treatment is interrupted or if the drugs are not working, patients have a much higher chance of developing (and spreading) drug-resistant tuberculosis. At the same time, health workers must track down and test anyone who came in close contact with patients before the disease was diagnosed, to be certain that no one else has been infected. There is no legal mechanism to determine which local health department "owns" a tuberculosis patient.

All this is made much more difficult by the patchwork of jurisdictions and the lack of coordination among health departments, which can easily lose track of patients who travel or relocate to another county or state. Tuberculosis is also most common in communities with the least stability. Besides the logistical problems, there are issues with funding on the local level. Extensively drug-resistant tuberculosis requires eighteen to twenty-four months of treatment and can cost more than half a million dollars. A local health department's entire budget can be depleted with just one case.

Reminiscent of a much earlier era, decisions about these matters are often left to the vagaries of local politics. In Jackson County, Ohio, voters in 2013 were asked to approve a tax to continue to fund the county's tuberculosis prevention and treatment program. In an effort to ensure approval, tax commissioners reduced the levy, leaving just enough to keep the program going. Voters still rejected it. As a result, the health department had to cut the program's public health nurse and a clerical assistant.[51] In 2019, health officials pleaded with the Texas legislature to increase the budget for the state's tuberculosis program to $27 million. Local health departments needed the money for testing, screening, and other tuberculosis services.[52] The Division of Tuberculosis Elimination at the Centers for Disease Control and Prevention

(CDC) routinely works with local public health departments to monitor tuberculosis outbreaks and to provide expert guidance. But it does not have the funding to help local departments pay for tuberculosis treatment, even where local resources are clearly inadequate.

. . .

An example from Atlanta illustrates the challenge for local health departments throughout the country. In 2008, an outbreak of a drug-resistant form of tuberculosis began with "patient zero" at a downtown Atlanta homeless shelter. Over a seven-year period, researchers learned, the drug-resistant genotype identified in patient zero had spread to at least nine other states and infected 120 people, 10 of whom died.[53] Atlanta's failure to contain its tuberculosis outbreak imposed tremendous costs on other cities across the nation, leading some to consider whether they could sue Atlanta to recover those costs.

Health officials in Atlanta faced a problem common to other large cities. The outbreak began in and spread through homeless shelters in the city—the perfect breeding ground for tuberculosis because of the cramped quarters and transient populations.[54] By the time patient zero was diagnosed, the homeless shelter where he had stayed could not provide a list of others who may have been exposed so that health officials could identify others who might be infected. This pattern repeated itself as more and more patients showed up at the city's large public hospital, Grady Memorial, with drug-resistant tuberculosis. New cases can be slow to develop in any event: the earliest symptoms include weight loss, fatigue, and a slight cough. Homeless populations have little access to medical care, even if they notice these early symptoms.

By 2014, it was clear that one shelter, known as Peachtree-Pine, accounted for most of the growing number of cases. A task force of health officials and community service providers attempted to work with the shelter's owner to gain control over the outbreak. But for several years, the owner had refused to cooperate with their efforts to trace the contacts of residents who had acquired tuberculosis. The task force also alleged that conditions specific to the Peachtree-Pine shelter made the spread of the disease easier.[55] The situation led to calls to shut down the Peachtree-Pine facility, which Atlanta mayor

Kasim Reed publicly lambasted as "one of the leading sites for tuberculosis in the nation." The director of the shelter denied the mayor's assertion, claiming that the facility was "100 percent compliant" with CDC protocol. She accused the mayor of conspiring with the business community to close the shelter.[56]

Eventually, the shelter was closed down after the city purchased the property using the legal mechanism of eminent domain. It was an unusual approach to solving a public health problem. The state's laws governing management of tuberculosis simply did not account for the nature of the disease and the social conditions of poverty in a highly mobile population. The resolution of the problem came far too late to protect residents of other states from Atlanta's problem.

• • •

Tuberculosis caught the nation's attention in dramatic fashion in 2007. That year, Andrew Speaker boarded multiple international flights, even though he had just been diagnosed with a drug-resistant form of tuberculosis and was told not to travel on airplanes because of his infectious state. A young, prosperous lawyer from Atlanta, Speaker was determined to keep his wedding date in Italy. That he could travel on three international flights despite being tracked by both state health officials and the CDC led to a public outcry and congressional hearings.[57] As an affluent attorney, Speaker was certainly not the usual face of tuberculosis. His story made the public aware not only that wealthy Americans can get tuberculosis, but that terrifying and deadly drug-resistant TB strains were present in America and much of the world. Congressional hearings revealed the precariousness of dividing authority between the federal government and state/local health departments. But Congress did nothing to clarify that authority.

After all, whose problem was he? The state of Georgia could not prevent his travel unless it served him with an isolation order and the possibility of arrest, which it had not done. The CDC, in charge of blocking air travel by anyone with a serious communicable disease, was not notified until after Speaker had left the country; at that point, the agency could only ban his return travel by air. Apprehended on May 25, 2007, as he attempted to sneak back into the US by car across the border with Canada—having flown through Prague to Montreal—Speaker then voluntarily entered the National Jewish Health Center in Denver. During two months of treatment, doctors removed a portion of infected lung. In late July, Speaker was declared noncontagious, and he flew home to Atlanta following his release from the hospital. Around the same time, passengers on the flight from Prague to Montreal sued Speaker for knowingly exposing them to drug-resistant tuberculosis.[58]

Speaker's escapade fueled uproar and outrage on both the left and the right about the trade-off between restricting individual liberty and protecting the public from human germ bombs.[59] Congress made its feelings clear with the title of its special hearing convened in June 2007: "The XDR [Extensively Drug-Resistant] Tuberculosis Incident: A Poorly Coordinated Federal Response to an Incident with Homeland Security Implications." As so often in the past, however, legislators did nothing to make such occurrences less likely in the future.

• • •

Charles-Edward Amory Winslow, an advocate for tuberculosis hospitals and president of the American Public Health Association in 1926, said, "If we really want to prevent preventable disease, we must supply the machinery, the fortifications and munitions of war, to use against the enemy." But "all these things cost money," he said, "and in order to secure them we must have in each community an aroused and organized public opinion," one that leads to each citizen's "cooperation in community efforts against preventable disease."[60] As both the Atlanta shelter outbreak and the Andrew Speaker incident illustrate, the war on tuberculosis in the first half of the twentieth century got us only so far, and the continuation of local control over contagious disease still poses distinct disadvantages for the rest of the nation. The plan to control tuberculosis proposed by Herman Biggs in 1912—isolation and treatment of TB patients by local authorities—is, in many respects, still the national playbook. Yet the interstate migration of tuberculosis germs, described by Ernest Sweet in 1915, occurs more rapidly than ever in today's mobile, jet-propelled population. There is no ray of light in Winslow's ominous remark that our policies force each community to "determine its own death-rate."[61]

Five-year-old Mary Kosloski, the 1955 March of Dimes
Poster girl from Collierville, Tennessee, meets seven-year-old
Randy Kerr of Falls Church, Virginia, the first polio pioneer
to receive the Salk vaccine during field trials in 1954.

6

THE FIGHT AGAINST POLIO

[P]eople, being human, forget. They forget the panic that swept whole communities when polio epidemics descended upon the nation each summer. They forget the crowded polio wards, the streets empty of children, the closed schools and playgrounds. . . . Yet, millions of people have not yet been vaccinated, neglecting to take advantage of the blessed protection which can be had with so little effort.

—*THE BALTIMORE AFRO-AMERICAN* (1958)[1]

On April 12, 1955, in Ann Arbor, Michigan, Dr. Thomas Francis Jr., director of the Poliomyelitis Vaccine Evaluation Center at the University of Michigan School of Public Health, made a stunning announcement: a vaccine developed by Dr. Jonas Salk and his colleagues at the University of Pittsburgh had been shown to be up to 90 percent effective in preventing polio. Nearly two years earlier, Salk had reported in a CBS radio interview a successful test of his vaccine on a small group of children. The next step before the Ann Arbor announcement had been a large-scale, controlled test that ultimately involved nearly two million children in forty-four states.[2]

Edward R. Murrow, who covered the event live for CBS, declared, "Today, a great profession made a giant step forward, and the news that came out of this room lifted a sense of fear from the homes of millions of Americans."[3] Lynne Seymour, eight years old in 1955, remembered her mother's reaction when she heard the news on the radio. Her mother, a nurse, "started jumping up and down, crying and laughing at the same time." The new vaccine "meant we wouldn't have to worry about polio anymore, and children wouldn't be in iron lungs and we could go back to the swimming pool."[4]

Fear of polio had haunted parents for generations. Doctors originally named the disease infantile paralysis because it primarily afflicted children, but adults contracted it as well. Franklin Roosevelt, the nation's thirty-second president, was diagnosed with infantile paralysis in 1921 when he was thirty-nine years old. Until the 1930s, medical experts could not pinpoint its cause (a virus) or how it spread. Polio spreads through contaminated food and water, but it can also spread person to person from airborne droplets from a cough or sneeze.[5] Outbreaks occurred throughout the first half of the twentieth century, but the worst followed the end of World War II. During the early 1950s, the nation averaged more than 25,000 new cases of polio each year. But the year 1952 had been especially bad: 58,000 new cases led to more than 3,000 deaths, and 22,000 victims were left with disabling paralysis. Few hospitals had the "iron lungs" needed to help patients who were unable to breathe on their own. No wonder Murrow extolled the announcement in Ann Arbor with such joy.

For Basil O'Connor, the vaccine announcement was an exceptionally triumphant moment because his financial ingenuity had brought it about. This day marked ten years after President Roosevelt's death; O'Connor had been his close associate. In collaboration with Roosevelt, O'Connor had established the National Foundation for Infantile Paralysis in 1938. His foundation followed the model of the National Tuberculosis Association from two decades earlier—organize private philanthropy across the nation to target a specific disease, to ease, if not end, the suffering associated with it. O'Connor's foundation had been wildly successful in amassing a war chest of donations through the March of Dimes campaign, its primary fundraising tool. Dime by dime in community campaigns across the nation, the foundation had raised millions of dollars to finance laboratory research for a vaccine, and it had funded the trials to establish Salk's vaccine as safe and effective. In 1949, O'Connor boldly proclaimed, "The conquest of polio is now in sight." A galvanized nation responded. According to historian David Oshinsky, by 1954 "two-thirds of the nation had already donated money to the March of Dimes."[6] O'Connor was so confident in the trial's success that the foundation paid $9 million for commercial production of the Salk vaccine so that millions of doses would be ready for distribution when the vaccine was approved—enough to inoculate eighteen million people by the following spring once the final evaluation was complete.[7]

It seemed fitting, then, when Edward R. Murrow asked Jonas Salk in April 1955, "Who owns the patent on this vaccine?" Salk replied, "Well, the people I would say. There is no patent. Could you patent the sun?"[8]

• • •

As events very quickly illustrated, not only was there no patent on the vaccine but there was no plan in place to oversee or coordinate its distribution. America's first nationwide vaccination effort was chaotic and politically divisive, as demand for the vaccine outpaced supply. Less than a month after the announcement in Ann Arbor, the *New York Herald Tribune* observed: "The Salk vaccine against poliomyelitis is a national blessing which has created a national emergency. Experts have confirmed the vaccine's general efficacy. The demand is far greater than the supply. Every child in America has a right to its protection."[9]

The US Public Health Service licensed six manufacturers to produce the vaccine, with the idea that local health departments would provide the new vaccine free of charge.[10] The National Foundation for Infantile Paralysis had purchased eighteen million doses to provide free to health departments but lacked any mechanism for getting the vaccines distributed equitably across the nation. In any event, eighteen million doses would not be nearly enough to satisfy the demand. Because vaccine producers were free to sell and distribute their product as they saw fit, a mad scramble ensued to purchase vaccine directly from the manufacturers. Doctors and pharmacists found themselves competing with school districts and city governments. Well-funded state and local health departments offered the vaccine much sooner than poorer localities could manage.

In cities large and small, parents impatiently awaited arrival of the vaccine. Picket lines in front of the mayor's office in New York City included mothers who were "angry because they felt that their children were in needless danger" and who protested the failure of the city to make enough vaccine available. Some carried signs that read "We demand Polio Vaccine."[11] Over the next two years, distribution problems only made anxiety and panic worse, as initial shipments were quickly used up and parents could rarely get reliable information about when new supplies would be available.

In Boston in March 1956, hundreds of parents pushed 3,248 children through record-breaking snow drifts to reach one of the city's vaccination centers. "By sled, baby carriage and piggyback," a news article reported, "pre-school children were lugged through yesterday's storm in Boston to receive Salk anti-polio vaccine." Dr. John Cauley, Boston's public health commissioner, reassured parents a new program would be devised for children who could not get shots that day. Because of the intense demand, he said, health officials would plan to "step up the program with increased facilities and personnel."[12]

As was true in Boston, most health departments nationwide did not have the staff or facilities for a mass vaccination campaign and had to improvise with the help of volunteers. New York City, though, had recently learned how to vaccinate a large population in a short time when it faced one of the last smallpox outbreaks in the country in 1947. In April of that year, the city's health department managed to vaccinate over five million New Yorkers in just twenty days. City officials appropriated $500,000 to purchase the vaccine and necessary supplies; the health department organized vaccine locations and volunteers to administer it after the first report of smallpox on April 5. The effort confined the outbreak to only twelve cases and two deaths, a result New York City's health commissioner Israel Weinstein called a "miracle." Dr. Hollis Ingraham, the state health director, said that without New York City's vaccination program, "the disease would have spread throughout the state and to other states."[13]

In 1940, shortly before the New York City smallpox outbreak, the nation's state and territorial health officers had debated their continued role in providing to the public immunizations against contagious disease. The association's president, Dr. William Grayson said that mass immunization for communicable disease had been "inaugurated by health departments in order to protect the public against epidemics," especially smallpox, but also with newly developed vaccines against diphtheria, pertussis (whooping cough), rabies, tetanus, and typhoid.

"It was originally thought that when a sufficient proportion of the population was immunized, the health department could withdraw from the field," Grayson said, and the public would go to private practitioners for vaccinations. "Yet today, after many years of this activity, we find a large part of the personnel's time occupied with mass immunization, and the public educated to demand it of health departments rather than private practitioners." He then posed this question: "Are we to continue this process as our obligation, or should we direct this responsibility to the family physician and relieve our time and money for development of other fields?"[14]

Grayson's question was left unanswered, but more important, his assumptions did not reflect reality in the many parts of the country without a local health department, or where state governments did not purchase vaccines to provide free to its citizens. Fifteen years later, the situation remained the same. As one consequence, when the Salk polio vaccine announcement came in April 1955, urban populations in areas with well-organized and financed health departments stood a better chance of getting it first, at least while the supply lasted and if some kind of orderly distribution could be managed.

When a polio outbreak in Chicago began in the summer of 1956, the city's medical society sent an urgent plea for volunteer doctors and nurses to give shots, and it also proposed that hospitals in the city become vaccination sites. Over eleven thousand people reportedly received the vaccine on a single day, July 24, in locations hastily set up by the municipal board of health and a newly opened center in Cook County Hospital.[15] Notwithstanding that effort, one week later "thousands of mothers and children stormed a city inoculation center," a newspaper reported, pushing and shoving when the doors opened to be sure they were vaccinated before supplies ran out.[16]

One month after the Ann Arbor announcement, US Surgeon General Leroy E. Burney held a conference on how the vaccine could be fairly distributed. The general agreement was that children should get it before adults because they were the most vulnerable.[17] That had been the intent of O'Connor's foundation when it distributed the first doses it had purchased to vaccinate schoolchildren in the first and second grades. But there was no plan or mechanism to ensure that children of any age got it first.

Predictably, not everyone shared this prioritization, and illicit markets for the vaccine arose. "It is too much to expect of human nature," the *New York Herald Tribune* opined, "that when the promise of release from [the fear of polio] appears, voluntary arrangements will hold against a mother's insistence on the protection of her children, or the greed of those who want to make money out of that emotion."[18] Wealthy parents found ways to get their children vaccinated first. What rankled more was that instead of children being the priority recipients, in some instances wealthy adults bought their way to the front of the line, with the cooperation of physicians who purchased vaccines directly from one of the manufacturers.

In response, in New York City in May 1955, a county medical society grievance committee called nine physicians before it to face possible disciplinary action. The city's health department took the lead in reporting transgressions, alleging that these doctors "had given the vaccine to five men and twelve women." Their actions were especially objectionable, a city official said, because a scarcity of the vaccine meant only half the city's schoolchildren in the first four grades would receive free injection before schools closed for the summer.[19]

In an effort to stop black market sales of the vaccine, New York City amended its sanitary code in May 1955 to impose a $500 fine and a possible year in jail for the unauthorized sale or possession of the Salk serum. But there is no record that such fines were ever imposed. Instructing a grand jury, New York judge Hyman Barshay told jurors, "If it is found that there is a black market in the vaccine, and the new law is not adequate," the jury should not hesitate to make recommendations for a stronger law "as a warning to all violators that the grand jury, the police, the district attorney and others in Kings County are on guard." The jurors' vigilance was necessary, Barshay said, because of the "emergency condition which affects the health of our children."[20]

Once again, it was up to state and local governments to make rules to address the illicit market in Salk vaccine. Few took the opportunity, or like New York City, could find an effective way to enforce rules if they did. A newspaper editorial noted that "states and localities have improvised their own distribution systems." These systems "are based on voluntary allocations and priorities, and are concerned more with the acquisition of and payment for the vaccine than with seeing to it that priorities are absolutely observed." The federal government, the editorial continued, was "the only authority capable of exercising national controls," but it had made "no serious effort" beyond advisory committees and reliance on voluntary cooperation. The licensing agreement to produce the Salk vaccine gave the federal government "no authority over allocation, over price, over violators of agreements." A national law was essential, the editorial stated, "to bring order out of this explosive situation" because the "parents and children of the nation demand it."[21] No such law would be forthcoming.

. . .

Oveta Culp Hobby was President Dwight Eisenhower's cabinet official in charge of the US Public Health Service and the National Institutes of Health. The Department of Health, Education, and Welfare was created in April 1953 as part of the Eisenhower administration's plan to reorganize the federal government, and Hobby was its first secretary. Hobby, a veteran Texas political actor and publisher of the *Houston Post*, had vigorously supported Eisenhower in Texas in the 1952 presidential election, but she had no background in public health.[22]

Six weeks after the public announcement that the Salk vaccine worked, Hobby submitted to the White House a plan calling for manufacturers voluntarily to allocate a certain amount of vaccine for each state, depending on the state's population of children. The Eisenhower administration planned to ask Congress for $28 million to purchase serum "to make sure children under 19 aren't deprived of the vaccine because it costs too much." But the plan otherwise left it to the states to set up mechanisms by which children would actually receive the vaccines. As the *Wall Street Journal* reported, "Vaccine makers, distributors, and medical groups would follow allocations and other procedures" recommended under the plan, "without direct Federal controls being imposed." Doctors and medical associations "would make certain [that] shots are given only to children in the priority groups" and would keep records on who received the vaccine. The plan "reflected the Administration's distaste for imposing Federal controls as well as its conviction that a cooperative set-up simply will work better." The *Journal* opined that "many Congressional critics are sure to challenge this Administration belief, of course, as they've been doing steadily since the vaccine was cleared for use April 12."[23]

When asked by a Senate committee why her plan had not been ready in April to coincide with the Ann Arbor press conference, Hobby blithely observed, "No one could have foreseen the public demand for the vaccine." Observers marveled at the secretary's response. The *New York Times* reported that Democrats attacked the plan as "too little and too late," while "Republicans staunchly defended Mrs. Hobby and chided the Democrats for 'injecting partisan politics' into the vaccine situation." The administration still opposed controls, the *Times* reported, because "federal controls would impede distribution because it would take so long to set up the enforcement machinery."[24]

The fact of the matter is that both the pharmaceutical industry and the Eisenhower administration believed in the primacy of private enterprise in producing and distributing the vaccine. Drug companies had lobbied Congress and the White House for months to have the matter left to the free market. "The polio vaccine being produced by the licensed six firms is their own property," an industry spokesman insisted. "It belongs to them." If the Salk vaccine were to be "socialized"—that is, if prices were set and distribution standards imposed by the federal government—drug companies claimed they would have no incentive to continue production.[25] While some congressional Democrats sought federal oversight from the beginning, the Eisenhower administration, and congressional Republicans generally, believed that the distribution of medical vaccines was not a legitimate government function.

Three months after the White House requested $28 million to purchase vaccine for needy children, Congress obliged with the Poliomyelitis Vaccination Assistance Act, the first federal involvement in immunization funding since the short-lived smallpox vaccination program that President James Madison signed into law in 1813. Congress directed the surgeon general to distribute the funds to states on a formula based on state per capita income. States needed to apply for the money with justification for the need. The grants could only be used to purchase polio vaccine, and the state must provide the vaccine free of charge. Congress exhorted the surgeon general to make "the most effective and equitable distribution and use of available supplies" of polio vaccine.[26] Leaving distribution of the funds in the surgeon general's hands, with relatively few strings attached, meant there was at least someone in the federal government who could attempt an equitable allocation throughout the nation.

. . .

Demand remained high for the Salk vaccine despite a serious problem that occurred within weeks of the Ann Arbor announcement. Cutter Laboratories in Berkeley, California—one of the six original licensees—had contaminated two batches of its product with live polio vaccine, not the inactivated vaccine designed by Salk. That meant the vaccine itself could cause polio. In early May, health officials received the first reports of polio in children who had been vaccinated, and the race was on to determine what had gone wrong. Seven-year-old Susan Pierce of Pocatello, Idaho, was thought to be the first child to die from a defective batch of the vaccine.[27] In all, more than two hundred thousand children in five states received the defective Cutter Laboratories vaccine. At least ten died, and many more were left with lifetime paralysis.[28]

University of Pennsylvania pediatrician Paul Offit described the Cutter incident as "one of the worst biological disasters in American history."[29] To ramp up production speed for the national vaccine program, Cutter used a glass filter, not an asbestos one, as had been used in Dr. Jonas Salk's laboratory. The glass filter allowed some live virus to slip through.[30]

Five-year-old Anne Gottsdanker of Santa Barbara received one such dose manufactured by Cutter Laboratories. Her parents had made sure she was at the front of the line to receive the polio vaccine. The shot was administered at the family home. Gottsdanker remembers being in a hospital bed, unable to move. "With polio, you have feeling in your limbs, but the muscles don't work," she said in 2005.[31]

Gottsdanker's parents eventually hired San Francisco attorney Melvin Belli to represent their daughter in a lawsuit. The jury trial against Cutter Laboratories, in a courtroom in Oakland, took four weeks. Occasionally, Gottsdanker remembered, Belli would call her in and have her attempt to walk in front of the jury. The jury awarded Gottsdanker $147,300 in damages.[32] Despite the injuries the company's product had caused, Cutter's sales more than doubled between 1955 and 1962, and its assets in 1962 were reported to be "80 percent greater than when the polio disaster had occurred."[33]

The Cutter incident threatened to shut down the vaccination effort entirely. The Public Health Service banned the continued distribution of vaccines produced by Cutter Laboratories while it turned control of vaccine safety "over to the polio experts," rather than leave safety testing up to commercial laboratories.[34] The Public Health Service and the National Institutes of Health jointly established an expert committee to evaluate and review all vaccine lots and advise on their safety for eventual use. A significant portion of this technical work fell to an obscure Atlanta-based agency, the Communicable Disease Center, the precursor of today's Centers for Disease Control.

Shortly after its organization in Atlanta in 1946, the Communicable Disease Center—a subsidiary branch of the Public Health Service previously responsible for malaria control in the Southeast during World War II—undertook polio as part of its surveillance of contagious diseases, and it had also organized the advisory committee that planned the field study for the Salk vaccine. That made the CDC a crucial contributor to solving the vaccine mystery. Within weeks, the CDC's polio surveillance program had established the cause of the Cutter Laboratories problem, the issue was corrected, and the inoculation program resumed.[35] By mid-May, just three weeks after discovering the problem, the Public Health Service approved vaccines made by Parke-Davis and Eli Lilly and recommended resumption of the mass vaccination program. Officials for the service acknowledged that, having completed a "plant by plant inspection of the five manufacturers in the reappraisal of previously cleared lots of vaccine," the inspectors would undertake application of "more refined standards and test data to materials on hand."[36] After the production problems were identified and corrected, no other cases of polio were associated with the Salk vaccine.[37]

But reassuring the public was no easy matter, and understandably, some parents resisted the surgeon general's reassurances. The New York Times reported in May 1955 that the National Foundation for Infantile Paralysis had obtained enough Parke-Davis vaccine to distribute in New York free of charge to the most vulnerable age groups. However, "as many as 30 per cent of city children who had applied for injections last month failed to turn up last week." As the *Times* speculated, much, if not all, of the absenteeism could be attributed to "nervous" parents who found themselves in a dilemma: "Millions of parents fear that if their children don't get the vaccine, they may get polio, but if they do get the vaccine, it might give them polio."[38] Parke-Davis was not Cutter Laboratories, but the damage had been done.

Ultimately, fear of polio and public confidence in the assurances of health officials fueled a new burst of demand for the vaccine. As evidence of the undiminished demand, supply shortages continued well into 1957. In March of that year, Surgeon General Leroy Burney told Congress that demand for the shots, which fell steadily between July and November 1956, accelerated again in the early months of the new year, creating new shortages. Burney reported the nation had used up "the entire backlog" of 26 million shots that were on hand at the beginning of that year, including the new supply of 10.5 million produced in the last three months. Burney acknowledged that "during the next two weeks the situation will be serious" but predicted that output would increase significantly after that.[39]

Despite irregular patterns of supply and distribution, problems in targeting vaccines to the most appropriate and neediest populations, and reluctant federal oversight that addressed the safety of supplies but not the means by which the vaccine reached the public, by 1957 clear signs of success appeared. In that year new reported polio cases in the United States fell to 5,600, one-tenth of the totals in the worst year of the epidemic. By 1961, when the Salk vaccine was largely supplanted by the Sabin oral vaccine, the United States reported 161 new polio cases.[40] Since 1979, no new cases of polio have originated in the United States.[41]

The lasting effects of the Cutter incident set in motion greater federal oversight and monitoring of vaccine production and safety. The National Institutes of Health's biologics laboratory expanded its work with vaccines. The CDC emerged as the primary government agency to monitor safety of vaccines, and its national polio surveillance program raised the agency's profile considerably. The nation's two primary health agencies divided their responsibilities—NIH would conduct

basic research, while the CDC investigated disease outbreaks, monitored vaccine safety, and helped states both to recognize and control
communicable diseases. From less than one hundred personnel in 1947
when Emory University donated land to the CDC for its headquarters,
the CDC would grow to become the largest federal agency outside of
Washington, DC, with more than ten thousand employees.[42]

• • •

It was a very good thing that by the summer of 1957, the nation's polio
vaccine supply problems had improved such that health officials could
find some breathing space—because the second influenza pandemic of
the twentieth century would soon reach America. In February 1957,
a new influenza A (H_2N_2) virus emerged in East Asia, triggering a
pandemic known to contemporaries as the "Asian flu." It was first reported in Singapore and Hong Kong that spring, spreading rapidly to
other East Asian nations and then to other continents.[43] By late summer,
cases of the new influenza strain appeared in coastal cities in the US.

For forty years, the 1918 influenza pandemic haunted scientists
and the public alike. No one could predict if or when the world might
see another. Scientists had made great strides in influenza vaccine research; indeed, it was a top priority. As terrible as the polio scourge
was, the 1918 flu pandemic had killed at least fifty million people
worldwide, including about 675,000 in the United States.[44] Despite
desperate attempts to create an effective vaccine in 1918, it would take
more than two decades to come up with one. But there was no way to
know if it would work against a new strain.

This time, a vaccine was ready. Fortuitously, Maurice Hilleman,
a doctor at the Walter Reed Army Institute of Research, happened to
read a *New York Times* article about the Hong Kong outbreak. He requested a sample from an army base in Japan, receiving the first specimens on May 17, 1957. Hilleman used those to devise a vaccine that
proved to be up to 70 percent effective. But vaccine manufacturers
were unable to produce it in sufficient quantities before the peak of the
pandemic—which meant, of course, a limited supply of vaccine, with
no mechanism to prioritize distribution in any equitable fashion.[45]

Under the headline, "The Great Epidemic—The Threat," *Newsweek* in August 1957 informed Americans, "Sometime this autumn,

about 17 million Americans will suddenly take to their beds" with what scientists then called the "Asian flu." The US Public Health Service warned Americans to expect a "temporary halt of a large part of the American activity this fall" if sufficient quantities of influenza vaccine were not distributed before the epidemic's expected arrival. *Newsweek* quoted Dr. Mayhew Derryberry of the Public Health Service, who "hoped there won't be panic." But "It's going to be a very difficult situation. We don't want to get people worried before the vaccine is ready, but we do want them to buy it when the epidemic strikes." One manufacturer intended to ship free vaccine to "each of the nation's 220,000 doctors." But the rest expected to charge doctors one dollar per shot. When the doctor's fee was added, the cost to patients to receive the vaccine was five dollars.[46]

Immediately above the dramatic *Newsweek* headline, a brief article with the heading "Special Medicine Report" is set in bold print and in a callout box to draw attention to it:

Who Gets the Vaccine First?

IF the U.S. Public Health Service's recommendations are heeded, the first flu-vaccine shots will go to 12 million "essential personnel": 3 million health workers, 5 million key defense production workers, 3 million transportation employees, 700,000 in communications, 500,00 utility workers, 300,000 police and firemen.

BUT the USPHS, despite some urging, refuses to establish Federal priorities. Last week, Dr. Leroy E. Burney, U.S. Surgeon General, said: "We think the ultimate decision as to who should get the vaccine is up to local communities."[47]

Expressing optimism that a better ability to treat secondary bacterial infections like pneumonia would make this flu less deadly than that in 1918, *Newsweek* reported that "modern antibiotics" should hold "the death rate to around 5,000."

That prediction turned out to be wrong. Although the 1957 flu pandemic was far less devastating than that of 1918, more than 116,000 Americans died, and twenty million Americans contracted it. The estimated number of deaths worldwide was just over one million.[48] But the prediction of fewer deaths in the US relied on the premise that

Hilleman's influenza vaccine would be more widely available than it ended up being. Manufacturing problems slowed production, and the decentralized mode of distribution meant that when producers finally sent bulk shipments, much of it went unsold or became unusable as a result of delays.[49]

Surgeon General Burney remained firm that the vaccine "is going to be distributed through normal commercial channels"—as had been used for the polio vaccine. The American Medical Association organized a network of local and state committees to identify locations where outbreaks might be particularly bad. The intention was to relay that information to the Public Health Service in the hope that it would "recommend to manufacturers the diverting of vaccine supplies from less needy localities."[50]

The Association of State and Territorial Health Officers met in Washington, DC, that August to discuss the threat. They could not ascertain whether the worst would hit during the usual influenza season, predominantly in the winter months, or in September as it had done in 1918. Though the influenza appeared to be spreading rapidly, no attempts were made to close the national border or to impose quarantines within states, a strategy that would be "useless because of the large number of travelers and the frequency of mild or inapparent cases." Neither were large groups dissuaded from gathering, such as those that congregated at college football games or church services. This was in part because so many who contracted this strain of flu had mild cases and also because of the widespread belief that school closings and curtailment of public gatherings should be a local decision based on local conditions. For all of these reasons the nation's strategy to mitigate deaths focused only on having enough supplies of vaccine.[51]

The epidemic swept the country in just over two months, with the opening of schools in September believed to be "a major factor in initiating community epidemics." Although by the end of October more than half of the nation's counties had been hit by the epidemic, and in one week alone an estimated one million Americans had been struck by the flu, the saving grace was a low overall death rate, estimated by the surgeon general to be less than 1 percent.[52]

• • •

Only ten years later, in 1968, the third influenza pandemic of the twentieth century hit the United States. It was another variation of influenza A; scientists referred to it as the "Hong Kong flu" because it had first been reported there. (But as with the "Spanish" flu of 1918, the perceived geographic origin often bore no relation to reality—the 1918 flu originated in the United States.) Estimated death rates were similar to the 1957 influenza pandemic: one million worldwide, and about a hundred thousand in the United States.[53]

Also like the 1957 experience, an effective vaccine was available, but demand overwhelmed supply and officials abandoned voluntary plans for priority distribution. Once again, the lack of a central authority for a nationwide vaccination campaign contributed to uneven distribution, and the highest-priority groups did not receive the vaccine first. This was now the third example, in less than fifteen years, that nationwide vaccine campaigns could not rely on an open market for vaccines with no way to control distribution. An article in *Science* that year explained, "Individual physicians are responsible for ensuring that high-risk groups—the aged and the chronically ill—receive the vaccine first." The federal government could "only recommend distribution to certain groups"; it could not control distribution of a product "sold on the open market."[54]

As historian George Dehner summed up,

The publicity campaigns in 1957 and 1968 had worked; many people knew about the vaccine and wanted to be inoculated, but the doses were unavailable when needed. If the federal government purchased the vaccine, then the manufacturers would be assured of a market, and the U.S. Public Health Service would be able to control its distribution. Increasingly, those in the field of public health began to push for just such an expanded role.[55]

The United States finally took that step in preparation for a feared flu pandemic in 1976. By then, scientists understood more about the genetic variations with influenza strains, and in 1976 it looked very much like something as bad as the 1918 pandemic was at hand.

. . .

A smiling President Gerald Ford was captured by national news media, shirt sleeve rolled up, receiving an influenza vaccine from the
White House physician. It was October 14, 1976, and the CDC
feared the beginning of a massive flu pandemic. Earlier that year, a
nineteen-year-old soldier, David Lewis, had died at New Jersey's Fort
Dix. An investigation identified a long-dormant strain of swine flu as
the cause. That a pandemic was imminent was an expectation shared
not just by CDC experts but by international health officials too.[56]

Citing the "strong possibility" of a swine flu pandemic, CDC director David J. Sencer sounded the alarm. "The administration can tol-
erate unnecessary health expenditures better than unnecessary deaths
and illness," Sencer wrote in a March 13 memo. President Ford knew
his greatest political risk lay in doing nothing, so he agreed to an unprecedented plan—the National Swine Flu Influenza Immunization
Program, a massive vaccination effort to prevent a pandemic. An advertising campaign urged citizens to "get a shot of protection," with
photographs of President Ford receiving the vaccine distributed to rally
support. "No one knows how serious this threat could be," President
Ford announced. "Nevertheless, we cannot afford to take a chance
with the health of our nation."[57]

Although some forty million Americans would be vaccinated, the
vaccination campaign was beset with difficulties from the start. One
vaccine manufacturer produced two million doses with the wrong viral strain.[58] But then surveillance by the CDC revealed that some swine
flu vaccinations created an increased risk of Guillain-Barré syndrome
(GBS). GBS is a relatively rare disorder marked by muscle weakness
and paralysis that often follows infection with a virus or bacteria. In
most years, one or two cases of GBS occur per million doses of flu vaccine administered. In 1976, however, that risk increased by a factor of
ten, for reasons that are still incompletely understood.[59]

When the expected pandemic did not materialize, the consequences
were predictably political. Held responsible for the unanticipated effects of the vaccine because of his aggressive promotion of the preventive effort, Dr. Sencer was removed as CDC director by the new
secretary of Health, Education, and Welfare, Joseph A. Califano,
shortly after the Carter administration took office.

Another consequence was an onslaught of multimillion-dollar law-suits and public unease regarding vaccination. In response to the vaccine panic, vaccine manufacturers—vulnerable to liability and expensive lit-igation—threatened to abandon the market.[60] Congress responded in 1986 with the National Childhood Vaccine Injury Act (NCVIA). The NCVIA set up a national reporting system and established a fund to compensate individuals injured by vaccines, a no-fault compensation system that functions much like workers' compensation laws. Vaccine manufacturers contribute to the fund and in return are protected from lawsuits over injuries from vaccines.[61]

The world may have escaped another influenza pandemic in 1976, but the fear of another catastrophic flu pandemic never eased among scientists. In 2005, Dr. Michael Osterholm, director of the Center for Infectious Disease Research and Policy, said: "Without a doubt, if you were to add up my entire public health career's concerns, worries, and—in some cases—nightmares, they collectively do not meet the con-cern, worry and nightmares that I have about the issue of an impending pandemic of influenza."[62] That same year, President George W. Bush committed unprecedented resources to protect the country against pan-demic flu. The president's *National Strategy for Influenza Pandemic* began a years-long readiness effort still underway when a novel coro-navirus, not influenza, spread across the globe in 2020.

· · ·

The epidemics Americans faced in the three decades after World War II changed some aspects of how the nation would respond to pub-lic health crises in the future. The increasing involvement of federal agencies in general, and the Centers for Disease Control in particular, became the focal point of public and political expectations about how, and the extent to which, the federal government would involve itself in the nation's health. Meanwhile, the power to act continued to rest in the hands of state and local public health authorities; that allocation of power did not change in the years between polio and the swine flu.

Perhaps most importantly, the intensive publicity focused on offi-cials struggling to formulate responses to epidemic disease amplified the imperfections of existing approaches in the eyes of the American public. This could be seen in the fears arising from the Cutter Laboratories tainted polio vaccines; it could be seen in the public and political reactions to the swine flu vaccine campaign twenty years later. By the late twentieth century, the focus of public health policies on the use of vaccines to fight epidemic disease met rising public skepticism about experts generally, public health experts in particular, and the safety of hastily developed vaccines above all.

These conflicting positions would color both public and official responses to the next epidemic the nation was about to confront.

ACT UP protest in front of the headquarters of the Food and Drug Administration in Rockville, Maryland, October 11, 1988.

7

THE AIDS EPIDEMIC

*The AIDS epidemic teaches us that it is essential for us
to rise above our differences as people, our differences as
gay and straight people, as men and women, as minorities,
as majorities, as Africans, as people of different religious
preference. The virus proceeds without these differences.
The virus spreads around without prejudice, and in order to
combat it, we have to rise above our prejudices. We have to
say there are things more important than this. In fact, that
lesson is a human lesson. It's a lesson that makes us better
people and makes the world a better world.*

—JAMES CURRAN, *Frontline*, 2006[1]

In June 1981, the CDC reported a strange new illness—five otherwise
healthy young men in Los Angeles had come down with an unusual
strain of pneumonia, and two of them had already died. Soon after
the first CDC account of the disease cluster in Los Angeles, hospitals
in New York City and San Francisco reported dozens of similar cases.
Doctors elsewhere in the country were seeing the same thing—a confusing variety of rare illnesses most often contracted by people with
weakened immune systems.[2]

Around the time of the CDC's first report, Dr. John M. Luce joined
San Francisco General Hospital's pulmonary and critical care team.
Luce was a young physician fresh from a fellowship. He described
what it was like to work that summer in a large public hospital. "I
thought I could predict the patients I would care for," he said. But in

addition to routinely treating "alcoholics, drug users, and poor people from the Mission District," Luce related, "my colleagues and I were confronted with young, white, gay men with diseases like Kaposi's sarcoma (KS), Pneumocystis pneumonia (PCP), and other opportunistic infections that bespoke an underlying immune deficiency."[3]

Because the patients were all gay men, Luce and his colleagues initially called the condition GRID, for "gay-related immune deficiency." At first, they thought that the condition might be drug related. Only later would it become clear that what they were seeing was, instead, a new, deadly virus, one that could be silently passed on to others and would become a predominantly heterosexual disease. The disease would come to be called Acquired Immunity Deficiency Syndrome, or AIDS.

Less than four years after the initial CDC report, physicians had reported 12,000 AIDS cases, and more than half of those had died.[4] By 1987, the first time President Ronald Reagan publicly spoke about AIDS, the US death toll was more than 20,000. More than 700,000 Americans would die from AIDS by 2020.[5] He couldn't know it then, but Dr. Luce had begun his hospital career at the start of a worldwide pandemic that has so far killed 40 million people around the globe.

• • •

Soon after the CDC published its first report of the mysterious illnesses in Los Angeles in 1981, CDC director William Foege appointed a thirty-person task force, drawn from various CDC divisions and specialties, to begin surveillance and epidemiologic investigations into the cause. Foege asked James Curran, at that time an epidemiologist in the CDC's Sexually Transmitted Disease Control Division, to chair the task force, an assignment that would last fifteen years. Curran and his team were soon overwhelmed with case reports that continued to grow. It was already clear that whatever it was, they were dealing with a fatal disease.[6]

It would take more than two years before scientists could identify the cause of AIDS, and by then it was clear that AIDS not only was present throughout the US but had likely been circulating the globe for some time. In 1983, two researchers at the Pasteur Institute in Paris, Françoise Barré-Sinoussi and Luc Montagnier, isolated a retrovirus never before seen in humans. This retrovirus, which would eventually be named HIV, for "human immunodeficiency virus," proved to be the missing link. For their discovery, the two received the 2008 Nobel Prize in medicine.[7]

Identifying the underlying cause of AIDS was just the first step in combatting the epidemic. As the experience with COVID-19 four decades later would demonstrate afresh, defeating a novel virus required combatting a potent combination of stigmatization, scientific uncertainty, public misconceptions and misinformation, and political inertia and denial.

On the scientific front, researchers still needed to learn how the virus spread, whether it was transient or lifelong, and whether those infected with the virus could pass it to others without themselves having any symptoms of AIDS. Most important of all from a public health perspective was the need to develop a reliable lab test to identify carriers. The mission was urgent: AIDS was a death sentence, usually within eighteen months of onset of symptoms, after terrible suffering.

Until these breakthroughs happened, no one at CDC could advise US health workers how to safely care for AIDS patients. Some healthcare workers refused to treat AIDS patients, and some hospitals turned them away. John Luce recalled one surgeon at San Francisco General who refused to operate on AIDS patients because "she believed HIV could be transmitted through unbroken skin."[8]

Journalists reported wildly varying theories about how the disease was transmitted, including that AIDS could by spread by casual contact. A study in Los Angeles, published in 1982, suggested that AIDS was sexually transmissible, but other scientists were skeptical even of that. Americans worried about contracting AIDS in schools, restaurants, and public restrooms. A *Life* magazine cover story about the high prevalence of AIDS in Belle Glade, Florida, quoted physicians there who speculated on the possibility of insect transmission. The CDC task force sent a team to investigate but could find no evidence that was happening.[9]

By far the worst outcome of scientific uncertainty was the too-late recognition that HIV had entered the US blood supply at some unknown point. In 1982, physicians began to report AIDS patients who were not gay but shared the common trait of hemophilia. By 1984, researchers believed 50 percent of hemophiliacs in the nation had become infected with HIV through tainted blood products.[10] Eventually, nearly half of all patients with hemophilia who had received blood transfusions developed AIDS. This meant also that intravenous drug users who shared needles could transmit HIV.

Even the path of the disease into the United States was something of a mystery, much as the gateway for COVID-19 would be disputed later. Researchers initially blamed Gaëtan Dugas, a gay flight attendant from Canada, for importing HIV and starting the AIDS epidemic in the US.[11] Later, scientists recognized that this conjecture was wrong, but lawmakers had already seized on the "patient zero" narrative because it provided a social group to blame and indulged a nativist impulse to protect the borders by excluding homosexuals. Even with the mounting evidence that AIDS was not a "gay disease," the stigma was firmly ensconced in the public mind.

More damaging still, the association of AIDS with homosexuality pervaded the White House and the halls of Congress. President Reagan and his domestic policy advisers believed AIDS predominantly affected the gay community and drug users, who "brought the disease upon themselves by engaging in immoral conduct."[12] Much of the president's reaction was influenced by religious conservatives' disapproval of behaviors seen as causative. Televangelist Jerry Falwell said that AIDS was God's punishment of America for tolerating homosexuality. Reagan would not even use the terms AIDS or HIV in public until 1987 (after 20,849 Americans had already died from AIDS).[13] Journalists were informed that officials would not answer questions about AIDS at press conferences. Throughout Reagan's first term, White House officials prevented his own surgeon general, Dr. C. Everett Koop, from addressing the subject.[14]

Nearly five years after the first cases were reported, Koop obtained permission to prepare a report on AIDS. Koop wrote it himself; he would not allow anyone from the White House to even see the report before he released it at a press conference in October 1986.[15] The thirty-six-page report, distributed to members of Congress, public health organizations, and journalists, described what was known about HIV and how it was transmitted. The report discussed condom use and sex education for school children. It was the start of a campaign strategy by the surgeon general to inform Americans how to protect themselves from AIDS. With no cure and no vaccine, Koop understood that educating the public was the only way to slow the spread. This task fell under the mandate of his office, Koop believed. He would later say, "If ever there was a disease made for a Surgeon General, it was AIDS."[16]

Koop followed up two years later with a pamphlet on AIDS mailed to every household served by the US Postal Service—114 million copies. It was the first time the US government had ever sent a health advisory directly to Americans.[17] "Understanding AIDS" was a candid discussion of sex-related preventive measures. "Some of the issues involved in this brochure may not be things you are used to discussing openly," Koop wrote. "I can easily understand that. But now you must discuss them." Koop explained how the AIDS virus could be transmitted, what types of condoms were safest, and what constituted risky behavior—"sex with someone you don't know well (a pickup or prostitute) or with someone you know has several sexual partners." Equally important, Koop emphasized ways people would not get AIDS: everyday contact with people in school, in the workplace, at stores or childcare centers, or at parties or in a swimming pool. AIDS could not be transmitted from a mosquito bite, saliva, sweat, or tears, or from clothes, a telephone, or a toilet seat.[18]

Koop put America on notice that "people who have died of AIDS in the U.S. have been male and female, rich and poor, white, Black, Hispanic, Asian and American Indian." His final message: "Who you are has nothing to do with whether you are in danger of being infected with the AIDS virus," Koop concluded. "What matters is what you do."[19]

The brochure's cover pictured Americans of all ages and races. Inside, a picture of Carole, last name not given, appeared with the quote, "Obviously, women can get AIDS. I'm here to witness to that. AIDS is not a 'we,' 'they' disease, it's an 'us' disease." AIDS counselor Sally Jue and volunteer Drew Sisselman were featured too. On the fifth page, Americans were introduced to a young Anthony S. Fauci, director of the National Institute of Allergy and Infectious Diseases and coordinator of AIDS research at the NIH. "You can't tell if someone has been infected by the AIDS virus by looking at him or her," Fauci states.

"But you aren't in danger of getting the disease unless you engage in risky behavior with someone who is infected."

A significant advance in controlling the spread of the AIDS virus came in 1985 with the development of a blood test for the presence of HIV. Until then, the concept of lab testing for a silent infection that spread asymptomatically was still relatively new. Testing campaigns would heat up in future years, but Koop introduced the subject in a short section of his pamphlet titled "Should You Get an AIDS Test?" Koop explained that the test "doesn't actually tell you if you have AIDS." Instead, it would show the presence of HIV, the virus causing AIDS. "The Public Health Service recommends you be confidentially counseled and tested if you have had any sexually transmitted disease or shared needles; if you are a man who has had sex with another man; or if you have had sex with a prostitute, male or female." You should also be tested "if you have had sex with anyone who has done any of these things." Hemophiliacs and anyone who received a blood transfusion between 1978 and 1985 were advised to get tested too. Scientists were able to develop a technique for killing the virus in blood products in 1985, making the blood supply safe for transfusions.[20]

At a news conference in advance of the mailing, Koop made it known that there had been no White House interference in the contents of the brochure, and he noted that Congress had not only authorized the national mailing but also, in the legislation itself, had "spelled out that its content was not to be subject to clearance" by any executive branch official. Congress thought this was necessary, the New York Times reported, because "Dr. Koop has often run into opposition from Administration officials outside the health department for his persistence in calling for the use of condoms by sexually active people not in monogamous relationships."[21] This would not be the last time that a part of the executive branch would try to contain a virus while being undercut by the White House.

Unexpectedly, the surgeon general became a media favorite and a widely recognized public figure. Koop had come to the job known as deeply religious and against abortion, delighting conservatives. He transformed the surgeon general's role by his insistent public presence and avuncular personality. He appeared on television in the kind of military uniform earlier surgeon generals had worn, a tradition that had fallen by the wayside decades earlier. Tall, authoritative, with a sharp sense of humor, he was especially memorable because he bore a slight resemblance to Colonel Sanders in the Kentucky Fried Chicken ads of the time. Journalists began referring to Koop as "the nation's doctor," an enduring moniker applied for the first time to the surgeon general.[22]

Another factor helped account for the relative openness to Koop's public activities by White House officials during Reagan's second term. Along with the rising numbers of infections and rising numbers of fatalities came the revelations that celebrities of every stripe had contracted AIDS. Actor Rock Hudson, a personal friend of Reagan's, came out as homosexual just before he died of the disease in 1985. Basketball star Earvin "Magic" Johnson opened up the sports world in the same way that Hudson had Hollywood, when Johnson announced in 1991 that he had contracted the disease. In 1993, star US tennis player Arthur Ashe died of AIDS, contracted from a transfusion of infected blood, further helping dispel the stigma.[23]

· · ·

And yet the public information campaign by the surgeon general came too late for the epidemic of fear gripping the nation. The "gay plague" label stimulated adverse social reactions and stigma, even though health officials had known years earlier that about half of those infected were not gay. Those diagnosed with AIDS, or merely suspected of it, were barred from schools and workplaces, treated with disdain, distance, and fear—even children who acquired AIDS through the nation's tainted blood supply. Bigotry and discrimination were salt in the wound to those who had just been given a death sentence.[24]

Ryan White was a thirteen-year-old hemophiliac from Kokomo, Indiana, who contracted AIDS in 1984 from a blood transfusion. The next year, he began a two-year court battle to be allowed to attend public school in Kokomo in person; as a seventh grader in that pre-Zoom, pre-internet era, he was required by the local school board to attend class from home by a telephone hook-up. Ryan eventually won the right to attend high school in person, but he and his family faced a vicious public reaction. Fellow students yelled insults at him in the halls and scrawled obscenities on his locker. The family's home and car were vandalized. When Jeanne White, Ryan's mother, went to the grocery store, cashiers would place her change on the counter to avoid any contact.[25]

In 1987, the White family moved about twenty miles away, to Cicero, a farming town where Ryan was accepted as just another student. The local school board sponsored public meetings about the disease and encouraged people to approach Ryan with compassion. When Ryan died in 1990, the *New York Times* pointed out that the difference between the two towns was not a stark tale of good versus bad. Not everyone in Kokomo had opposed Ryan's returning to school: "For every parent who pulled a child out of school in protest, there were 20 who did not. Nor was everyone in Cicero pleased to welcome a boy with AIDS. The difference was time and education about the disease."[26] Some parents in Cicero had talked to their children about AIDS, explaining that Ryan did not pose any danger to them because of the way the disease was transmitted. Peggy and Jerry Lockwood told their daughters: "You don't have to be afraid. Go up and talk to Ryan. He's a nice boy. There's nothing to worry about."[27]

By the time Ryan entered hospice care in his senior year of high school, it seemed as if not only the whole town but the whole nation was rooting for him—Ryan had become the sympathetic public face of AIDS. He lived longer than his doctors had predicted but died one month before his high school graduation. More than 1,500 people attended his funeral, including then First Lady Barbara Bush, Elton John, and Michael Jackson.[28]

If Ryan had won some measure of acceptance, schoolchildren elsewhere did not. Negative public perception and misinformation about AIDS produced harmful results in communities all over the United States. In New York City, for instance, the decision to allow a second-grade student with HIV to attend classes at an elementary school in Queens led to a boycott in which more than eleven thousand students were kept home by their parents on the opening day of school.[29] By December 1986, a *Los Angeles Times* poll reported that about 50 percent of adults supported mandatory testing for people considered to be in a high-risk group, while 29 percent supported tattoos to identify HIV virus carriers.[30]

Actions by state and local health officials highlighted the tension between protecting the public and protecting individual rights—in this case, maximizing public safety by identifying those with AIDS and those who were HIV-positive and tracing their contacts for testing, while safeguarding the privacy and interests of the actual and prospective patients.[31] Many state and local measures were ineffective at best, counterproductive at worst (in some cases not by design, but as a result of the combination of lack of information and political reactions). Legal scholar Wendy Parmet described the "epidemic of fear" that led some officials to consider quarantine for AIDS victims and for those who were HIV-positive, despite the fact that HIV is not transmitted through mere proximity with someone who is infected.[32] In Texas, for example, the state health commissioner proposed adding AIDS to the list of diseases subject to quarantine but ultimately withdrew the plan after a backlash from civil rights groups.[33]

As recently as 2017, a Georgia legislator asked in a public meeting whether people with HIV could be legally quarantined.[34] It was all the more noteworthy because the legislator, Dr. Betty Price (who lost her seat in 2018), was an anesthesiologist and the wife of Dr. Tom Price, who served for a short time as secretary of the Department of Health and Human Services (HHS) under President Donald Trump. "What are we legally able to do?" Price asked Dr. Pascale Wortley, director of the HIV/AIDS program at the Georgia Department of Public Health. "I don't want to say the 'quarantine' word, but I guess I just said it." According to a recording posted on CNN, Dr. Price continued: "It just seems to me it's almost frightening the number of people who are living that are potential carriers—well, they are carriers—with the potential to spread" HIV. "Whereas, in the past, they died more readily, and then at that point, they are not posing a risk. So, we've got a huge population posing a risk if they're not in treatment."[35]

Some states also targeted HIV patients through criminalization of behavior believed to be associated with spread of the disease. Before 2000, thirty-eight states passed laws criminalizing behavior that risked transmitting HIV. These statutes varied in specifics, but they all agreed that the accused would be deemed culpable if they had unprotected sex while knowing they were infected with HIV/AIDS.[36]

One example was the prosecution of Adam Donald Musser in Iowa in 2006. Musser was convicted for having unprotected sex when he knew he was HIV-positive without disclosing that to his partner.

The state needed to prove only that Musser knew he was infected and that he intended to engage in unprotected sex. Musser was sentenced to twenty-five years in prison, even though his partner was not infected.[37] Musser was paroled to work release in 2012, but he was arrested again in 2015. He pleaded guilty to two misdemeanor counts of reckless exposure to infectious disease and was sentenced to serve a year on each count.[38]

In June 2008, Nick Rhoades had a one-night sexual encounter in Cedar Falls, Iowa, with twenty-two-year-old Adam Plendl. Rhoades was HIV-positive and on antiretroviral medications. He said he wore a condom, but he did not tell Plendl he was HIV-positive. Plendl found out and went to a hospital for evaluation. The hospital called police, as it was required to do when treating the victim of a sex crime, and three months later Rhoades was arrested and charged with criminal transmission of HIV, a felony. Despite the fact that Plendl's hospital tests showed no infection, Rhoades spent nine months in the Black Hawk County Jail, unable to post a quarter-million-dollar bond. In May 2009, Rhoades pleaded guilty and was sentenced to twenty-five years in prison. He served four months in the Clarinda Correctional Facility before a public pressure campaign led to his resentencing. Rhoades's original sentence was reduced to time served and five years on probation—and a lifelong requirement that he register as a sex offender.[39]

Rhoades set out to have his conviction overturned. His first attorney never told him that the statute on criminal transmission of HIV requires proof that the HIV-positive person intentionally set out to infect the victim. The attorney also failed to contact Rhoades's doctor, who told his new lawyers that by 2008, Rhoades's viral load was "nondetectable," meaning that it was unlikely, if not impossible, that Rhoades could transmit HIV. The Iowa Supreme Court in 2014 sent the case back to the district attorney in Black Hawk County. Rhoades was allowed to withdraw the guilty plea, and the charge was dismissed.[40]

Rhoades eventually sought to recover damages for wrongful imprisonment. By 2016, he was unemployed and living in Des Moines, struggling to outlive the stigma associated with the original case. Even though the requirement that he register as a sex offender was lifted in 2014, Rhoades claimed that prospective employers doing background checks still found him on the state sex offender registry. "This conviction has put me on the sex offender registry, it's ruined my reputation," he told the *Des Moines Register*. "I spent over a year in jail or prison and I just need some sort of means to get my life back on track."[41]

But the Iowa Supreme Court rejected Rhoades's claim, pointing out that they never said he was actually innocent, only that there was insufficient evidence to support the original guilty plea. And that, the justices decided, meant Rhoades was not eligible for compensation because he had not been wrongfully imprisoned. Even though Rhoades was ultimately cleared, his life was disrupted and his future cast very much in doubt by the eagerness of the state to attack a public health problem by routing it through the criminal justice system.

• • •

In stark contrast to inaction by the federal government and harmful actions by many states based on prejudice and misinformation, some states adopted measures designed to help meet the needs of AIDS patients. For example, some states barred health and life insurance providers from asking about HIV status and sought ways to provide financial support for AIDS patients, a substantial number of whom, especially in the earlier years, relied on Medicaid for palliative care or treatment. As of 1988, only seven states reported that they had spent no public money on AIDS programs at all.

By 1986, the National Academy of Sciences reported that the lack of resources to address the epidemic was seriously straining hospitals in the worst-hit cities.[42] A national solution was needed, including more money for research and drug development, more money to support state and local governments caring for destitute AIDS patients, and a public commitment to combat AIDS while respecting civil rights.

The game changer came in 1987 with the formation in New York City of ACT UP, the AIDS Coalition to Unleash Power. ACT UP chapters soon organized in cities throughout the nation. More confrontational than other AIDS-related organizations, ACT UP directed its efforts toward political results. The group operated on the theory that pressure was needed to force the government and medical researchers to seek a cure and not just palliative or intermediate measures.[43]

ACT UP protesters occupied Wall Street, locked themselves to politicians' desks in the halls of Congress, organized protests at the CDC and NIH, and, in one of the more audacious moves, temporarily shut down the Food and Drug Administration. Some of the protesters at the FDA building lined up on the ground holding mock tombstones that said "Dead from FDA red tape." They wanted the FDA to give AIDS patients access to an experimental drug, AZT, that held promise of prolonging lives. Within a few months, the FDA changed its policy to allow access to experimental drugs.[44]

In a 2019 story for National Public Radio, Nurith Aizenman summed up what advocates had achieved: "They ultimately forced the government and the scientific community to fundamentally change the way medical research is conducted—paving the way for the discovery of a treatment that today keeps alive an estimated half-million HIV-positive Americans and millions more worldwide." As the title to Aizenman's story put it, it was a lesson in "how to demand a medical breakthrough."[45] A book and documentary by David France called *How to Survive a Plague* compellingly portrays the successful political activism by groups like ACT UP.[46]

James Curran said that one of the most difficult things for those at the CDC was "feeling like the communities that were at greatest increased risk didn't trust us because we worked for an administration which wouldn't mention the word 'AIDS.' We worked for an administration which had some anti-homosexual agendas."[47] Curran set out to change that, becoming the CDC's point person with AIDS activists and meeting frequently with organizers in Atlanta and New York. CDC director William Foege said that Curran was "a master" at dealing with scientists, academics, politicians, and other groups. But most important, said Foege, "he was comfortable with patients and the gay community." Activists were understandably suspicious of a government they perceived to be ignoring them, and they watched their friends die. "But somehow Jim Curran did not lose his way, and the gay community began to trust him."[48]

Curran was himself the target of some ACT UP protests. Activists once chained themselves to his office door at the CDC. Another time, he received twenty thousand postcards at his home with a target on his face. But Curran expressed nothing but admiration for the activists he engaged with for more than a decade, because he could appreciate the absolute urgency that motivated them: "They were constantly going to funerals. And we would be reminded of that because we would go to a meeting and ask, what happened to Bill? Well, he died."[49]

. . .

Likely influenced by the public attention that ACT UP generated, Congress by the early 1990s had taken two important steps. First, Congress provided $30 million to help states buy AIDS drugs after AZT became available in 1987. Second, and by far more consequential, was legislation prompted by the plight of Ryan White. Social mistreatment had turned Ryan into a national figure, and even President Reagan became acquainted with Ryan before he died from AIDS at the age of eighteen.[50] In 1990, shortly after Ryan's death, Congress enacted the Ryan White Comprehensive AIDS Resources Emergency Act (CARE Act), the most sweeping legislation for any epidemic in the country's history.

The CARE Act provided critical financial assistance to AIDS patients and to the hospitals treating them. Many AIDS patients lacked health insurance or the resources to pay for care. Urban hospitals also became overwhelmed as the epidemic got worse. As the legislation explained,

> It is the purpose of this Act to provide emergency assistance to localities that are disproportionately affected by the Human Immunodeficiency Virus epidemic and to make financial assistance available to States and other public or private nonprofit entities to provide for the development, organization, coordination and operation of more effective and cost-efficient systems for the delivery of essential services to individuals and families with HIV disease.[51]

Congress provided grants to state and local agencies to support prevention and treatment programs—on the condition that states conducted contact tracing of anyone who tested positive for HIV. Congress also recognized that AIDS createed housing issues. The 1991 Housing Opportunities for People with AIDS Act was intended to address housing needs by providing short- and long-term rental assistance as well as grants to develop and operate specialized housing for people with AIDS.[52]

The 1990 Americans with Disabilities Act (ADA) required "reasonable accommodations" for persons with disabilities, although it remained an open question whether the ADA would apply to HIV status. In 1998, the US Supreme Court ruled that it did.[53] The case involved Sidney Abbott, who had been infected with HIV since 1986. When she went to her dentist in Bangor, Maine, for an examination in 1994, she disclosed her HIV status on her patient registration form. The dentist, Randon Bragdon, found a cavity during the examination and then told Abbott about his policy against handling the cavities of HIV-positive patients in his office. He did not decline outright to fill the cavity, but he told Abbott he would do so only in a hospital setting where additional safety precautions were available.

Abbott turned down that offer and instead sued Bragdon, alleging discrimination because of her disability in violation of the Americans with Disabilities Act. Writing for a 5–4 US Supreme Court majority, Justice Anthony Kennedy held that HIV infection, even when asymptomatic, constituted a disability under the terms of the Americans with Disabilities Act. However, the court remanded the case to the lower court for further consideration of the question whether Bragdon unlawfully discriminated against Abbott by refusing to treat her in his office. The court would not accept Bragdon's position that his belief in a significant risk to his health and safety sufficed to justify his policy, given the possibility that the weight of medical evidence suggested otherwise.[54]

The Supreme Court's decision meant that HIV-positive Americans—more than one million at the time—could claim the law's protection against discrimination in "major life activities." Employers, with very few exceptions for some medical providers, cannot ask about or require HIV tests. Equally important was the Supreme Court's stance on science: medical professionals cannot substitute their own idiosyncratic judgment of the risk of treating a person with HIV in lieu of "objective, scientific information," in particular, the views of public health authorities.[55]

Still, employment discrimination against people with HIV has persisted, a significant problem since the 1980s. In 2012, Chance Cox, a machine operator at Gregory Packaging, a Newnan, Georgia, firm producing fruit juices, was the subject of rumors among his coworkers that his skin condition was indicative of AIDS. It was not, but Cox believed he could best address the situation by disclosing to management that he was, in fact, HIV-positive. Despite the fact that his medical circumstances had not affected his job performance, Cox was fired. Cox filed a complaint with the Equal Employment Opportunity Commission (EEOC), which in turn sued Gregory Packaging for discrimination in violation of the Americans with Disabilities Act. The case settled in 2015 with Cox receiving a $125,000 payment and the company agreeing to present training against disability discrimination at the plant.[56]

In 2016, the EEOC sued Diallo's, a nightclub in the Houston, Texas, area, after the club fired an employee who failed to provide proof that she was not HIV-positive. The club's owner, Leila Roberts, allegedly told employee Felicia Parks that she had heard a rumor that Parks was HIV-positive. Anticipating a possible negative effect on the club's business, Roberts insisted that Parks provide documented proof that she was not HIV-positive or face termination of her employment. When Parks did not, Roberts fired her. Parks complained to the EEOC, which filed suit in federal court on her behalf. A court ordered Diallo's to pay Parks more than $89,000 in back pay and compensatory damages, and $50,000 in punitive damages.[57] Connie Wilhite Gatlin, the EEOC senior trial attorney who handled the case, observed that "Employers may no longer rely on outdated and meritless assumptions about HIV to discriminate against employees. A demand for disability-related information without any legitimate reason is simply illegal."[58]

Even if civil rights laws increasingly protected persons living with HIV/AIDS, changing public opinion is another matter entirely. According to a 2012 survey by the Kaiser Family Foundation and the *Washington Post,* one in five Americans said they would be "uncomfortable working with someone who is HIV-positive or has AIDS," 26 percent would be uncomfortable "if their child's teacher was HIV-positive," and 44 percent would be uncomfortable "if their food was prepared by someone with HIV." The study also found that 27 percent of respondents did not know that HIV *cannot* be transmitted by sharing a drinking glass. Another 17 percent didn't know that the virus cannot be picked up by touching a toilet seat. These last two figures, according to the report, were "almost exactly the same share as in 1987."[59]

. . .

Antiretroviral drugs improved markedly in the 1990s, saving the lives of millions throughout the world. A positive HIV test no longer means a death sentence if people with HIV take an expensive pharmaceutical combination for the rest of their lives. A vaccine remains elusive, however. In 1997, President Bill Clinton announced a national goal of an AIDS vaccine within ten years, and the NIH's Vaccine Research Center opened two years later. Clinton's goal at least stood a better chance than the misguided optimism of former HHS secretary Margaret Heckler, who in 1984 announced that a vaccine for AIDS could be available for testing within two years.[60]

Without a vaccine, future presidents faced an unending epidemic, one they could only hope to control through behavior-based education and services offered by state and local health departments, including voluntary testing programs. Despite the significant strides made by Congress and the Clinton administration during the 1990s, those efforts remained hamstrung by ongoing conservative political winds and the policies that conservatives had previously secured. Congress outlawed federally funded needle-exchange programs in 1988. The year before, Senator Jesse Helms spearheaded legislation to prohibit the use of CDC funds for "AIDS education, information, or prevention materials." The measure also prohibited any activities that would "promote or encourage, directly or indirectly, homosexual sexual activities."[61] Over the next decade, a growing racial disparity in new HIV infections led Black congressional leaders to declare a "state of emergency" in 1998 after meeting with CDC leaders.

Major shifts in policy occurred during the George W. Bush presidency. The CDC was directed to prioritize abstinence messaging, and information about condoms was removed from federal government websites.[62] In 2004, a group of scientists, including Nobel Prize and National Medal of Science recipients, members of the National Academy of Sciences, and former senior advisers to administrations of both parties, published a statement decrying what they saw as a systematic misrepresentation of scientific knowledge for political goals.[63] Four years later, the same group published a report detailing the Bush administration's "abuse of science."[64] Nonetheless, Republican members of Congress sponsored audits of all federally funded HIV/AIDS programs, prompted by disagreements about content, not financial probity. Starting in 2003, Congress began to audit topics of NIH-funded research and to reevaluate grants related to HIV/AIDS.[65]

When Barack Obama became president in January 2009, federal engagement again shifted back toward a greater allocation of resources for HIV prevention and treatment. In 2009, the Obama administration increased sex education funding by nearly $190 million and drastically reduced abstinence-only education program funding.[66] The long-standing travel ban on HIV-positive foreigners entering the country was finally rescinded. Congress discontinued the ban on needle exchanges in 2009, when Democrats controlled Congress. The ban was reimposed in 2012 after Republicans regained control.[67] A bipartisan agreement on needle exchanges was reached in 2015, in time for then Indiana governor Mike Pence to approve the state's first syringe exchange program in response to what was at the time one of the worst outbreaks of HIV in the nation. In one rural Indiana county, 235 people were infected with HIV from sharing needles for intravenous drugs.[68]

Facing an alarming number of new HIV infections, particularly in the South, President Donald Trump in his 2019 State of the Union Address pledged to end AIDS in the US by 2030. When President Trump made his pledge, more than one million people in the country were infected with HIV, with likely hundreds of thousands more undiagnosed.[69]

. . .

For Jim Curran, the COVID pandemic provided eerily disturbing parallels to lessons we should have learned from AIDS. With any novel disease, scientists need time to unravel what causes it and how it spreads, while at the same time communicating to the public how they can best protect themselves. That communication is key, but political leaders can interfere with the scientific messaging or influence it in counterproductive ways. Falsehoods and myths circulated widely during COVID, just as they had with AIDS, but in the age of social media, falsehoods, myths, and outright lies can be exponentially amplified.

In the early years of AIDS, Curran said, the main problem was neglect—a lack of money from Congress and "nonexistent federal leadership" at the top. But during the COVID pandemic, Curran said, "there was direct interference: moving competent people out of their jobs, trying to silence Fauci, and lying about facts and science."[70]

Curran had left the CDC in 1995 to become dean of Emory University's Rollins School of Public Health, where he continued community outreach to and advocacy for people with AIDS. He also teaches hundreds of students each year. "When I talk to our students," he said, "I say that public health is always political because it involves populations of people and you have a lot of different stakeholders. But it shouldn't ever be partisan during an epidemic."

The HIV/AIDS epidemic of the 1980s offered a glimpse of the future and taught policy makers and the American people important lessons about confronting novel viruses. The first lesson, perhaps, was that novel viruses surely would come. The second lesson was the importance—indeed, the imperative—of communicating scientific knowledge clearly and frequently to allay public fears, combat prejudice, and debunk unfounded misconceptions. Perhaps a third lesson was the value of informed leadership from the White House and the CDC all the way down to school boards and town councils. Finally, testing for HIV demonstrated the value of the use of lab tests to detect silent killers in asymptomatic carriers. The US would have to relearn all of these lessons in the twenty-first century.

*A protester in front of the White House in October 2014
advocating for mandatory quarantine for medical workers
returning from Ebola-affected countries in West Africa.*

8

EBOLA IN DALLAS

It sometimes seemed that Dallas was ground zero
for the unhinging of our entire nation.
—EDITORIAL, *The Dallas Morning News* (2015)[1]

September 30, 2014, was a chaotic day for Dallas mayor Mike Rawlings and for county judge Clay Jenkins, the top elected official in
Dallas County. The CDC had just confirmed that Dallas was home
to the first case of Ebola diagnosed at a hospital in the United States.
Thomas Eric Duncan, the Dallas Ebola patient, had had no symptoms
before or during his flights from Liberia but became ill five days after
arriving at Dallas-Fort Worth International Airport. Were more cases
out there? If so, how would they be found, and how could Dallas
prevent an Ebola outbreak from spreading further? The immediate
burden fell to Jenkins and Rawlings, and in the months to come, they
would find the most difficult job to be managing the public panic that
gripped the city.

America was already on edge over the possibility that Ebola
might come to its shores. Throughout the summer of 2014, Americans watched with growing alarm as a health disaster unfolded in West
Africa, eventually claiming more than eleven thousand lives in the
countries of Guinea, Liberia, and Sierra Leone. Fear of the disease was
understandable—Ebola virus disease is among the most horrific contagious diseases known to humanity. Spread by contact with an infected
patient's blood or other body fluids, the virus has an average mortality

rate of about 50 percent and can go as high as 90 percent, with no known cure.[2] At the time, there was also no vaccine.[3]

In fact, the Ebola virus had already come to the nation before Thomas Duncan was diagnosed in Dallas. Four Ebola-stricken American aid workers had been evacuated from Liberia to the US for medical care, amid significant controversy. Dr. Kent Brantley arrived at Emory University Hospital in Atlanta in early August, the first American medical worker evacuated to the US for treatment. When Brantley arrived at Dobbins Air Reserve Base on a special containment flight, a high-security detail escorted the ambulance carrying him to Emory amid bomb threats and demonstrators who objected to Ebola being brought intentionally to the US. Nancy Writebol, a missionary, arrived at Emory a few days later, followed by Dr. Ian Crozier. A fourth repatriated American, a doctor, arrived at the National Institutes of Health on September 28, the day before the Dallas announcement.[4]

Two months before Thomas Duncan was diagnosed with Ebola in Dallas, CDC director Tom Frieden warned Congress the Ebola virus would "inevitably" enter the country, carried unknowingly by a traveler exhibiting no symptoms. If that were to happen, Frieden said, America would rely on the oldest tools in the public health playbook: Isolate a contagious sick person to prevent further spread, and find out if that person might have exposed anyone else to the disease. Because carriers of Ebola are not contagious before they exhibit symptoms, others exposed would need to be monitored to see whether they would develop the disease and isolated if they got sick.[5] Frieden did not emphasize an important detail: local authorities would be in charge of those tasks.

When Duncan's lab test confirmed Ebola, Governor Rick Perry flew to Dallas along with Dr. Thomas Lakey, commissioner of the Texas Department of State Health Services (DSHS), to meet with local officials and CDC representatives. Jenkins and Rawlings were stunned to learn what was expected of them. Much of the public "and all of official Dallas" expected the CDC to take charge of matters.[6] But that's not what happened. The CDC can only advise state and local governments and cannot make or carry out the difficult decisions that outbreak emergencies require.

The first task was to figure out who would lead the Dallas response. Mayor Rawlings was one possibility because the hospital treating the

Ebola patient was within Dallas city limits. But Dallas did not have its own health department, so it had no lab capabilities, epidemiologists, or authority to issue any public health orders. The Dallas County health department had that purview, and as an arm of county government, it answered to Jenkins. As a second possible response leader, Jenkins would have a wider jurisdictional authority if Ebola spread beyond the Dallas city limits, as the county's health department was responsible for a larger population that included twenty-six cities. The third possible leader was the state's chief health officer, Dr. David Lakey. By fortunate coincidence, he was an infectious disease specialist. But he was based in Austin, not Dallas, and he was not an elected official who could direct law enforcement or disburse local tax money.

Frieden and Lakey suggested that Jenkins should take charge.[7] Lakey had worked with Jenkins just two years earlier, when a West Nile virus outbreak in Dallas killed twenty people. Jenkins had demonstrated a calm, collaborative leadership style and had an excellent relationship with both Lakey and Mayor Rawlings. Jenkins also understood that addressing this emergency would be immensely important not only to Dallas but also to the nation, which was alarmed at the prospect that Ebola might spread. Dallas is the ninth-largest city in the US, with a population of nearly 1.5 million people and another million in Dallas County. Together with Fort Worth and Arlington, Dallas constitutes the fourth most-populous metropolitan area in the nation. Nearly seventy-five million passengers pass through Dallas-Fort Worth International Airport each year. The possibility of a spreading contagion seemed imminent. CDC director Frieden attempted to calm fears that the Dallas outbreak could widen. He was "confident that the U.S. won't suffer a widespread Ebola outbreak." He understood that people were scared: "It's a deadly virus, but you have to go back to basics—the bottom line here is we know how to stop it."[8]

Even before lab tests confirmed Duncan had Ebola, detective work was already underway. The Dallas County health department began to identify anyone who had been in contact with Duncan. Finding them quickly was essential to calm an alarmed populace. But predicting who might develop Ebola was tricky. Ebola could be passed from person to person through body fluids, but only from someone who already showed symptoms. That fact, at least, favored the contact tracers: unlike HIV (and later COVID-19), Ebola did not spread asymptomatically.

Scientists already knew a lot about Ebola from decades of work in Africa—as did many Americans from Richard Preston's 1994 book *The Hot Zone,* which describes a near catastrophic Ebola virus accident at a lab in Reston, Virginia, and details all too vividly the gruesome death brought on by the virus. But there was no test to determine whether someone exposed to the disease would go on to develop it, and the incubation period from exposure to symptoms could be as long as three weeks. This meant that preventing spread of the disease required monitoring persons with potential exposure for up to twenty-one days.

To make matters worse, Duncan initially had been misdiagnosed. Duncan's fiancée took him to the Texas Health Presbyterian Hospital emergency room on September 25, when he first experienced fever, abdominal pain, and diarrhea. Although he told emergency staff that he had traveled from Liberia, the possibility of Ebola apparently didn't register, and they diagnosed him with sinusitis, gave him antibiotics, and sent him back to the apartment where he was staying. Three days later, on September 28, he returned to Texas Presbyterian by ambulance after his symptoms grew worse. This time, doctors suspected Ebola. Because he had symptoms of Ebola before his first trip to the emergency room, anyone who had come into contact with him then, and for the intervening days, was at risk and needed to be identified and located.

Anthony Fauci, director of the National Institute of Allergy and Infectious Diseases at the National Institutes of Health, told reporters he "wouldn't be surprised if a close contact of Mr. Duncan also came down with the illness," but he urged a "rational" view. "The crux of preventing an outbreak in Dallas or anyplace else is to do exactly what the CDC and Dallas is doing—monitoring patients on a twice-a-day basis," he said on Fox. If they develop a temperature, "then you isolate them and you put them under the protocol of caring for an Ebola patient."[9]

Clay Jenkins, the Dallas County judge, told me his first concern was what to do with the family left behind, now that Duncan was in critical condition in the hospital's ICU.[10] Health officials had ordered Duncan's fiancée, Louise Troh, her thirteen-year-old son, and two nephews to stay in their cramped apartment.[11] Police cordoned off the entire apartment complex after a press scrum descended on the area. One image captured a friend leaving a bag of food outside Troh's apartment door, which had a quarantine sign taped to it. It would take five days for authorities to get the necessary permits to remove soiled bedding and other hazardous waste from the apartment. While the family was still there, cleaning crews in HAZMAT gear eventually removed mattresses, the television, and a PlayStation, among other items, cutting them apart to fit into specially designed hazardous-waste barrels.[12]

In an effort to help relocate the family as well as to calm anxieties in the neighborhood, Jenkins visited the family on October 3, without wearing protective gear. "There's zero chance you're going to get Ebola from being near an asymptomatic person," Jenkins told journalists. He drove the family to a home in an undisclosed location provided by the Catholic bishop of Dallas. "I had to convince them to leave their house and go to a place they'd never seen before, and I wanted to treat them with the same compassion that I would want Louise to treat my family member or me if my family were going through this," Jenkins said. "We have treated the people who are . . . waiting to find out whether they've got the terrible disease the way we ourselves would want to be treated. I think that is by definition what an elected official should be doing."[13]

Meanwhile, health department epidemiologists searched for others in the community who may have had contact with Duncan. The possibility that Ebola had already spread to others added urgency to the task, but it was otherwise a routine job. Contact tracing is a cornerstone of communicable disease control, a frequent undertaking in containing tuberculosis, HIV, and other diseases. Normally, tracking down everyone who has come into contact with someone diagnosed with an infectious disease falls to the local health department—in this case, Dallas County's.

Commissioner Lakey and CDC director Frieden decided to separate "community" contacts from healthcare workers at Texas Health Presbyterian Hospital. It made sense for hospital officials to do this contact tracing internally because they could determine which employees had come into contact with Duncan and could monitor them. The hospital also could identify everyone who had been in the emergency room with Duncan on his first visit, as well as the ambulance personnel who brought him back. The healthcare contacts eventually numbered 122, two-thirds of them designated as "no known exposure" because their brief interactions with Duncan were unlikely to have included contact with body fluid.[14]

Dallas County epidemiologists were in charge of locating and monitoring the non-healthcare contacts. They soon identified more than fifty people, including ten patients who had ridden in the ambulance after Duncan. Twenty-two of these were designated as having "high risk" or "some risk." The high-risk category included those who had visited or were living in the apartment where Duncan was staying. Only the four people at the apartment were placed under a health department order forbidding them to leave their residence, where, according to a news report, a police officer was posted outside "after they failed to comply with a request to stay put."[15] Louise Troh's son and two nephews had gone to school the day after Duncan was taken back to the hospital, according to Jenkins.[16]

Other community contacts with less risk were told about symptoms to look for and what to do if they developed. They had to check their temperatures twice a day for the next twenty-one days. Contacts in the higher-risk groups had "direct active monitoring," meaning that at least one of the two temperature checks was done in person, at their residence, by a member of the monitoring team, while the second temperature was reported by phone. Self-monitoring was deemed appropriate for the "no known exposure" group, which included hospital workers wearing personal protective equipment (PPE) at the time of possible exposure.[17]

• • •

Then the worst-feared scenario happened: Thomas Duncan died of Ebola on October 8 in Dallas. Within one week, two nurses at Texas Health Presbyterian Hospital—Nina Pham and Amber Vinson, both in their twenties—were diagnosed with Ebola. On October 12, Pham checked herself into the hospital after she discovered she had a low fever. Mayor Rawlings visited the neighborhood where Pham lived to inform residents. Meanwhile, Amber Vinson had flown to Cleveland,

Ohio, her hometown, to prepare for her upcoming wedding. She began to feel ill and registered a low temperature while she was there but was given clearance to fly back to Dallas on October 13. Two days later, Vinson tested positive for Ebola.[18]

The blowback over Vinson's travel was immediate—for the CDC for clearing Vinson to fly back to Dallas, and for Texas health officials who had allowed hospital workers to self-monitor for symptoms, with no movement or travel restrictions. Dozens more contacts now needed to be identified and monitored, and not just in Dallas. Health officials in Ohio, where Vinson had traveled, contacted hundreds and monitored their movements. The Ebola outbreak that began with a single patient became the most complex contact tracing effort the United States had yet seen.[19]

As Jenkins recalled later, panic took off "exponentially" after Pham and Vinson contracted Ebola. He faced calls to quarantine all hospital employees and their families, to shut down public transportation, even to declare a state of emergency for Dallas County. Mayor Rawlings faced much the same, as he would have authority to declare an emergency within Dallas city limits. Both Rawlings and Jenkins resisted stricter quarantines for hospital workers in favor of lesser measures, with support from Frieden and Lakey. They needed public confidence in Dallas hospitals and needed healthcare workers to keep working. Jenkins also nixed calls to declare an emergency. "The main reason," he said, "is when you've got a situation where people are already scared to death, where people are already convinced that they're all going to die, calling a state of emergency is just an unnecessary additional stressor on an already stressful situation." The federal and state partners supporting Jenkins all thought about it in the same way, he said. They were not just fighting an outbreak in inner city Dallas, Jenkins said, "they said the team down there is fighting America's Ebola outbreak."[20]

Despite the low risk of contracting the disease casually, communities around the nation reacted with draconian measures. Ohio instituted quarantines; some schools banned children from attending because of a lack of geographical understanding of Africa and where the Ebola outbreak originated; false alarms sounded in hospitals everywhere. At least six schools in Texas and Ohio were closed for disinfection because some students (or their parents) had been on the same flight as Vinson.[21] The bridal shop Vinson visited struggled to stay in business but eventually closed its doors as customers stayed away. Kevin Thomas, in his book *Global Epidemics, Local Implications,* described the worsening stigma and acts of discrimination against the Liberian community in Dallas, and in African immigrant communities elsewhere in the nation.[22]

Social media amplified rumors that Ebola could be spread through the air or could mutate to do so. Dr. Frieden and Dr. Fauci, in hearings before Congress and in press interviews, repeated the scientific community's confidence that Ebola transmission was not airborne. "You've probably read in the papers about the concern that it's going to change into a respiratory virus, spread over and destroy the world," said Fauci. "As a scientist and as a physician, I can say it's very, very unlikely that that would happen. It may change a bit, but unlikely to change so much."[23]

Both nurses survived. Amber Vinson was treated at Emory Hospital; Nina Pham at NIH. CDC and hospital officials initially blamed them for improper use of the personal protective equipment necessary to treat Ebola patients. A national nurses association fired back, citing improper training and lack of equipment. A nationwide scramble for scarce PPE was well underway by then. Texas Presbyterian Health would later settle a lawsuit over disclosing the nurses' names to the public and failing to provide proper training for them.[24]

• • •

As the nation absorbed the news that two Dallas nurses were infected with Ebola, attention turned to the hundreds of US health workers returning from volunteer stints treating Ebola patients in West Africa. Several state governors publicly denounced CDC quarantine guidance as inadequate and imposed their own, more stringent requirements. Led by New Jersey governor Chris Christie, other governors followed suit, criticizing the Obama administration for allegedly failing to protect the nation.[25] These state governors—from both political parties—squabbled publicly with the CDC and the federal government about who was in charge, whether to close the borders, and which persons should be quarantined. Some political analysts concluded that the governors feared political fallout from their constituents should their state fail to take an aggressive approach, after Governor Christie had done so.[26] Eventually, twenty-three states would adopt Ebola quarantine rules that were stricter than what CDC guidance called for. The CDC acknowledged that while its guidance "established a baseline standard, states had the authority to apply restrictions that exceeded CDC's recommendations."[27] It could hardly do otherwise; the CDC needed to retain good working relationships with the governors and health departments of those states. Those governors were also each represented in Congress by two US senators. The CDC is dependent on funding via annual appropriations by Congress, so it has strong incentives not to rock the boat at the state level.

Then came, as one journalist put it, "New York's one-man pandemic scare."[28] Dr. Craig Spencer returned to New York City on October 17, after treating sick patients in the West African country of Guinea. Back in the city, he went bowling with friends, rode the subway, ate at a restaurant—then was diagnosed with Ebola on October 23. Spencer contacted the health department immediately after he registered a low-grade fever. Officials redoubled their efforts to inform the public of symptoms to watch for. Ebola did not spread to anyone else, but many critics demanded to know why Spencer had not isolated himself at his Harlem apartment after his return. Dr. Spencer survived and went on to work on the front lines of the COVID outbreak in New York City six years later.

The announcement about Spencer posed an immediate problem for another volunteer who returned from West Africa the next day. After serving with Doctors Without Borders in Sierra Leone, nurse Kaci Hickox landed at Newark Liberty International Airport in New Jersey. New Jersey governor Chris Christie, publicly repudiating the quarantine standards issued by the CDC for returning health workers, ordered Hickox into quarantine. In a widely publicized series of events, Hickox spent nearly four days in a plastic tent outside Newark airport. With the exception of one slightly elevated temperature from a forehead scan that registered normal on a different device, Hickox never experienced symptoms and, indeed, never developed Ebola. In media interviews, however, Christie said Hickox was "obviously ill" and led what Hickox described as "a fear campaign" against her.

Hickox was allowed no visitors until three days later, when attorney Norman Siegel insisted he be allowed to speak with her. Siegel was a former director of the New York Civil Liberties Union. Friends in the medical community alerted him to Hickox's plight.[29]

New Jersey officials eventually transported Hickox to her residence in Maine, where health officials filed a court petition to require strict home confinement for three weeks. With Siegel's help, along with supporting documents from medical groups, Hickox challenged the most stringent aspect of the state's request. Judge Charles LaVerdiere agreed that state health officials had not shown home confinement was medically necessary to protect the public, but he left in place a less restrictive alternative—directly observed temperature monitoring, which Hickox had already agreed to. The decision was a victory for medical groups who argued that automatic three-week quarantines discouraged healthcare workers from traveling to Ebola-stricken countries, while New Jersey, Maine, and other states contended that such restrictions were necessary to protect public health. Judge LaVerdiere acknowledged the "misconceptions, misinformation, bad science and bad information being spread from shore to shore in our country with respect to Ebola." But he also recognized "whether that fear is rational or not, it is present and it is real."[30]

Another challenge to quarantine orders in Connecticut received less attention. Yale University's Legal Services Organization filed a class-action lawsuit against the governor of Connecticut and state public health officials over the state's treatment of residents affected by Connecticut's Ebola quarantine policies.[31] The complaint sought damages on behalf of Connecticut residents who were quarantined for up to three weeks with police officers posted outside their residences.[32] One plaintiff, Assunta Nimley-Phillips, alleged that she had received no written quarantine order and no information about her legal right to challenge it, while two Yale graduate students—Laura Skrip and Ryan Boyko—were confined to their apartments for three weeks after returning from Liberia, despite not having come into contact with Ebola patients there. The lawsuit was dismissed on the grounds of governmental immunity.[33] Health officials generally cannot be held liable for reasonable actions taken in a good-faith belief of public necessity. It was easier to assume any traveler from Liberia was at risk of developing Ebola than to prove someone had potentially been exposed to body fluids from an Ebola patient.

With the support of the ACLU, Kaci Hickox later sued Governor Christie and the New Jersey Department of Health for better civil rights protections in quarantines ordered by the state. She agreed to a settlement that spelled out a patient "bill of rights," which, among other things, ensures that anyone placed in quarantine has a right to an attorney and a right to a hearing to challenge the state's justification. As one journalist put it, "Her case reflected both the hysteria stirred up by Ebola at the time and the haphazard, varying rules governing public health emergencies across the country."[34] Hickox continued to advocate for change in public health quarantine laws by speaking at conferences and writing editorials. "It is my hope," she said, "that in the future civil liberties are fairly balanced with public health concerns, and quarantine policies are based on science and evidence instead of fear."[35] The "famous Ebola court case" involving Hickox continued to occupy academics for years to come.[36]

• • •

But Kaci Hickox was not the first person involuntarily quarantined for Ebola. That had already happened in Dallas, though few knew about it because the situation was intentionally kept from public view. At the request of Commissioner Lakey, a judge in Dallas ordered that a homeless man, with no symptoms and (at best) only an attenuated risk of exposure, should be quarantined. That man was locked inside an unused ward at Texas Health Presbyterian Hospital for nearly three weeks, against his will, and prevented by armed guards from leaving. The problem was that Texas law permitted no such thing.

I discovered the case while researching how public health officials handled the Ebola outbreak in Dallas. I uncovered an odd set of records in an obscure county court database that described a court-ordered quarantine not mentioned in any of the reports I had read.[37] Through a review of those court records, police reports, and interviews, I pieced together a troubling story.

As health officials searched for Dallas residents who may have encountered Thomas Duncan, they wanted to locate ten people who had ridden in the ambulance after Duncan, concerned about whether the ambulance's glucose monitor had been adequately cleaned. One of those ten, whom I refer to as X, a homeless day laborer, was the last to be found. Authorities located him outside NorthPark Mall. He had not heard of the Ebola incident at Texas Health Presbyterian and told the contact tracer, "I'm glad you found me."[38] X willingly accompanied the health department employee to Texas Health Presbyterian Hospital for evaluation, but after waiting all afternoon to see a doctor and not registering a temperature, he grew tired of waiting and left. He was under the impression he could leave and understood that the hospital did not, in fact, have the authority to detain him.

A media frenzy ensued after authorities told reporters they were seeking a man who had ridden in the ambulance after Duncan, including inaccurate reports that a "homeless man" with Ebola was on the loose in Dallas, hiding from authorities. Spearheading the effort to locate X, Jenkins and Rawlings met with more than forty police officers and sheriff's deputies outside the mall where they had last seen X.[39] Four Dallas police officers found him the next day in a nearby parking lot. According to the Dallas Police Department incident report, X was taken into custody without issue and transported to Parkland Memorial Hospital.

The story is murkier than the police report indicates, however. In reality, the purpose of locating and detaining X was to serve him with a DSHS control order prepared the day before. This control order was different from any used for community contacts, even for the family who had lived with Duncan. It did not offer ways for X to have his temperature checked twice a day or to report any symptoms. Instead, the order required that he stay at Texas Health Presbyterian Hospital until the Ebola incubation period had passed. He had to provide blood samples and cooperate with invasive testing. The order included the threat of criminal prosecution if he did not comply.

X would not agree to be locked in a hospital. According to the police report, officers explained to X that his health was a concern. His response included a string of vulgarities and the comment "I don't give a f*** about Ebola." The police, apparently under orders to take him into custody if he refused to go voluntarily, transported him to Parkland "for evaluation." But Texas public health law does not warrant forcibly arresting someone who is not sick and has no symptoms of a contagious disease. Instead, officers seem to have relied on Texas mental health laws to arrest X and take him to Parkland for evaluation. Even that seems pretextual—under Texas law, depriving someone of liberty for a mental health evaluation requires much more than their using colorful language.[40]

Whatever the justification for arresting X, to keep him under quarantine required a court order "for the management of a person with a communicable disease," a process used primarily for noncompliant tuberculosis patients in an actively infectious stage. Under Texas law, public health officials can request such an order if a person "is infected with or is reasonably suspected of being infected with a communicable disease that presents a threat to public health."[41] The health department must detail "the basis for its opinion that the person is infected with or is reasonably suspected of being infected with a communicable disease that presents an immediate threat to the public health."[42] But merely having (potentially) been exposed to Ebola doesn't fit the criteria. Ebola can be diagnosed and transmitted only when symptoms appear, and X had no symptoms then or later. Texas law does not permit health officials to order confinement just to see whether symptoms will appear.

On October 9, Judge Dale Tillery granted the state's quarantine application.[43] X would live in a deserted wing at Texas Presbyterian, under guard, for the next three weeks, even though Texas law was clearly in X's favor. Judge Tillery could hardly do otherwise in the dilemma he faced. The request was filed on behalf of Dr. Lakey, the top public health official in the state, and the lead attorney on the court papers was the state's attorney general, Greg Abbott.[44] On the other hand, Judge Tillery had available to him a guide to Texas communicable disease law, known as a "bench book," explaining the circumstances in which a person can be quarantined against his will. The bench book instructed judges that when health officials seek court enforcement of a control order, their main responsibility is "to ensure that the proper balance is found between the protection of public health and the protection of individual liberty rights."[45]

By all accounts, Judge Tillery is a well-respected, hardworking, and conscientious jurist. He went out of his way to make sure X was treated well during his quarantine, at one point ordering hospital officials to provide him with a television, according to a person familiar with the episode. Yet the documents filed in the case did not establish the state's right to take away X's freedom. Perhaps the best explanation for what happened to X is fear—fear that if authorities did not force X into quarantine he might develop and spread Ebola, and they would be blamed for doing nothing. That X's quarantine was illegal under Texas law "didn't matter," one person involved in the court proceedings told me. "They were too scared. And that's what happens when you're so scared. The rule of law goes out the window."

Philip Haigh, an aide to county judge Clay Jenkins, explained X's case was kept "under tight wraps because we didn't want people to know about it and we didn't want people to think we were arresting people left and right." Jenkins also explained, "This was bigger than Dallas. This is America's Ebola crisis. If we go and arrest this person, then in the next Ebola outbreak in Cincinnati or New York, you're going to have a lot of people who won't come forward. If they think they'll be jailed, they won't come forward. And they have to come forward. The repercussions would be tremendous."[46]

X lacked the social media following and contacts with the medical community that might have attracted the attention of the ACLU, as Kaci Hickox's situation did. No journalists reported on X's court-ordered quarantine or the legal issues it raised, but some instead informed the nation of every detail about his personal life that could be gleaned.[47] Kaci Hickox did not know it, but her lawsuit for a patient bill of rights for New Jersey spoke for X too.

By October 20, 2014, officials informed all of the community contacts that their monitoring period was over, and they were no longer at risk of contracting the disease. X was released from confinement. Not a single community contact ever developed Ebola. Louise Troh and three others who had been in the cramped apartment with Duncan were also declared Ebola-free and released from the health department's communicable disease control order. Troh released a statement expressing relief and gratitude that none of her family members showed any sign of illness.[48]

Monitoring continued for 149 others in Dallas—mostly healthcare workers and community contacts of Amber Vinson and Nina Pham. Ohio officials monitored 153 people who had been on the flight from Dallas to Cleveland with Vinson, along with nearly two dozen others in Ohio, including family members and the owner of the bridal store she had visited. Passengers on Vinson's return flight to Dallas—132 in all—were contacted by phone. Frontier Airlines contacted 750 additional passengers on five other flights that used the same plane afterward. Six crew members on the flight to Dallas were put on a three-week paid leave.[49] But for the Dallas residents who had first come into contact with Thomas Duncan, normal life resumed.

• • •

The spread of Ebola to health workers at an American hospital brought an immediate response from Congress. It held the first of several hearings just weeks after Thomas Duncan's death and immediately after news that a second Dallas nurse had contracted Ebola. Dr. Fauci, representing the NIH, and Dr. Frieden, from the CDC, testified before a congressional oversight committee examining the US public health response to the Ebola outbreak. Republican members of the committee expressed frustration that the Obama administration had not closed the US borders to all travelers from West Africa. Other members countered with the example of Andrew Speaker, who, in 2007, while infected with multi-drug-resistant tuberculosis, had managed to elude restrictions on his travel and entered the country through Canada.

Another concern was whether US hospitals could diagnose and treat Ebola patients, given the failures at Texas Presbyterian. Texas Representative Pete Sessions, a member of the House GOP leadership, complained that "CDC seems to take this as an academic or statistical exercise." Because the spread of Ebola in Dallas "is a scary thing to many Americans," Sessions said, "I think the federal government should respond in kind."[50]

Dr. Daniel Varga, CEO of Texas Presbyterian Hospital, appeared at the hearing by video link from Dallas. He admitted that Texas Presbyterian should have diagnosed Thomas Duncan correctly on his first visit to the emergency room and that he erroneously reported that Duncan had not told medical staff that he had traveled from Liberia. But Varga maintained that the nurses who became infected had made no mistakes in putting on and removing protective gear; he could not account for how they might have contracted Ebola. Tim Murphy, a Republican representative from Pennsylvania, directed his closing remarks at Dr. Frieden, Dr. Fauci, and the director of Customs and Border Protection: "So having listened to all your testimony. I appreciate Dr. Daniel Varga's statement of honesty that we made mistakes. I didn't hear that from any of you, and that troubles me." Democratic Representative Henry Waxman, of California, noted that "while Presbyterian Hospital in Dallas clearly had made mistakes, most other U.S. hospitals would have struggled as well to respond to Ebola."[51]

Congress would hold several more hearings about America's Ebola response and preparedness, but media coverage dramatically dropped off after the November midterm elections. One analysis reported that television news outlets aired nearly a thousand segments on Ebola in the four weeks before the midterms, but only fifty in the two weeks afterward. The Republican Party had developed a plan in early October to make the federal government's response to Ebola a central part of its midterm elections strategy, a strategy not needed after election day.[52]

· · ·

With no additional cases of Ebola in Dallas, media attention shifted from there, and with it the attention of Congress. Committee hearings hammered on the responsibility of the federal government to maintain adequate stockpiles of PPE and asked the Department of Health and Human Services to designate hospitals by region with the capability to handle highly contagious diseases like Ebola. In the following years, three expert commissions published critiques of the response by both states and the federal government. In one, an independent panel reached two conclusions that should have served as a wake-up call before the COVID-19 pandemic. Federal health agencies, the report warned, are "not configured or funded to respond to a prolonged public health or medical emergency." The report also noted, "Federal, state, and local governments applied different—and, at times, conflicting—policies and authorities for specific response measures."[53] If there were other lessons learned at the national level, Congress did not see the need to put them into law.

The story was different in Texas, however. In December 2014, a task force appointed by Governor Rick Perry issued a 174-page report explaining how Texas could have handled Ebola better. One of the "critically important" recommendations was to change the state's quarantine laws because, the report claimed, Ebola had proven them to be inadequate to protect the public.[54] Health officials could not enforce quarantine orders against someone who had merely been exposed to a disease but had no symptoms, when that disease cannot be spread before symptoms appear. Commissioner Lakey helped write the report, and he surely had X's case in mind.

The following March, Charles Schwertner, a Republican representing Georgetown, Texas, and also a surgeon, introduced legislation to overhaul Texas infectious disease law. Senate Bill 538 mirrored the wish list from the task force report almost exactly.[55] While Texas was successful in stopping the spread of Ebola, Schwertner said, "the event exposed weaknesses in our state's ability to handle infectious disease outbreaks." His legislation would better equip the state to handle a similar emergency in the future. Schwertner hoped his bill could be "a model for the rest of the country."[56]

Two provisions on the subject of quarantine in the lengthy bill practically amounted to an admission that Dr. Lakey and Attorney General Abbott had illegally quarantined X. The first proposal would make it easier to enforce health department orders without a court order. Dr. Lakey had been frustrated that while he could order a person who had potentially been exposed to Ebola to stay home, authorities could enforce the order only after the person had already broken it. Texas law should be changed to allow police officers to enforce the order without first going to court. Strengthening quarantine law in this way was "critically important," according to the task force.

The second proposal added a category of those who could be subject to involuntary quarantine. The state now would be able to confine anyone who had potentially been "exposed to" a contagious disease, not just anyone who was already ill. Dr. Lakey had claimed to have the power to issue quarantine orders to anyone exposed to Ebola. But the law would need to be amended to make that true. Accordingly, Senate Bill 538 applied Texas quarantine law to anyone who "has been exposed to a communicable disease," rather than only to persons "infected with" or "reasonably suspected of being infected with" a communicable disease that presents a threat to public health. No one who might have come into contact with Thomas Duncan could have been "reasonably suspected of being infected with" Ebola. Exposed to Ebola, perhaps. But that's not what the law said when Louise Troh's family was ordered not to leave their apartment and when X was confined by court order.

Despite nearly unanimous support in the state senate and the endorsement of the Texas Medical Association, Schwertner's bill never made it out of a House committee. Dr. Lakey would not get the quarantine law changed to have the authority he thought was needed.

SB 538 also would have centralized control over a public health emergency and given the state health commissioner broad power to take action, displacing local officials. The bill's sponsors believed the potential for conflict between state and local officials ought to be resolved in favor of the state. John Dahill, the executive director of the Texas Conference of Urban Counties, opposed the bill because it substituted state control for local control of infectious disease emergencies: "Officials in Austin don't have the same breadth of knowledge of local communities as do local health departments, local health authorities, and county judges and mayors."[57]

An editorial by the *Dallas Morning News* thought SB 538 was "overkill." It would grant the governor extraordinary powers to declare an "infectious disease emergency" and supersede the authority of county officials to respond to public health emergencies. "Recall the overreaction by New Jersey governor Chris Christie during last year's Ebola scare," the paper warned, "to understand how badly such authority could go awry."[58] Others opposed it for fear it could infringe on the civil liberties of anyone merely suspected of being contagious.[59]

If Texas law didn't change much, political leaders in the state had nonetheless gained valuable experience for the future. The Ebola episode in Dallas exposed two problems—confusion about who was in charge and confusion about what the law allowed. As a newspaper editorial summed up, "We learned that comfortable assumptions about preparedness crumble to dust in the presence of real-time emergency, and that some scenarios can't really be understood until they have been endured. Most of all, we learned a lot about the chaotic, reason-eroding effects of pure, unharnessed panic."[60]

At the 2015 Atlantic Health Forum, after Americans had mostly forgotten about the events in Dallas, Anthony Fauci reminded the audience that the Ebola crisis in West Africa continued. Fauci also conveyed his concern about new and emerging diseases. He was especially concerned that the next pandemic could be a respiratory virus that spreads more easily than Ebola: "The thing that's the most concerning is something that would spread by the respiratory route," he said. "We have a history of pandemics, and that's the reason why at the NIH we are trying to develop a much better influenza vaccine."[61] The next pandemic would indeed be a fast-spreading respiratory virus, as Fauci feared, but it was not influenza.

The US Navy ship Comfort *passes the Statue of Liberty as it enters New York Harbor in New York City, March 30, 2020.*

9

A CORONAVIRUS PANDEMIC

> *Pandemics bring out the worst in society, for some reason. They expose the fault lines of communications and leadership and politics and haves and have-nots in this horrific way that we're now seeing.*
>
> —ERIC SCHMIDT, former Google CEO[1]

The United States Navy hospital ship *Comfort,* with a thousand hospital beds and a crew of 1,200, sailed past the Statue of Liberty in New York harbor in the early morning hours of March 30, 2020. Earlier that month, New York City had become the epicenter of the US coronavirus outbreak, and its medical centers were overwhelmed. President Trump ordered the *Comfort* to New York City from its home port in Virginia with a mission to help local hospitals, as a "70,000-ton message of hope and solidarity to the incredible people of New York."[2] The *Comfort* had seen emergency service in Puerto Rico following Hurricane Maria in 2017, but this was only the second time the *Comfort* was ever dispatched to an American mainland city. The first time had also been to New York City, after the terrorist attacks of September 11, 2001.[3]

With less fanfare, the navy's other hospital ship, *Mercy,* had arrived at Los Angeles three days earlier from its home base in San Diego. The *Mercy* was now the largest hospital in Los Angeles. As the ship docked, California governor Gavin Newsom was on hand, declaring, "The spirit of collaboration and cooperation is alive in this state."[4]

The *Mercy*'s captain, John R. Rotruck, said, "Although we have never responded to a pandemic, this is the type of mission that we train for, as our ship is uniquely outfitted for humanitarian assistance and disaster relief."[5] In the meantime, US naval ships in other parts of the world began to report outbreaks of COVID-19 onboard. Aboard the aircraft carrier *Theodore Roosevelt,* more than a quarter of its 4,800 sailors fell ill and were placed in isolation in Guam.[6]

Before the deployments ended, both *Mercy* and *Comfort* had treated fewer patients than expected. But the symbolism of the US military's most advanced hospital ship passing the Statue of Liberty brought hope to the residents and health workers of New York City. For the rest of the nation, however, the sight evoked fear and trepidation. Americans had seen images of overburdened facilities and exhausted hospital workers in Italy, France, and Great Britain, and they had seen US residents rush home before travel from Europe had shut down completely. The chaos abroad, first in Wuhan, then in Europe, was coming here.

When pandemics strike, a federal official had warned in 2007, they can reshape nations.[7] Indeed, the COVID pandemic humbled rich and poor nations alike, as scientists struggled to understand how it spread and what treatments, if any, might reduce its severity.

Just the year before, in 2019, the Johns Hopkins Center for Health Security had ranked 195 countries on their readiness to confront a pandemic.[8] The United States topped the list. Ominously, though, America received the lowest possible score for public confidence in government. Stunningly, the nation ranked 175th for access to healthcare, ahead of just nineteen other countries. What surprised public health experts the most during the pandemic was the nation's slow, inconsistent response and its high rate of infections and deaths, which led the world throughout the first year, even though the US represents just 4 percent of the global population. "I don't think we've ever failed on this scale," said Joe Smyser, head of a national healthcare nonprofit. "The level of failure is almost inconceivable."[9]

• • •

In September 2007, Massachusetts State Police Major Timothy Alben submitted his eighty-page thesis to the Naval Postgraduate School in

Monterey, California, the last step in earning his master's degree in security studies. Over the previous eighteen months, Alben had joined a cohort of police officers, firefighters, state emergency management employees, and even some elected officials for a unique program designed to train public servants to respond to emergencies. The degree required each student to choose a topic for in-depth research. The majority of Alben's classmates chose topics related to terrorism and how to respond to it. "We were only a few years removed from 9/11," he explained, and "the 9/11 Commission's report was part of the readings that we had to do before you even got to the program."[10]

Alben chose a different subject from his classmates, one he saw as equally essential to homeland security—how to prepare communities for a future pandemic. On a plane ride to California at the start of the program, Alben read John Barry's 2004 book about the 1918 pandemic, *The Great Influenza.*[11] "I was just riveted by it," Alben said.

> The one thing that stood out to me in Barry's book, I think I carry it with me to today, is his description of one week in October of 1918 in the city of Philadelphia, where they had over five thousand people die. They were dragging them out to sidewalks and leaving the bodies there to be picked up. As bad as 9/11 was, as bad as Pearl Harbor was, it was nothing like that in my viewing. How would we deal with such an event today? What's the strategy? How would you rally the American people behind anything at that point to try to mitigate it?[12]

Alben set out to do just that—study ways to gain public cooperation in a fight against a pandemic. It was an unusual subject choice for a Massachusetts state trooper, but not so unusual for elected officials and public health experts at the time. The anthrax attacks after 9/11 raised alarm bells in Congress about the threat of bioterrorism, perhaps a weaponized smallpox. Every city in the nation needed to be prepared to respond to "dirty bombs." But as yet, the nation had no national security agenda to combat naturally occurring biologic threats like pandemic flu. In 2005 President George W. Bush came to recognize pandemic disease as a national security threat.[13] Bush ordered federal agencies to come up with a plan for a nationwide response to a naturally occurring outbreak, and he called on Congress to fund the nation's readiness.

Congress responded the next year with the Pandemic and All-Hazards Preparedness Act, convinced after Hurricane Katrina that the US must be better prepared for a public health emergency, whether from a terrorist attack or from a natural event.[14] With both the White House and Congress now mandating preparations for pandemic influenza, agencies at all levels of government produced an enormous number of emergency response plans. Alben reviewed these closely and mastered the already immense academic literature on pandemic preparation. The difficulty was how to say something new about it.

To Alben, the plans all shared a major weakness—they relied on the development and distribution of effective vaccines, which could take a year or more. In the meantime, the nation would have to rely on measures to slow or delay the spread of a virus—the time-tested strategies of fighting a pandemic through "community mitigations and interventions," such as "school closures, event cancelations, limited travel, quarantine and work at home plans."[15] But restrictive measures like these require citizens to go along with them. It would not be a good use of police officer time, for example, to settle disputes between customers and business owners, break up house parties and arrest curfew violators, watch the homes of persons under quarantine, or issue citations for failure to wear a face mask. Public health experts had long since moved to a cooperation model from the more coercive tactics of a century before and the authoritarian power reflected in quarantine laws. "It's all about trust," according to public health expert Ruth Bernheim. "If you get to the point you are locking people up, you've already lost."[16] Public health interventions like these would require unprecedented levels of public trust.

But how to earn that trust? The need for voluntary cooperation was not a new insight, but Alben's idea came from his training and experience in law enforcement. Pandemic planners should borrow from the "community policing" model and look at the problem from a law enforcement perspective. Community policing is a law enforcement strategy to create stronger bonds between police and local residents. The model encourages officers to engage with the communities they serve to identify concerns and develop solutions together, avoiding the too-late phenomenon of a police presence only after a crime is committed.[17]

The key element to the community policing concept, Alben learned, is transparency and effective communication by government officials under stressful circumstances. Gaining public confidence in a pandemic, Alben predicted, would prove to be far more challenging to elected officials than putting together a pandemic plan. It would not matter what the law said or what any plan required unless community members chose to comply.

Alben was right. Elected officials would find responding to COVID-19 far more difficult than anyone contemplated. Utter confusion prevailed about who had what authority and how to use that authority to slow the pandemic. When El Paso, Texas, experienced a tidal wave of new cases in November 2020, the highest-ranking county official issued a limited business closure order, which the mayor of the city promptly overruled on the grounds that it was unnecessary. County police tried to enforce the lockdown, while city police announced they would not. Soon enough, the state attorney general was leading an effort in state court to strike down the county order as illegal under Texas law. The president of the El Paso Chamber of Commerce, David Jerome, summed up the tug of war: "One thing almost worse than being closed down is being confused about whether you are closed down. I'm a big fan of fifty experiments in democracy but not when it comes to a pandemic."[18] At that time, the city of El Paso had more people hospitalized with COVID-19 than most states. With all their beds full, hospitals resorted to airlifting coronavirus patients to other cities. The National Guard helped move bodies into mobile morgues.[19]

Mitigation strategies varied wildly from state to state and city to city, starting with a confusing and bewildering variation in what qualified as a "nonessential business" to be shut down temporarily. In Florida, Texas, Maine, and other states, police officers stopped travelers at state lines to inform even returning residents they must quarantine for two weeks. A partisan divide emerged over face masks; some sheriffs announced they would not enforce local ordinances because they believed them to be unconstitutional.[20] Major retailers like Walmart adopted face-mask policies to protect their employees, but some governors sued cities to stop face-mask ordinances meant to support those business policies. Public health officials were threatened and attacked.[21] Armed protesters appeared in state capitols to intimidate lawmakers, urged on by a presidential tweet to "liberate Minnesota."[22] More peaceful protesters complained of government invasion of personal liberty.

To be fair, the coronavirus moved too fast for the aspirational community involvement Alben envisioned. In a matter of months, COVID-19 spread from Wuhan, China, throughout the world. Within weeks, long before the *Comfort* sailed past the Statue of Liberty, the virus had spread across the entire continental United States. In those first weeks, no one seemed to know who was in charge of doing anything about it. Returning cruise ships, many ravaged by COVID, needed permission of local mayors to dock and let passengers disembark. On both US coasts, local officials delayed or turned away cruise ships with American citizens aboard, as the federal government negotiated with governors and mayors to aid them. The city of Costa Mesa, California, and the governor of Alabama refused to allow the federal government to set up quarantine facilities for Americans evacuated from Wuhan and from cruise ships. The early months of the COVID pandemic brought many such examples of state and local governments refusing to host quarantined Americans who had returned from overseas.

For nearly the entire first year of the pandemic, the federal government left states to their own resources and encouraged governors to make their own decisions—or to do nothing. Governors scrambled to compete on the open market with hospital systems and healthcare facilities for critical medical supplies, adequate testing, and other resources. Long-term care facilities were mostly left on their own to find personal protective equipment for caregivers. Some of the worst situations during COVID, though, did not result from inadequate federal leadership, as damaging as that was. Instead, state laws thought to be adequate for a public health emergency fell short of the need.

• • •

In all of the pandemic planning that had gone before, no one expected all fifty state governors to rule by emergency decree so extensively and for so long—well over a year. The governors of California and New

York were the first to declare states of emergency in the first week of March 2020. One after another, governors of every other state followed suit, along with the District of Columbia, the Commonwealth of Puerto Rico, and all US territories. These emergency declarations gave governors the power to issue pandemic control measures (or not, if the governor did not see the need for them). Emergency declarations also empowered governors to invoke crisis standards of care for healthcare facilities, contract for emergency supplies and personnel, and enforce laws against price gouging, among other measures.

Emergency declarations are a management power granted by state legislatures to respond to short-term disasters like hurricanes, fires, and earthquakes. In a state of emergency, governors have extraordinary powers not available to them in "normal" times. They have broad discretion to take actions to protect life, property, public health, and safety, including the authority to commandeer resources, order evacuations, prevent price gouging, and enact curfews. Governors can set aside the normal processes of state government and suspend laws.[23] There may not be time for the state's legislature to convene during an emergency, and in any event the legislative process is slow, not designed for quick action.

Never before in US history had all fifty states simultaneously declared states of emergency for a pandemic or for anything else. Such use of emergency powers proved that existing public health laws were inadequate for this pandemic and prompted considerable antagonism toward state governors by one camp or another. Even proponents of local decision-making and serious skeptics of the federal government found cause for concern about the seemingly unlimited authority exercised by state governors.

That existing law would be so unclear and inadequate to meet the emergency surprised almost everyone, including the governors themselves. The COVID-19 pandemic exposed a significant gap in state legislation. Public health laws enacted over the years by state legislatures were meant to control local outbreaks; these laws did not specifically authorize the type of broad mitigation measures that governors and health officials in both red and blue states believed were necessary to protect the public. State and local laws for quarantine and isolation, some dating back a century or more, had never been applied to control the behavior of more widespread populations, regardless of known exposure to a contagious disease. One would search the statute books in vain for terms like "social distancing" and "nonessential business." That is one reason why governors relied on emergency declarations, which were not designed for an emergency lasting more than a few weeks and which have few "guardrails" to constrain arbitrary or excessive actions.[24]

In the year following the state declarations of emergency, governors collectively issued thousands of executive orders covering matters ranging from restaurant regulations to driver's license renewals to restrictions on nonessential medical care.[25] Some executive orders followed CDC guidelines, as those became available; others did not. Business closures were the most controversial by far. What was an essential business? Grocery stores obviously qualified; nail salons usually did not. Governors had no ready-made lists, so they created their own. No two lists were the same; the differences among them often reflected economic and constituent priorities. In Georgia, for example, tattoo parlors were among the first businesses to reopen, while comparable businesses in other states remained shuttered.[26] Few legislatures had included any direction on business closures in the statutes granting emergency authority to governors, although in Georgia (again) gun sales could not be restricted.[27] The US Department of Homeland Security advised state and local governments to consider gun stores as "essential services" allowed to operate under emergency declarations. The National Rifle Association sued California and New York when their governors listed gun stores as nonessential.[28]

The National Governors Association shared information via frequent conference calls, and they brought in legal experts to advise on many urgent questions. One of the first questions was whether governors could legally enter collective bargaining agreements with each other for greater purchasing power in the medical supplies market. Legal analysts concluded that they could, and regional coalitions began bidding for medical supplies as a group in an effort to keep prices from spiraling further upward as other states bid against each other. Governors in the Northeast also found it helpful to coordinate with each other on business reopenings and quarantine requirements. The relatively small geography of those states required such coordination;

otherwise, one state's efforts to slow the virus in its population could be quickly undermined by its citizens driving down the road to take advantage of another state's different approach.

In response to the political backlash against pandemic emergency orders and concerns about executive overreach, legislatures in more than half of the states enacted laws permanently restricting public health powers.[29] Some of these new laws require governors to seek legislative approval of emergency declarations. Other laws withdraw specific pandemic measures from the governor's control, such as business closures and stay-at-home orders. At least seventeen states banned vaccine mandates or requests for proof of vaccination by businesses. Nearly a dozen state legislatures passed new laws banning mask mandates. In Arkansas, the legislature banned all local governments—including public schools—from implementing mask requirements at any time in the future. The law went into effect before a surge of the hyper-infectious Delta variant swept the state, which still has one of the lowest vaccination rates in the country. (Governor Asa Hutchinson said he regretted signing the law and now believes it is unconstitutional.)[30]

Some state legislatures made only temporary changes to public health emergency law. Kansas, for example, enacted legislation to sunset after the COVID pandemic. Among other things, the Kansas legislature told citizens they need not cooperate with contact tracers. Legislatures in all fifty states considered hundreds of different proposals to reform state public health emergency law in one form or another. Lobbyists pushed agendas too: the National Rifle Association pushed legislation to keep gun stores open during a pandemic. Understandably, advocates for laws limiting the kinds of emergency measures officials can put in place believe "they are a necessary check on executive powers and give lawmakers a voice in prolonged emergencies."[31]

Discord between state and local governments throughout the pandemic added to the confusion about the legal authority of governors. From the nation's earliest decades, city and county governments had been able to decide what measures were necessary to protect their residents from disease. In a break from this tradition, Republican governors in a number of states used their emergency authority to preempt more protective measures that cities wanted to put in place. Governors and local officials disagreed about whether there should be in-person schooling, whether church services could be held in person indoors, which businesses should remain open or operate with restrictions, and more. In Texas, Dallas County health officials abandoned plans to prioritize vaccinations in mostly Black and Latinx neighborhoods, after the state's health commissioner threatened to slash the county's vaccine allocation. County officials sought to remedy a problem seen nationwide: vaccination distribution centers tended to be set up in white, wealthier neighborhoods, making it more difficult for minority communities to access them. The Dallas County plan had sought to help the very communities that had been hardest hit by COVID, but local authorities were thwarted by partisan forces.[32]

In Georgia, residents of Tybee Island, a community of about three thousand residents near Savannah, ordered its beaches closed on March 20, 2020, out of fear that visitors could bring COVID. The community had no hospital, and only a single two-lane highway connected it to the mainland. But in early April, Governor Kemp ordered all Georgia beaches to reopen, catching local officials by surprise. Tybee Island mayor Shirley Sessions objected that reopening Tybee's beach would put "the health of our residents, staff and visitors" at risk. She expressed her fury in a statement soon after the governor's announcement: "As the Pentagon ordered 100,000 body bags to store the corpses of Americans killed by the Coronavirus, Governor Brian Kemp dictated that Georgia beaches must reopen, and declared any decision makers who refused to follow these orders would face prison and/or fines." Glynn County commissioner Allen Booker called the governor's move "stupid and crazy at the same time."[33] The town already had two hospitalized city employees and at least six first responders in quarantine.[34]

It is one thing for legislatures to take away the independent public health authority that city and county governments have long held. It is quite another, however, for a governor to do so, using emergency powers to single-handedly take back that delegation of authority. Executive orders intended to be enforced statewide overlooked the fact that urban and rural America experience epidemics differently, especially when infections spike in densely populated areas.

Even proponents of local decision-making and skeptics of the federal government found cause for concern about the seemingly unlimited authority exercised by state governors, given that disaster laws were not designed for an emergency lasting for more than a few weeks and have few guardrails to constrain arbitrary or excessive actions. But the quick succession of permanent changes to state law in reaction to COVID-19 threaten to make state law for future pandemics even more chaotic than it already is.

. . .

Unsurprisingly, litigants turned up in droves to state and federal courts to challenge pandemic measures. Sometimes the parties were different branches of the same government: legislators sued the governor, claiming that pandemic orders exceeded the governor's authority. Most such cases came from states with divided government—a governor of one party and a legislative majority of the other. Courts typically upheld the broad use of emergency powers, with notable exceptions. The Wisconsin Supreme Court ruled in March 2021 that the state's emergency law did not permit the governor to issue successive emergency declarations during the pandemic—although by then, the governor had done so for a full year.[35]

Far more lawsuits were filed by private citizens and organizations, many hundreds throughout the country, asking judges to strike down COVID measures as violations of individual constitutional rights and liberties. Chief among them were face-mask requirements, which drew more controversy than other COVID mitigation measures.

Federal officials early in the pandemic downplayed face coverings as a protective measure, even while images from China and other nations showed the public wearing them. For weeks the CDC—concerned primarily by the need to conserve the nation's severely limited supplies of personal protective equipment—told Americans they need not wear a face covering if they were not sick.[36] Surgeon General Jerome Adams would come to regret a tweet he sent on February 29, 2020: "Seriously people—STOP BUYING MASKS!" The rest of the tweet explained that "if healthcare providers can't get them to care for sick patients, it puts them and our communities at risk."[37] The clear implication was that the average person did not need one.

But as scientists understood more about how COVID was spread, it became clear that even rudimentary cloth coverings could be of substantial benefit. Reversing course in early April 2020, the CDC recommended the use of cloth face coverings to slow the spread of COVID-19, especially in public settings such as grocery stores, where social distancing is difficult. The CDC estimated that up to 35 percent of people infected with the coronavirus have no symptoms and therefore may unknowingly infect others. Masks reduce the chance of infected people transmitting the respiratory droplets that contain the virus. Again, however, a clear partisan divide emerged. Many never understood that face masks protect others; instead, they saw requiring masks as an invasion of personal liberty. I heard one caller to a local radio station say that he would not wear a mask to the store because he "wasn't afraid." "But if you're afraid," he said, "then wear one." But fear for oneself was not the issue. Protecting others was.

Some state and local governments mandated the use of face masks in specific settings, typically in retail establishments and on public transportation. In several states, including Michigan, New York, and Rhode Island, governors ordered that all employers provide face masks and require employees to wear them if the employees would be in close contact with others.[38] But in July 2020, business leaders in the private sector led the way toward a national masking policy when large retailers, including Walmart, CVS, and Lowe's, announced face coverings would be required in all stores.[39]

Anti-mask protesters sometimes disrupted city and county commission meetings when face masks were under consideration. In Idaho, Ada County commissioner Diana Lachiondo excused herself from an August 8 meeting of the Central District Health Board, which had planned to vote on a mask mandate for the four counties it covered. The reason she gave shocked those viewing the public meeting on Zoom. "My 12-year-old son is home by himself right now, and there are protesters banging outside the door," she said. "I'm going to go home and make sure he's okay."[40] Demonstrators went to other board members' homes as well, and hundreds gathered outside the Central District's building where some of the board members were in their offices. When the board delayed the vote to the following week, protesters tried to storm the building. Demonstrators attended the rescheduled meeting as well, but this time police barricades were up. The health board approved the face covering order on August 11. Before then, some cities within the district had already enacted face-mask mandates of their own, including a public health order signed in July by the mayor of Boise, Idaho, Lauren McLean.[41]

As face-mask ordinances multiplied around the country, lawsuits challenging them followed. Judges let them stand, as courts consistently rejected claims that mask mandates violate rights and liberties guaranteed by the federal constitution. Whether imposed by private businesses or government officials, no court has recognized a "right" not to wear a face mask in public settings when government officials with authority to do so have mandated their use to mitigate the spread of COVID. With a virus spread through respiration, especially when a significant percentage of contagious people have no symptoms, courts routinely upheld masking requirements as a necessary public health measure. So long as the face-mask requirement applied to everyone and allowed exceptions for medical need, such as for persons with breathing problems, government officials could mandate that they be worn.

Some litigants claimed that wearing a face mask would identify them with a political position with which they disagreed. But face-covering requirements regulate conduct, not speech, and for decades, health and safety ordinances of all kinds have restricted individual freedoms. Indoor smoking bans in restaurants and other retail establishments, for example, are designed to protect the health of employees and patrons, not the smoker, and courts routinely have upheld such ordinances as within the police power of the state. There is no fundamental right to be a health threat to others, especially if reasonable steps can reduce that threat. The nation's courts had little difficulty fitting mask mandates into this traditional power of state and local governments to protect population health and safety.

Residents in some cities faced the opposite problem: The governor of their state not only refused to mandate any rules on face coverings but also prohibited local governments from doing so. Governors in Florida and Texas ordered local governments to rescind face-mask ordinances, backing that up with threats of lawsuits against the cities. In Idaho, Lieutenant Governor Janice McGeachin issued an executive order barring local face-mask ordinances when Governor Brad Little was out of town. Governor Little quickly rescinded the order when he returned.[42] McGeachin repeated the stunt in October 2021, issuing a ban on COVID-19 vaccine or testing mandates for public schools while the governor was on an official trip to the border region. Governor Little promptly reversed it.[43] Just two weeks earlier, the *Washington Post* reported that COVID deaths in Idaho had reached record highs and morgues were running out of space, "another grisly illustration of what happens when a state fails to contain infections."[44]

In Georgia, Governor Brian Kemp sued the city of Atlanta over its face-mask policy. In July 2020, the mayor of Atlanta, Keisha Lance Bottoms, had required that masks be worn within the city limits. Three county health boards have jurisdiction in the metro area as well but could not implement rules for all of Atlanta. Hartsfield-Jackson International Airport lies within the city limits of Atlanta. For a brief time that summer, travelers passing through the world's busiest airport were required to wear face masks in the terminals and in security lines. Governor Kemp's lawsuit put a stop to that, exposing thousands of travelers to unnecessary risk that they would not face in other major US airports. Although the lawsuit was ultimately dropped and Governor Kemp granted cities some authority to impose localized restrictions, the Atlanta airport reverted to a mask-optional zone. President Joe Biden ended this confusion on his first day in office, ordering that face masks be worn in airports and all forms of public transportation.

As schools reopened in the fall of 2021, the mask wars of the prior year moved to the classroom. Even though courts rejected such claims, many Americans continued to believe that they had a right not to wear face masks because they personally objected to them. Some governors, including Ron DeSantis of Florida and Greg Abbott of Texas, stoked this belief by banning local schools from adopting mask mandates. School mask policies divided communities into two camps: parents who objected to mask mandates because of the inconvenience to their children, and parents who demanded mask policies so that their children could attend school safely. The Centers for Disease Control and Prevention recommended students and teachers wear masks indoors at school, regardless of vaccination status.[45] Before the CDC's updated guidance, the 67,000 doctors of the American Academy of Pediatrics also "strongly" recommended children wear masks in school.[46] With low vaccination rates in many areas, and no vaccine available for children under twelve, the stakes were particularly high.

Who sets mask policies for schools? As schools reopened in fall 2021, in more than half of all US states school districts could decide for themselves, according to the National Academy for State Health Policy. Seventeen states required school masking statewide, regardless of local preference. At the opposite end of the spectrum, more than a dozen states claimed the authority to prohibit mask mandates in any school.

State governors who banned local school districts from requiring masks claimed to vindicate a right of personal choice on behalf of constituents. Tennessee governor Bill Lee, for example, ordered Memphis-area schools to allow students to opt out of a mask mandate, claiming "parents are THE authority and will be the ultimate decision-makers for their individual child's health and well-being." Attorney Brice Timmons, representing parents who supported the school mask requirement, pointed out the obvious: "The sentiment that parents know what's best for their kids is nice, but the way he has framed this is as though parents' decisions about their children only affect their children." When a parent makes a decision for a child to opt out of a school mask requirement, Timmons said, "they're making decisions for other people's children, and the decision they're making is that their comfort matters more" than the safety of all children in that classroom.[47]

Face-mask requirements were only one of many public health measures challenged in court. Hundreds of lawsuits disputed social-distancing measures, including temporary business closures and limits on the size of gatherings. Judges generally upheld these measures, citing *Jacobson v. Massachusetts,* the US Supreme Court case about smallpox vaccination from more than a century ago. *Jacobson* recognized that a state's duty to "guard and protect . . . the safety and health of the people" includes the responsibility of citizens not to endanger others: "Real liberty for all could not exist under the operation of a principle which recognizes the right of each individual person to use his own, whether in respect to his person or his property, regardless of the injury that may be done to others."[48]

Only a handful of cases reached the US Supreme Court during the first year of the COVID pandemic, but the court would weigh in on three of them, all having to do with religious liberty. The first one came from California, when a church group objected to restrictions on in-person worship. Although the court declined to intervene, Chief Justice John Roberts took the unusual step of issuing a concurring opinion that explained that the Constitution "entrusts" health decisions primarily to politically accountable officials.[49] Quoting from the *Jacobson* case, Roberts recognized the extraordinary situation facing all elected officials and wrote that courts should give deference to them during a public health emergency:

> Our Constitution principally entrusts "the safety and the health of the people" to the politically accountable officials of the States "to guard and protect." When those officials "undertake to act in areas fraught with medical and scientific uncertainties," their latitude "must be especially broad." Where those broad limits are not exceeded, they should not be subject to second-guessing by an "unelected federal judiciary," which lacks the background, competence, and expertise to assess public health and is not accountable to the people.[50]

It was the Supreme Court's first foray into state and local efforts to control COVID-19. Chief Justice Roberts used the case to provide broad guidance to lower courts. *Jacobson v. Massachusetts* counsels judges to afford wide latitude to the judgment of health experts, so long as such measures are neutral, generally applicable, and justified by a medical necessity. But while judges must defer to the need to protect public health, they must also be vigilant against abuses of public health powers.

After Amy Coney Barrett replaced Justice Ruth Bader Ginsburg on the court, however, the balance tipped toward a far less deferential approach to restrictions on religious worship. In two subsequent cases, one from New York and the other again from California, the Supreme Court enjoined state orders restricting religious services, even though the measures applied equally to secular gatherings. The new court's revised approach showed it to be far less willing to defer to state officials when religious liberty was at stake.

• • •

If school mask policies proved controversial, a backlash against vaccine mandates topped the scale just as the nation shifted to a "pandemic of the unvaccinated" with the arrival of the more easily transmissible Delta variant in mid-2021.[51] Regions of the country with low vaccination rates were hit hard, with some states seeing case rates and hospitalization rivaling the worst months before vaccines became available. Urgent efforts to vaccinate more people met with limited success in some areas, keeping the virus in circulation to the detriment of the medically vulnerable and those unable to be vaccinated.

Executive orders became a tool in the vaccine wars. First on the stage was Florida governor Ron DeSantis. His ban of so-called vaccine passports prevented businesses in the state from requiring any documentation of a person's vaccine status, a measure later ratified by the state's legislature.[52] Any business requesting vaccine documentation of a patron could be hit with a $5,000 fine for each occurrence. For good measure, DeSantis put the cruise ship industry on notice that no ship departing from the state could require proof of vaccination for passengers. Cruise lines, in response, threatened to bypass Florida ports if ships were not allowed to require vaccinations; they said that federal law applied, not state law.[53] Legal experts agreed—the federal government regulates international commerce; Florida's claim to the contrary was "political buffoonery."[54] A federal judge ruled that cruise ships could ignore the Florida law. Norwegian Cruise Lines faced millions of dollars in fines if it held to its vaccination policy, which it said was the safest way to resume its business.[55] The irony of DeSantis's stance would not be lost on the Holland America Line. In March 2020, one of its cruise ships carrying nearly 200 sick people, four of whom died, needed a place to dock and was headed to South Florida. DeSantis objected, leaving the ship in limbo for two weeks before the White House brokered a deal to permit the ship to land at Port Everglades.[56]

Fierce debates continued about whether businesses could legally mandate vaccines as a condition of employment. The Biden administration responded in two ways. First, a federal mandate required nursing homes and other health facilities to ensure their workers were vaccinated against COVID-19, or risk losing Medicare and Medicaid reimbursements. Second, Biden announced a "soft mandate" for businesses with more than 100 employees. Employers must ensure employees are vaccinated or are tested weekly, a policy already in place for federal employees. A federal vaccine requirement as a workplace safety measure is unprecedented, but the option of weekly testing for those unable or unwilling to be vaccinated increases the likelihood the measure will survive judicial scrutiny. States have long required vaccines for schoolchildren as a condition for attending public school, and the judiciary has consistently upheld those mandates.[57] In August 2021, the US Supreme Court let stand a lower court ruling that upheld Indiana University's vaccination requirement for students.[58]

· · ·

One problem begging for a national solution was the hodgepodge of state policies on the quarantine of persons entering the state. The debate ignited after a motorcycle rally in Sturgis, South Dakota, allegedly became a "superspreading" event. The Sturgis Motorcycle Rally bills itself as the largest motorcycle rally in the world. While most other states prohibited large gatherings and required travelers across state lines to quarantine for fourteen days, Governor Kristi Noem refused the pleas of health officials to cancel the rally or to put in place any restrictions at all. Some 460,000 people from across the nation attended the ten-day rally in August 2020. Then they went home.

While precise numbers are elusive, evidence suggests that COVID infections spread from that rally throughout the nation. An early estimate by four American economists set the number of infections from the rally at a quarter of a million, a figure Governor Noem disputed even while admitting the rally led to 124 new cases in South Dakota and one death.[59] In neighboring Minnesota alone, fifty-one Minnesotans contracted COVID at the rally in Sturgis and then spread it to at least three dozen others. Four of them were hospitalized and one died, a man in his sixties who had attended the rally.[60] The Minnesota Health Department study relied on genetic sequencing, a resource few other state health departments could replicate. And most local health departments in other states had already given up on contact tracing, at least outside of nursing homes and other care facilities. Still, health officials in more than twenty states reported COVID cases brought there from the rally.[61]

On the other hand, when protests broke out after George Floyd's death in Minneapolis in May 2020, some public health experts were criticized for a perceived double standard. Some of the same experts who called for limitations on public gatherings, including protests over business restrictions and prohibitions on large religious gatherings, supported Black Lives Matter protests. Whether the massive demonstrations throughout the nation contributed to the spread of COVID is likely impossible to establish.[62]

If residents of some states objected to lax COVID policies in other states, there was little they could do about it. But governors could guard their state lines by requiring entering travelers to quarantine. In the early weeks of the pandemic, the governors of Texas and Florida were the first to do so, ironically, considering their refusals to take other public health measures. But they weren't alone in their fear that the exodus from New York City in March 2020 would bring COVID to their doorstep. As journalist Todd Gillman put it, "From interstate checkpoints to arrests for golfing without quarantining first, emergency powers are being put to the test."[63] Texas governor Gregg Abbott justified his quarantine order by claiming "many early cases of COVID-19 in the State of Texas were caused by people who transmitted the virus to Texans after traveling here from other states." Abbott's March 26 order singled out travelers from New York and New Orleans, specifically. Three days later he added other states and cities and imposed a mandatory fourteen-day quarantine for "roadway travelers coming to Texas from Louisiana."[64] At the Texas line, state troopers stopped travelers coming from Louisiana to inform them of the quarantine. Such scenes were eerily reminiscent of a century ago, when Louisiana sued Texas over its yellow fever quarantines, as described in chapter 2.

More states soon followed the lead of Texas and Florida, mandating quarantines for out-of-state travelers and returning residents alike. Ahead of the July 4 weekend, Chicago and Pennsylvania announced new travel quarantine measures for arrivals from fifteen states, joining New York's order aimed at travelers from states where out-of-control spread of the coronavirus threatened other parts of the nation.[65] NPR aired a thought-provoking segment just before the holiday period began, leading with, "If you're traveling this holiday weekend or if you have guests coming your way, there's a good chance you live in a state affected by a mandatory 14-day travel quarantine."[66]

In a limited way, these states tried to replicate the federal government's attempt to keep the virus out of the nation. The United States first banned travelers from China, then Europe, then Brazil, and the list grew. President Trump ordered the Mexican and Canadian borders closed, except for returning US citizens, nationals, and most green-card holders. But this strategy was a leaky sieve, as thousands upon thousands of US travelers returned home from abroad at the same time non-US nationals were banned. Federal authorities ordered the first planeload of US citizens evacuated from Wuhan into a mandatory two-week quarantine at a US military base. For a while, federal quarantine orders also applied to arriving cruise-ship passengers. But when thousands of travelers rushed home from Europe in April, the CDC's website merely advised, "If you have traveled internationally in the past 14 days, stay home and monitor your health."

The federal government could have set uniform standards for travel within the country based on a given location's infection rate, an authority it has had since the Epidemic Diseases Act of 1890.[67] Instead, we ended up with a crazy assortment of state quarantine rules directed against other states with higher infection rates. Texas and Florida wanted to protect themselves from a virus rampant in New York City. The tables turned when infection rates skyrocketed in other regions. New York imposed its own restrictions on travelers to protect its hard-won gains from one of the most stringent lockdowns anywhere. The problem, left unresolved in the yellow fever era, had appeared again. We had to ask what Congress meant more than a century ago when it gave the federal government the authority to prevent the spread of contagious disease from one state into another.

• • •

While changing state law would cut down on some of the confusion over who is in charge of public health emergency measures at the local level, Congress must pay attention as well. Even if law reform efforts in the future succeed in bringing some cohesion to state law, it would still be far better to fight epidemics as one nation, rowing in the same direction, with the superior financial and scientific resources of the federal government.

President Biden showed that it was possible for the federal government to assume a greater role in the nation's defense, but the standard to measure against was not high. In March 2020, President Trump told state governors that they were on their own to secure critical medical supplies, when the federal government should have used its immense contracting authority to keep the scramble for limited supplies from driving up market prices. Leading by example matters, too, but it can't be legislated. If President Trump had endorsed face masks rather than made fun of people who wore them, perhaps public opinion on face masks would not have devolved into a Republican-Democratic divide. If President Trump had joined all former living presidents in a public-service announcement urging Americans to get vaccinated, rather than getting vaccinated in secret, perhaps that divide would have been lessened as well.

Missteps early in the pandemic by the CDC in supplying states with COVID tests did not help. While the initial federal response to COVID-19 could have been better, together Congress and the executive branch accomplished much that helped. Operation Warp Speed produced effective vaccines in massive quantities in record time. No other nation achieved this. It was never a given that scientists could produce a safe and effective vaccine for COVID-19. There had never been a vaccine for a coronavirus before, despite scientists' familiarity with SARS (severe acute respiratory syndrome) and MERS (Middle East respiratory syndrome). The federal government spent an enormous sum to make it happen, and the FDA served an essential role in determining whether the vaccines were safe and effective. Distribution problems marred the vaccine's rollout, but state governments were in charge of that; our prior history taught us to expect an uneven performance there. In the initial rollout, some states quickly and efficiently distributed vaccines to their residents. Others performed abysmally. Whether because of poor record keeping or poor planning, in some states unused vaccines expired and had to be thrown out while health officials struggled to meet the demand.

Congress also passed legislation in the first months of the pandemic to support hospitals and to provide financial relief to Americans harmed by job losses and facing eviction. These measures included the Families First Coronavirus Response Act (March 18), the CARES Act (Coronavirus Aid, Relief, and Economic Security Act; March 27), and the Paycheck Protection Program and Healthcare Enhancement Act (April 24). Nonetheless, administrative bungling slowed getting money to those who needed it; it was jarring to see so many Americans across the country waiting in line for food at makeshift programs for the hungry. Congress also put in place a temporary moratorium on housing evictions and authorized $47 billion for emergency rental assistance. But states were in charge of disbursing the money, and some states had distributed only a fraction of their allotment by the time the federal eviction moratorium ended in August 2021.[68]

And while President Trump declared when he signed the CARES Act that it "should alleviate any concern uninsured Americans may have" about seeking treatment for the coronavirus, some gaping holes remained.[69] Some uninsured COVID victims were hit with substantial bills they could not pay, and studies suggested many others avoided testing and treatment entirely because they feared the cost. Preexisting health disparities for the poor and uninsured were further exacerbated by the pandemic. One study found that "one-third of COVID-19 deaths and around 40% of infections were linked to a lack of health insurance," and for "every 10% increase in a county's uninsured rate, the researchers found a 70% increase in COVID-19 infections and nearly a 50% increase in deaths from COVID-19."[70] As Sara Rosenbaum, a professor of health law and policy at George Washington University stated, "This is not the way you deal with uninsured people during a public health emergency."[71]

· · ·

After thirty-two years of service, Timothy Alben retired from the Massachusetts State Police in 2015, well before COVID was on the horizon. I wondered what he thought about the nation's response, given his observations nearly fifteen years earlier about the need for public cooperation in a national emergency like a pandemic. When I caught up with him, I asked what had surprised him the most. "The inconsistency of messaging," he said. "You have to have political leadership that's on the same page and promoting the same message from the top down" to gain public cooperation with stringent mitigation strategies.

The problem started with a lack of presidential leadership, Alben said. From there, it cascaded downward to state governors:

> When you have governors in Massachusetts and New York doing one thing, and Texas, Florida, and Georgia doing something completely different, that is the complete opposite of what I said in my thesis. There needs to be transparency and consistency of messaging and projection of leadership that gives people faith in what you're saying. And if you don't have that, it's just not going to work. You can't get the community to come along, if they don't know which message to listen to.[72]

Alben had foreseen the problem and studied possible solutions, but he could only watch the chaos unfold.

• • •

Many challenges we experienced with COVID-19 were not new, and it was possible to predict certain government failures. We endured the pandemic with inadequate laws and poor coordination among various levels of government. We provided inadequate support to hospitals, medical providers, and care givers, as earlier generations had done in the past. We ignored clear lessons from past outbreaks, leaving ourselves vulnerable to missteps and missed opportunities in our response to COVID-19.

Add to these challenges the distrust of authority at any level of government. Some communities have a long history of distrust of public health agencies and the federal government. A few years before COVID hit, the *New York Times* reported that less than one-third of Americans said they trusted public health officials to share complete and accurate information during outbreaks. The same article stated that "only 14 percent trust the federal government to do what's right most of the time."[73] Especially in the age of social media, rumors and disinformation can cause panic—or a false sense of security—and prevent effective health measures.

America's COVID response exposed a weakness of our federalist system—we don't have a *national* defense to a pandemic. One single state or local government's failure could mean the more rapid spread of a virus anywhere in the nation. State and local officials have limited medical and scientific resources to understand the transmission of complex diseases and to form independent judgments about the best means to control their spread. But two other considerations must remain in the balance. First, a vast, geographically diverse nation will experience a pandemic at different times and in different ways, so a one-size-fits-all policy may do more harm than good, especially in more rural areas. Second, a bad national policy is worse than no national policy at all. States remain the "laboratory of democracy" in this country for reasons that include a more responsive local government.

We depend on good leaders and need effective governance to protect us from pandemics, find a cure, produce and deliver a vaccine if possible, and mediate the inevitable conflict that arises amid the stress of a pandemic. Facing COVID, elected officials, like everyone else, were limited by constraints on their knowledge, authority, and capacity. The result was a patchwork approach that deepened divisions in America and allowed hundreds of thousands of us to die.

*An installation that included more than seven hundred thousand
white flags covering twenty acres of the National Mall in an
art memorial for COVID-19 victims by Suzanne Brennan
Firstenberg entitled* In America: Remember. *There was one
flag for every American who had died from COVID-19.*

EPILOGUE
Law for the Next Pandemic

We need to remember that pandemics can be deeply
divisive, and the political response profoundly reflects
on the kind of society we want and aspire to be.

—LAWRENCE O. GOSTIN[1]

After a long year made more difficult by the COVID-19 pandemic, the Emory Law School graduating class gathered at the Georgia World Congress Center in May 2021 to receive the degrees they had earned. Their medieval-era academic regalia now included the face masks they had grown accustomed to wearing. Seated wide apart in a cavernous exhibition hall, some saw friends for the first time in more than fourteen months. I myself had not seen students or most of my colleagues in person since March 2020, when Emory University switched to remote teaching while students were away on spring break. By the time we gathered for this graduation program, nearly six hundred thousand Americans had died of COVID. But there was reason for optimism that the end was in sight. Vaccines had just become more widely accessible to broader swaths of the population. Yet to come was a third surge that summer, raising the number of dead Americans to well over seven hundred thousand. By September, COVID-19 had killed approximately 1 in 500 Americans.[2]

As the ceremony unfolded, Emory President Greg Fenves congratulated the students on their perseverance and achievements in the face of unprecedented disruptions to the usual course of study. Then he introduced Dr. Anthony Fauci, who appeared from Washington, DC, via recorded video. By that May, Fauci had become for most Americans the face and voice of all that we know about COVID-19. Emory had awarded him an honorary doctorate in 2003, but this year he received the President's Medal, the highest honor Emory University bestows. Fenves presented the medal on behalf of not only the university but also "a deeply grateful nation."[3]

Appearing on large video screens in the exhibition hall, Fauci acknowledged that the graduates and their families, like everyone in the country and around the world, had come through an extraordinary year, one that had "changed the landscape of all our lives." His message was simple: "Such times call upon all of us to work together."[4]

> If there are any lessons that we have learned from this pandemic, they are: one, science will provide a solution to this pandemic, as we have seen with the rapid and successful development of multiple safe and highly effective vaccines. And two, societal divisiveness is counterproductive in a pandemic. We must not be at odds with each other, since the virus is the enemy. Not each other.[5]

Fauci concluded with a caution: America must be ready for more disease outbreaks that are sure to come. There will come a day, he said, when we once again will need "collective commitment, tireless efforts, passion, and resilience" to defeat a pandemic.[6]

Among the law school graduates that day was an older student named Suman Malempati. "Older" because he, like Fauci, was also a medical doctor—Malempati had spent two decades as a pediatric oncologist. While he had found medicine rewarding, he chose to leave his career and enter law school because he wanted to do more—to help right the wrongs he observed in the world his patients lived in. He could "no longer stand on the sidelines without being part of the fight for a more just world."[7]

In his three years as a law student, Malempati pursued his commitment relentlessly. The former physician worked with the Southern Poverty Law Center reviewing medical records of immigrant detainees. He helped devise policies that would benefit children in Georgia's foster care system. He advised tenants facing eviction proceedings and contributed to litigation for environmental justice. In recognition of this service, Emory Law School bestowed its public service award on Malempati.

But on that commencement day, Malempati received yet another honor—election by his peers as the "most outstanding student" in the class of 2021. The only student invited to address the audience from the stage of dignitaries, Malempati said that when he had graduated from medical school twenty-five years earlier, he was impossibly shy, terrified to ask questions or speak up in rounds of six to eight doctors during his residency. He would have been terrified to speak before the crowd of people in front of him. But Suman assured his classmates that, like him, they would learn to do things they didn't think they could, because "you are never too old to stop learning. That's what my dad used to say."[8]

Then he paused at the mention of his father. He knew that many of his classmates had been affected by COVID, and his own family had suffered grief. "I ended the fall semester last December with a father who was healthy, and active, and working, and who I saw every weekend when he would often play and dance with my 3-year-old daughter." But in only a few weeks, everything changed: "I started the spring semester in January with my father in ICU struggling to breathe, not sure if he would make it to the next day. My dad fought for his life for the next three months, and I was at his bedside on April 7 when he took his last breath."[9]

Suman did not dwell on his personal loss. Instead, he used the final moments of his address to remind his classmates that the profession they were entering was responsible for justice, and that injustice and inequality can be repaired. Recalling the words of one of his professors, Suman said:

> Law is made by people, and it is made for people, supposedly as a way to organize ourselves into a fair and just society. Which means if it is not working that way, we can change it. We have to believe that's where we are headed—toward justice and equality. We can't change inequality and injustice unless we believe it can happen.

"If we all remember to think, question, and believe," Malempati concluded, "not only will we make my dad proud, we will make the world a better place."[10]

. . .

If the world is to be a better place, we must heed the words of Drs. Fauci and Malempati. Our laws have not adequately organized our society to balance justice and public health efficiently when pandemics arise. Preparation for the next pandemic and changes to the law must go hand in hand.

The divisiveness Fauci referred to that day brought to mind many ugly episodes over the preceding year. Asians suffered hate crimes because of the link between the virus and China. Armed militants invaded a state capitol to threaten lawmakers because of social-distancing measures. City council meetings devolved into screaming matches over mask mandates. A Georgia vaccination site was forced to close after protesters threatened workers.[11] Public health workers received death threats, and the ongoing harassment led many to quit a seriously underpaid but essential role.[12] And then there was the partisan divide. Taking cues from political leaders, Americans divided largely along party lines over the acceptance of face masks and vaccinations—and even over whether COVID was a hoax.

Most shameful of all was another divide in American society. A great, wealthy nation, with scientific expertise envied by the world, failed its most vulnerable citizens. The high death toll in communities of color and among residents of nursing homes, extended-care facilities, and prisons will be the most lasting, ignoble record of America's pandemic response. To make matters worse, the economic burden of social-distancing measures, including school closures and business restrictions, fell most heavily on minority communities and the poor. Americans did not share equally the sacrifices necessary to combat COVID.

But we knew from America's past plagues that epidemics tend to produce social conflicts. We knew that the poor and disfavored groups often suffer the most, both from the disease itself and from the inevitable economic consequences. Fauci's address at Emory served as a reminder that we are still grappling with problems we have seen many times before. For some of these, law provides no remedy; nor will changing our laws provide the solution. Laws alone will not stamp out bigotry and ignorance. At the end of the day, a deliberative democracy relies on elections to hold the government accountable.

Laws can, however, lead to better governance during an epidemic, and legislation can address one of the most critical problem described in this book—our overreliance on local resources to contain outbreaks. Our nearly three thousand state and local public health agencies can't handle a pandemic on their own, even if they were better funded. They barely hold their own to contain local outbreaks of everyday diseases, which easily can and do spread to other regions. The duty that elected state officials owe to their constituents to protect their health is not a duty they owe to residents of other states.

A greater federal role is essential, especially in a pandemic: distributing supplies, equalizing resources available to rich and poor states, and, above all, offering a unified and trustworthy message based in science. There are some specific changes we can make now to respond better in the future, but it will be up to Congress to make them. My wish list would include the following:

Congress should clarify the provision from the 1944 Public Health Service Act authorizing federal rules to prevent the spread of contagious disease across state lines.[13] In a pandemic emergency, there should be minimum standards for control measures that apply nationally, especially for interstate travel. Any state could exceed the floor if it chose. If a state failed to act, however, the federal government could take steps designed to protect the residents of other states. The CDC relied on the 1944 act to authorize the eviction moratorium put in place in September 2020 by President Trump. The US Supreme Court blocked the Biden administration's effort to extend the moratorium, with the majority expressing skepticism that the 1944 act's language in fact authorized the CDC's action.[14] Surely Congress can take the time to revisit this critical provision from the 1944 Public Health Services Act to meet the needs of a new century. If Congress understood that this law actually dates back to 1890 and that it was consolidated into the 1944 act long after the yellow fever era (described in chapter 2) prompted it, would Congress feel a greater sense of urgency?

The CDC must have greater insulation from political control to increase confidence in its recommendations and emergency standards for the nation. One way to achieve this independence might be the Federal Reserve model. Not only are the Federal Reserve's directors relatively free from political control during their appointed terms, but the governance structure is divided regionally. If the nation's primary health agencies (CDC, NIH, FDA, and the US Public Health Service) were to be coordinated under such a model, the public might find federal guidance during a pandemic more acceptable. This model also could make interagency coordination easier at the federal level, and could reduce the effect of both lobbying and uneven political representation on the distribution of federal funds and medical supplies.[15]

Congress must ensure that the nation can rapidly produce and distribute essential medical supplies. The national pandemic influenza stockpiling program proved woefully inadequate for such basic supplies as masks and protective equipment for front-line workers. States should not be left to secure what they need on their own because richer states always win out. In addition, Congress must ensure that the costs of testing and treatment during an epidemic are covered—and covered equitably. Contagion cannot be stopped if people avoid seeking healthcare because they are afraid of the cost (or in the case of noncitizens, because they are afraid seeking healthcare will adversely affect their immigration status).[16] Congress should commit in advance to cover individual healthcare costs necessary to stop a pandemic. It is also essential to provide financial assistance when asking individuals to sacrifice for the common good.

The items on my wish list are not intended to take away the independence of states or to displace local decision-making. But one need not be a die-hard fan of the federal government to recognize that there are some emergencies local governments cannot handle on their own, and there also must be a fair way to distribute scarce supplies and resources among states that is not based solely on wealth or political clout. Many state health departments are underfunded and understaffed in normal times and lack the scientific expertise to advise state governors and coordinate an effective response. This is where the weakness of a decentralized system of national health defense becomes clear. Only the federal government can coordinate a truly national defense against a pandemic, and only it can coordinate the fair distribution of aid and limited supplies.

Our experience with yellow fever, the 1918 flu, polio, and AIDS taught us that ignorance, misinformation, fear, and panic can override reason in populations, meaning that issues become "political" as constituents demand governmental response. In the midst of an epidemic, public panic puts significant stress on conventional governmental processes, policies, and institutions—and may even cause them to fail, notwithstanding medical expertise and institutions that are among the best in the world. During the outbreak of a deadly disease, the public may overestimate the degree of risk, leading to poor decision-making and uninformed pressure on their leaders. This could contribute to inequitable allocation of medical resources, ineffective and economically harmful prevention measures, and deep suspicion of government's ability to control the spread of disease.

The opposite reaction—underestimating the risk—can lead to its own set of problems, as we saw during COVID, when many states declined to follow the advice of health officials and consequently suffered from out-of-control infection. Other states, understandably, then make demands based on those perceived failures—to control the interstate spread of disease before it reaches them.

Presidential leadership matters enormously, another lesson available to us from past epidemics. In March 2017, Dr. Fauci warned President Donald Trump's administration that it would undoubtedly face infectious disease emergencies that no one could foresee. Fauci was merely repeating a message he had delivered to the five preceding presidents he had served. Their varied responses demonstrate the way leadership at the top can make a difference for better or for worse. Ronald Reagan ignored AIDS until he couldn't any longer, while Clinton increased investment in AIDS research, and George W. Bush launched the President's Emergency Plan for AIDS Relief, an effort to address the global epidemic in HIV/AIDS. Likewise, presidential leadership has been instrumental in helping to create a stronger public health system, from Franklin Roosevelt's signing of the Public Health Service Act to Dwight Eisenhower's brokering a deal to overcome an intransigent Congress and provide funding to establish the CDC.

Congressional leadership, or its absence, also matters. In the past three decades, the United States has faced a series of unexpected pandemics: the emergence from Southeast Asia of an avian flu (H5N1) with a mortality rate between 33 and 60 percent, followed in 1999 by the first appearance in the Americas of the West Nile virus, which is now endemic to the United States.[17] George W. Bush faced not only the devastating terrorist attacks of 9/11 but also a novel coronavirus known as SARS, for which there is still no vaccine. Just months after President Barack Obama took office, the country faced a new influenza known as H1N1, which quickly spread around the world and eventually killed 12,500 Americans, most of them younger than sixty-five.[18] That pandemic was largely forgotten after Ebola broke out in West Africa early in President Obama's second term. And while Ebola preoccupied the American public, another obscure virus, known as Zika, caused widespread disease throughout South America, eventually coming to Puerto Rico, Florida, and Texas.

All of these health emergencies captured the attention of Congress, but none of them led to any significant change in public health policies or law, with one exception: the Pandemic and All-Hazards Preparedness Act of 2006, which was designed to help prepare the nation for pandemic flu and other public health emergencies.[19] The law required reauthorization every five years, but in 2018 Congress failed to do so. As a result, critical funding for emergency preparation programs lapsed until Congress finally renewed the act in June 2019—just months before COVID-19 made its first appearance.[20] Congress must assess how well the Preparedness Act worked in practice during COVID-19 and then revise it as needed. Better yet, Congress should pass a bill introduced in the Senate in 2021 that would allocate two billion dollars over the next four years to create a "Disease X" program, designed to develop vaccines, therapies, and other countermeasures for novel virus threats, of which COVID-19 was only the latest.[21]

• • •

As I listened to the speakers during that commencement ceremony in May 2021, I reflected on Fauci's concern about future pandemics. Even before COVID hit, the US had struggled to control all kinds of contagious diseases. HIV and tuberculosis remain significant problems in America and around the globe. Local health departments reported fewer new cases during the COVID pandemic, but epidemiologists are certain that infections have been missed. Health officials were too overwhelmed with COVID to keep up with existing HIV and tuberculosis patients, let alone offer testing, contact tracing, and other programs that have kept these diseases barely contained.

Present dangers demand attention. They include the following:

- Hepatitis C, a leading cause of death from infectious disease in the United States. New infections increased fourfold from 2010 to 2018, with as many as five million Americans estimated to have hepatitis C.[22]
- The Zika virus, which may reemerge as a threat in the US. Scientists developed a vaccine in 2018, but no commercial producer has been willing to make it.
- The CDC warned of outbreaks of Legionnaires' disease, a serious type of pneumonia, as buildings reopened after COVID.[23] State and local health departments take the lead in investigating outbreaks, set safety standards, and identify the steps necessary to clean up the source of infection. Health departments reported nearly ten thousand cases of Legionnaires' disease in the US in 2018, but that number is likely undercounted when milder cases aren't diagnosed.[24]
- An increasing number of bacteria are now completely resistant to existing antibiotics, rendering them useless for some infections. Every year, nearly three million antibiotic-resistant infections occur in the US, killing more than thirty-five thousand people.[25]

And then there is hepatitis A, a highly contagious but vaccine-preventable liver infection common in developing countries. Hepatitis A is linked to poor sanitation—the virus usually spreads from ingesting food or drink contaminated by a minuscule amount of fecal matter, but it can also spread from person to person through close contact. Drug users and people who are homeless are most at risk of contracting the disease and then spreading it to others. In 2018–19, a hepatitis A epidemic spread relentlessly across two-thirds of the country from local outbreaks that began in California in 2017.[26] In less than two years, nearly forty thousand acute cases from that strain were reported across the nation, a more than 1,000 percent increase in cases from 2015.[27] An estimated 37,000 people required hospitalization, and 376 died.[28] Local health officials adopted the strategy recommended by the CDC to vaccinate those at highest risk. The CDC spent nearly $10 million to help local health departments meet the crisis, including the purchase of 150,000 vaccines.[29] In urban areas with large homeless populations, local officials installed more restrooms and stepped up cleaning efforts in existing ones. San Diego County, for example, opened handwashing stations, distributed hand sanitizer, and even washed down streets with a bleach solution. Efforts to contain hepatitis A in California that year, extensive as they were, did not protect the nation.[30] The virus spread from city to city and state to state—no local health department was able to break that chain on its own.

As the hepatitis A outbreak readily demonstrates, even if one city or state does a good job controlling a local outbreak, neighboring states with poor resources or a lack of political will to address problems can undermine all that progress. It is one more illustration that the nation's public health defense relies primarily on state and local governments to contain outbreaks that respect no jurisdictional boundaries. When local jurisdictions fail, the entire nation is at risk. The everyday disease outbreaks that local health departments deal with are not generally divisive or partisan—those departments are simply forced to contain them with inadequate preparation or funding.

• • •

Not only does the United States have the most fragmented public health system in the world, but most states retain antiquated public health laws that do not serve us well. Many of the laws on which we rely during a public health emergency were created on the fly in the midst of frightening epidemics, rather than soberly crafted afterward. Once a threat subsides, we become complacent as a society, and our elected representatives become complacent as well. State and federal officials and agencies lose the sense of urgency to implement reforms.

Another tendency has been to leave it to courts to set boundaries for what government officials may require in an epidemic emergency, but judges are not well positioned to make these calls. During the COVID pandemic's first year, Chief Justice John Roberts reiterated, "Our Constitution principally entrusts 'The safety and the health of the people' to the politically accountable officials of the States."[31] Elected officials are responsible for the health and safety of their constituents. Citizens who object to restrictive COVID mitigation measures can sue about them, and sometimes win. But when elected leaders take no action, or worse—prevent actions deemed necessary based on medical and scientific consensus—the judiciary cannot intervene. The only remedy for poor governance and failure to protect the nation's most vulnerable citizens is a political solution—the next election.

America's experience with plagues past and present shows that effective disease control is not just a public health task of containing pathogens, but also a summons to thoughtful law and reasoned governance. History proves that democratic governments like ours have inherent weaknesses in their ability to control epidemics, especially if coercive measures become the last line of defense while awaiting a vaccine or a cure. Most voters generally do not choose their elected representatives based on their ability to handle emergencies, let alone a public health emergency like an epidemic. Democratic processes can fail, especially when the question is who pays, rather than who suffers—a lesson we should have learned from the early years of the AIDS epidemic.

America has faced many serious outbreaks of contagious disease throughout its history and will do so again. COVID-19 has provided us with just one more installment from which to learn. Effective response to epidemic threats will always require political choices, as law professor Lawrence Gostin notes in the epigraph to this chapter. The political choices we make now, before the next plague in the nation, "profoundly reflect on the kind of society we want and aspire to be."

Yard sign thanking healthcare workers, Atlanta, Georgia, 2021.

ACKNOWLEDGMENTS

This book was made possible by a generous grant from the Carnegie Corporation of New York. The statements made and views expressed are solely the responsibility of the author.

I also thank the Robert Wood Johnson Foundation for introducing me to the work of state and local health departments. In 2014, they funded a summer in residence in El Paso, Texas, at both the CDC quarantine station and the regional office of the Texas Department of State Health Services located there. I would not otherwise have met the many dedicated public health professionals in the Paso del Norte region, especially my mentors, Dr. Mary A. Anderson and Dr. Miguel Escobedo.

The dedication page lists my grandparents. I wish I could ask them about the 1918 flu and what life was like before a polio vaccine became available. My paternal grandfather survived polio as an infant and always walked with a limp.

This book is also dedicated to Ray C. DuVarney, professor emeritus at Emory University. Ray died before the book was published, but he had the good grace to warn me that could happen as yet another year went by without a finished manuscript. Ray was a physicist, but he was also interested in and insanely knowledgeable about *everything*. He was especially helpful discussing the topics in this book. Ray once suggested the title "Plagues, Trains, and Automobiles" for one of the chapters. That would have been perfect.

I owe a special debt of gratitude to Helene Atwan at Beacon Press, and to my agent, Jessica Papin. The original plan would have seen the book published before the COVID-19 pandemic hit. Given what we have learned from that experience, I think it is a better book, and I appreciate their patience in seeing the project through.

I received excellent editorial assistance from Gary Hauk, Ulrike Guthrie, and Edward Shoemaker. While I was on leave to write the book, William and Mary School of Law generously hosted me for two semesters, and I benefited from another semester at the Department of Public Health Sciences at New Mexico State University. Emory Law School provided unstinting support, and Emory's library professionals earned star ranking, as always. I benefited from the research assistance of Emory Law students Joshua Brennan, Jack Dewinter, Patrick C. Diaz, Catherine Grady, Sama Kahook, Andrew Salman, and Nicholas Smith. Brandon Goldberg, a former research assistant who had since graduated from Emory Law, also pitched in to help. Mary E. Hilpertshauser at the David J. Sencer CDC Museum in Atlanta could not have been a better resource.

Colleagues at Emory's Rollins School of Public Health--especially James Curran and Carlos del Rio—helped with my research and inspire me daily. My work has drawn inspiration from many fellow legal scholars, but especially Wendy Parmet and Lawrence Gostin. Frederic E. Shaw, former editor in chief of the *Morbidity and Mortality Weekly Report* and *Public Health Reports,* and a CDC veteran, provided countless helpful tips and introductions. I also want to thank the public health professionals who let me interview them, follow them around, and learn from their work, even if their names did not make it into the book.

I take responsibility for any errors in the book but submit in my defense that they crept in unseen and unexpectedly—like a plague.

NOTES

Author's Note: There are many more excellent books and articles devoted to the topics in this book than I have cited in each chapter. If you would like to read more on any particular subject, I provide an online bibliography at my website, plaguesinthenation.com.

PREFACE

1. Michael Levenson, "Scale of China's Wuhan Shutdown Is Believed to Be Without Precedent," *New York Times*, Jan. 20, 2020, https://www.nytimes .com/2020/01/22/world/asia/coronavirus-quarantines-history.html.

2. Centers for Disease Control and Prevention, "Quarantine and Isolation," Apr. 23, 2019, https://www.cdc.gov/quarantine/index.html.

3. World Health Organization, "The Classical Definition of a Pandemic Is Not Elusive," https://www.who.int/bulletin/volumes/89/7/11–088815/en, accessed May 26, 2021.

4. Lawrence K. Altman, "Is This a Pandemic? Define 'Pandemic,'" *New York Times*, June 8, 2009, https://www.nytimes.com/2009/06/09/health/09docs .html.

5. *Merriam-Webster*, s.v. "epidemic," https://www.merriam-webster.com /dictionary/epidemic, accessed Aug. 23, 2021.

6. Centers for Disease Control and Prevention, "Principles of Epidemiology," May 11, 2020, https://www.cdc.gov/csels/dsepd/ss1978/lesson1/section11.html.

7. Victoria R. Green and Matthew B. Barry, *FDA Warns of Youth Epidemic of E-Cigarette Use*, CRS Insight, Oct. 23, 2018, https://fas.org/sgp/crs/misc /IN10986.pdf.

8. Cynthia J. Stein and Graham A. Colditz, "The Epidemic of Obesity," *Journal of Clinical Endocrinology & Metabolism* 89, no. 6 (June 2004): 2522–25.

9. Polly J. Price, "Do State Lines Make Public Health Emergencies Worse? Federal Versus State Control of Quarantine," *Emory Law Journal* 67, no. 3 (2018): 542.

CHAPTER 1: AMERICA'S FIRST PLAGUES

1. Sims v. State, 72 Tenn. 357, 360 (Tenn. 1880).
2. St. Louis Historical Society, "The Pest House," http://slphistory.org/pesthouse, accessed Sept. 13, 2021.
3. David Monagan, "Isolated Reminders of Old Epidemics," *New York Times*, Apr. 9, 2000, https://www.nytimes.com/2000/04/09/nyregion/isolated -reminders-of-old-epidemics.html.
4. Monagan, "Isolated Reminders."
5. John Duffy, "Smallpox and the Indians in the American Colonies," *Bulletin of the History of Medicine* 25, no. 4 (1951): 325.
6. Quoted in Elizabeth A. Fenn, *Pox Americana: The Great Smallpox Epidemic of 1775–82* (New York: Hill and Wang, 2001), 23.
7. Michael Willrich, "'The Least Vaccinated of Any Civilized Country': Personal Liberty and Public Health in the Progressive Era," *Journal of Policy History* 20, no. 1 (2008): 79.
8. Willrich, "'The Least Vaccinated of Any Civilized Country,'" 79.
9. Fenn, *Pox Americana*, 29.
10. Declaration of Independence, National Archives, reviewed July 24, 2020, https://www.archives.gov/founding-docs/declaration-transcript.
11. James W. Ely Jr., *The Guardian of Every Other Right* (Oxford: Oxford University Press, 1992), 26.
12. Wilson v. Alabama G.S.R. Co., 77 Miss. 714 (Miss. 1900); Phoenix v. Commissioners, 12 How. Pr. 1 (Sup. Ct. N.Y. 1855).
13. *Sims*, 72 Tenn. at 360.
14. Prichard v. Commissioners, 126 N.C. 908 (N.C. 1900).
15. *Prichard*, 126 N.C. 908.
16. "Gun Quarantine Being Enforced," *Atlanta Constitution*, Jan. 18, 1905, 4.
17. Matthew Gramling, "Pox and Pig Iron: A Public Health Crisis in Antebellum Bartow County," Etowah Valley Historical Society, Oct. 19, 2020, https:// evhsonline.org/archives/49553.
18. *State Board of Health Bulletin* 11, no. 3 (Nashville, TN, Oct. 20, 1895): 33.
19. "Shot by a Quarantine," *Atlanta Constitution*, Sept. 7, 1895, 2.
20. Montgomery, Alabama Municipal Code Sec. 14–103, https://library.municode .com/al/montgomery/codes/code_of_ordinances?nodeId=COOR_CH14HESA _ARTIIICODI, accessed Sept. 14, 2021.
21. Commissioners v. Powe, 51 N.C. 134 (1858).
22. *Commissioners*, 51 N.C. at 136–37.
23. Charles E. Rosenberg, *The Cholera Years: The United States in 1832, 1849, and 1866* (Chicago: University of Chicago Press, 1987), 1.
24. Quoted in Rosenberg, *The Cholera Years*, 3.
25. Rosenberg, *The Cholera Years*, 36–37.
26. Walter J. Daly, "The Black Cholera Comes to the Central Valley of America in the 19th Century—1832, 1849, and Later," *Transactions of the American Clinical and Climatological Association* 119 (2008): 144.
27. Daly, "The Black Cholera Comes to the Central Valley of America in the 19th Century," 145.
28. Rosenberg, *The Cholera Years*, 60, 116.

29. "The Death of James K. Polk," *The Polk Home Blog*, https://jameskpolk.com
    /history/the-death-of-james-k-polk, accessed Sept. 14, 2021.
30. Fenn, *Pox Americana*, 31.
31. Rosenberg, *The Cholera Years*, 19–20.
32. "Almshouse & Pest House," Maryland State Archives, Dec. 16, 1991, http://
    msa.maryland.gov/megafile/msa/stagsere/se1/se5/003000/003300/003301
    /pdf/msa_se5_3301.pdf.
33. Multonborough v. Tuftonborough, 43 N.H. 316 (N.H. 1861).
34. Otis v. Town of Strafford, 10 N.H. 352, 355 (1839).
35. Gabriel Loiacono, "William Larned, Overseer of the Poor: Power and Precari-
    ousness in the Early Republic," *New England Quarterly* 88, no. 2 (2015): 223.
36. Loiacono, "William Larned, Overseer of the Poor," 233.
37. Alan D. Watson, "Combating Contagion: Smallpox and the Protection of
    Public Health in North Carolina, 1750 to 1825," *North Carolina Historical
    Review* 90, no. 1 (2013): 44.
38. Solomon v. Tarver, 52 Ga. 405, 406 (1874).
39. *Multonborough*, 43 N.H. at 318.
40. Inhabitants of Kennebunk v. Inhabitants of Alfred, 19 Me. 221, 224 (1841).
41. Charles E. Rosenberg, *The Care of Strangers: The Rise of America's Hospital
    System* (Baltimore: Johns Hopkins University Press, 1995), 4.
42. Rosenberg, *The Care of Strangers*, 4, 18.
43. Ory's Syndics v. David, 9 La. 59 (La. 1836).
44. *Ory's Syndics*, 9 La. at 62–63.
45. Fenn, *Pox Americana*, 32.
46. Kiona N. Smith, "How Ben Franklin Went from Anti-Vaxxer to Advocate,"
    Forbes, Jan. 20, 2021, https://www.forbes.com/sites/kionasmith/2021/01/20
    /how-ben-franklin-went-from-anti-vaxxer-to-advocate.
47. "Jonathan Edwards," Princeton University, updated Nov. 26, 2013, https://
    pr.princeton.edu/pub/presidents/edwards/index.html.
48. Gordon Wood, ed., *John Adams: Revolutionary Writings 1755–1775* (New
    York: Literary Classics of the United States, 2011), 99.
49. Wood, *John Adams*, 96, 104.
50. Wood, *John Adams*, 102.
51. Wood, *John Adams*, 107–8.
52. Smith, "How Ben Franklin Went from Anti-Vaxxer to Advocate."
53. Benjamin Franklin, *Writings* (New York: Literary Classics of the United
    States, 1987), 1402.
54. Fenn, *Pox Americana*, 33.
55. "Report of the Committee of the Philadelphia Medical Society," *American
    Journal of the Medical Sciences* 2, no. 3 (May 1828): 241.
56. New Hampshire State Board of Health, *1882 Annual Report* (Concord: Par-
    sons B. Cogswell, 1882), 52.
57. Thomas Y. Simons et al., "Report of the Committee of the Board of Health
    of Charleston," *American Journal of the Medical Sciences* 9, no. 17 (1831):
    115–16.
58. New Hampshire State Board of Health, *1882 Annual Report*, 142, 285–86.
59. New Hampshire State Board of Health, *1882 Annual Report*, 142.

60. New Hampshire State Board of Health, 1882 *Annual Report*, 286.

61. Erin Blakemore, "Over 200 Years Ago, a Bold Smallpox Experiment in a New England Town Proved the Success of Vaccines," *Washington Post*, Feb. 27, 2021, https://www.washingtonpost.com/health/smallpox-vaccine-children-test/2021/02/25/54dd7ac8-76d1-11eb-9537-496158cc5fd9_story.html.

62. "A Proclamation," *Louisville (GA) Gazette and Republican Trumpet*, Aug. 19, 1800.

63. Rebecca F. Green, "'Simple, Easy, and Intelligible': Republican Political Ideology and the Implementation of Vaccination in the Early Republic," *Early American Studies* 12, no. 2 (2014): 322–27.

64. Watson, "Combating Contagion," 45–46.

65. Gramling, "Pox and Pig Iron."

66. Acts and Resolutions of the General Assembly of the State of Georgia, 1897, 101.

67. "Small Pox in Atlanta," *Christian Index*, May 11, 1882, 8.

68. "Small Pox in Atlanta."

69. "Vaccine Virus to Be Applied," *Atlanta Constitution*, Dec. 1, 1897, 7.

70. Morris v. City of Columbus, 102 Ga. 792 (Ga. 1898).

71. *Morris*, 102 Ga. at 796.

72. *Morris*, 102 Ga. at 798.

73. Michael R. Albert, Kristen G. Ostheimer, and Joel G. Breman, "The Last Smallpox Epidemic in Boston and the Vaccination Controversy, 1901–1903," *New England Journal of Medicine* 344, no. 5 (2001): 3751.

74. Jacobson v. Massachusetts, 197 U.S. 11, 38 (1905).

75. *Jacobson*, 197 U.S. at 27.

76. Commonwealth v. Jacobson, 183 Mass. 242, 248 (Mass. 1903) (emphasis added); Karen L. Walloch, *The Antivaccine Heresy: Jacobson v. Massachusetts and the Troubled History of Compulsory Vaccination in the United States* (Rochester: University of Rochester Press, 2015), 189, 194.

77. "Small Pox in Atlanta."

CHAPTER 2: YELLOW FEVER AND THE SHOTGUN QUARANTINE

1. "Fruits of Local Quarantine," *Washington Post*, Oct. 10, 1898, 6.

2. "Did They Run Away from Yellow Fever?," *New York Times*, June 9, 1855, https://www.nytimes.com/1855/06/09/archives/did-they-run-away-from-yellow-fever.html.

3. "Death of Bishop Gartland," *New York Times*, Sept. 26, 1854, 1; Rita DeLorme, "Humanizing a Legend: Bishop Francis X. Gartland, the Man," *Southern Cross*, Dec. 6, 2007, https://archives.diosav.org/sites/all/files/archives/S8743p03.pdf.

4. Joseph Waring, "The Yellow Fever Epidemic of Savannah in 1820," *Georgia Historical Quarterly* 52, no. 4 (1968): 402.

5. Chuck Mobley, "Davenport House Stylishly Dispenses History of 1820 Yellow Fever Epidemic," *Savannah Morning News*, Sept. 28, 2013, http://www.savannahnow.com/article/20130928/NEWS/309289814.

6. Linda Jones, "Church of the Yellow Fever Martyrs Museum," *South Reporter*, Mar. 1, 2001, http://msgw.org/marshall/church/yfmartyr.php; "Yellow

Fever Martyrs Church and Museum," https://yellowfevermartyrs.com, accessed June 3, 2021.

7. Jones, "Church of the Yellow Fever Martyrs Museum."

8. "Yellow Fever," Yellow Fever Martyrs Church and Museum, https://yellow fevermartyrs.com/yellowfever, accessed Sept. 14, 2021.

9. John R. Pierce and Jim Writer, *Yellow Jack: How Yellow Fever Ravaged America and Walter Reed Discovered Its Deadly Secrets* (Hoboken, NJ: John Wiley & Sons, 2005), 1, 7.

10. K. David Patterson, "Yellow Fever Epidemics and Mortality in the United States, 1693–1905," *Social Science and Medicine* 34, no. 8 (Apr. 1992): 857–58.

11. "Judgments Must Be Paid," *Atlanta Constitution*, Mar. 23, 1901, 3.

12. Pierce and Writer, *Yellow Jack*, 69.

13. Bennecke v. Insurance Company, 105 U.S. 355, 361 (1881); Globe Mutual Life Insurance Company of New York v. Wolff, 95 U.S. 326, 328 (1877).

14. "Way Down South," *Chicago Daily Tribune*, Apr. 8, 1879, 9.

15. A search of ProQuest Historical Databases (thirteen leading newspapers) between 1878 and 1910 returns more than 250 articles using the term "shotgun quarantine."

16. P. J. Moran, "Greenville and the Yellow Fever," *Atlanta Constitution*, Sept. 16, 1897; "Terrified South Ties Up Traffic," *Chicago Daily Tribune*, Aug. 29, 1905; "Fight on Quarantine," *Washington Post*, Aug. 9, 1905.

17. "The Foolish Shotgun Quarantine," *Washington Post*, Oct. 17, 1897, 6.

18. "Fruits of Local Quarantine," *Washington Post*, Oct. 10, 1898, 6.

19. "A Big Scare in Texas," *New York Times*, Sept. 7, 1897, 1.

20. "A Southern View of the Case," *Washington Post*, Oct. 24, 1898, 6. See also "Columbus Bars Montgomery: There Is a Shotgun Quarantine Maintained at Some Points," *Atlanta Constitution*, Oct. 19, 1897, 2.

21. "Yellow Fever: Still Spreading in Memphis—The Shotgun Quarantine," *Washington Post*, Aug. 23, 1879, 1.

22. John H. Ellis, *Yellow Fever & Public Health in the New South* (Lexington: University Press of Kentucky, 1992), 46–47, 57.

23. Reprinted in *Annual Report of the Surgeon-General of the Marine-Hospital Service for the Fiscal Year 1898* (Washington, DC: Government Printing Office, 1899), 754.

24. Polly J. Price, "Epidemics, Outsiders, and Local Protection," *University of Pennsylvania Journal of Constitutional Law* 19, no. 2 (2016): 388–89.

25. *Annual Report of the Surgeon-General of the Public Health and Marine-Hospital Service for the Fiscal Year 1906* (Washington, DC: Government Printing Office, 1907), 182.

26. "Today's Notices," *Daily Democrat* (Natchez, MS), Oct. 12, 1905, 3.

27. Magee v. Town of Osyka, 45 So. 836 (Miss. 1908).

28. St. Louis & S.F.R. Co. v. Roane, 46 So. 711, 712 (Miss. 1908).

29. "Death of Jurist Is Deeply Mourned," *Jackson Daily News*, July 25, 1922, 8.

30. *Roane*, 46 So. at 712.

31. "Oxford Notes," *Jackson Daily News*, May 7, 1908, 2.

32. "Jackson Will Not Take Down Bars," *Vicksburg Evening Post*, Oct. 16, 1905.

33. Marshall Scott Legan, "The War of the Waters: The Louisiana-Mississippi Quarantine War of 1905," *Journal of Mississippi History* 50, no. 2 (1988): 89–110.
34. "Brunswick Ready for Quarantine," *Atlanta Constitution*, Sept. 12, 1899, 1.
35. "State Health Board Ends Quarantine," *Vicksburg Evening Post*, Oct. 23, 1905, 1.
36. "The Shotgun in Alabama," *Atlanta Constitution*, Sept. 27, 1888, 2.
37. "Yellow Fever," *Journal of the American Medical Association* 45, no. 10 (1905): 722–23.
38. Louisiana v. Texas, 176 U.S. 1, 22 (1900).
39. "Louisiana Against Texas Treatment," *Atlanta Constitution*, Oct. 16, 1899, 1.
40. H. Campbell Black, "The Police Power and the Public Health," *American Law Review* 25 (1891): 181.
41. R. R. Co. v. Husen, 95 U.S. 465, 472 (1877).
42. *Louisiana*, 176 U.S. at 23.
43. Morgan's Steamship v. Louisiana Board of Health, 118 U.S. 455, 464 (1886).
44. *Morgan's Steamship*, 118 U.S. at 464.
45. Margaret Warner, "Local Control Versus National Interest: The Debate over Southern Public Health, 1878–1884," *Journal of Southern History* 50, no. 3 (1984): 407–28, 413.
46. Act of June 2, 1879, 21 Stat. 5, An Act to Prevent the Introduction of Contagious or Infectious Diseases into the United States.
47. Jerrold M. Michael, "The National Board of Health: 1879–1883," *Public Health Reports* 126 (2011): 127.
48. Ellis, *Yellow Fever*, 79–80, 118.
49. Warner, "Local Control Versus National Interest," 412.
50. Warner, "Local Control Versus National Interest," 412.
51. Molly Caldwell Crosby, *The American Plague: The Untold Story of Yellow Fever, the Epidemic That Shaped Our History* (New York: Berkley Books, 2006), 15.
52. "Yellow Fever Conditions," *Wall Street Journal*, Oct. 1, 1897; "Effect of Yellow Fever," *Wall Street Journal*, Sept. 2, 1898; "The Yellow Fever Situation," *Wall Street Journal*, Aug. 1, 1905.
53. "Unify Quarantine Throughout the Land," *Atlanta Constitution*, Dec. 17, 1897, 1; "State Quarantine Ineffectual," *Washington Post*, Dec. 14, 1900, 1.
54. "Quarantine in the Gulf States," *New York Times*, June 3, 1884, 5.
55. 26 Stat. 31, Epidemic Diseases Act of 1890.
56. 51st Congress, Sess. 1, Ch. 51, Mar. 27, 1890, An Act to Prevent the Introduction of Contagious Diseases from one State to Another, 26 Stat. 31. Preceding this was an act of Aug. 1, 1888, which concerned only the establishment of federally operated port quarantine stations. Act of Aug. 1, 1888, 25 Stat. 355, An Act to Perfect the Quarantine System of the United States.
57. 26 Stat. at 31, Act of March 27, 1890.
58. 26 Stat. at 31, Act of March 27, 1890.
59. "Quarantine Folk Will Meet Today," *Atlanta Constitution*, Nov. 17, 1898, 2.
60. "Wanted—a National Quarantine Law," *Atlanta Constitution*, Oct. 17, 1899, 6.

61. "Governors Disagree," *Washington Post*, Nov. 10, 1905, 1.

62. "The National Quarantine Law," *Atlanta Constitution*, Apr. 7, 1906, 8.

63. *Annual Report of the Surgeon-General of the Marine-Hospital Service for the Fiscal Year 1898*, 753–54.

64. *Quarantine Powers: Hearing before the House Committee on Interstate and Foreign Commerce*, 55th Congress (1898), 39, 46.

65. US Department of the Treasury, *Annual Report of the Surgeon-General of the Public Health and Marine-Hospital Service for the Fiscal Year 1883*, at 284 (describing effects of local shotgun quarantines).

66. 58 Stat. 703. The 1890 Epidemic Diseases Act was unchanged through 1944, when the Public Health Service Act of 1944 modernized the US Public Health Service and coordinated its various functions. The key language from the Epidemic Diseases Act, however, was retained—federal intervention is authorized whenever specified contagious diseases threatened to spread "from one state . . . into any other State."

CHAPTER 3: BLACK DEATH ON THE WEST COAST

1. "The Bubonic Plague in San Francisco," *New York Times*, Nov. 3, 1902.

2. "The Plague Spreading: More Cases of Yellow Fever in Jacksonville," *New York Times*, Sept. 2, 1888.

3. "State Plague Is Unchanged: Some Districts Improve While Others Increase; San Francisco Man Shot When Refuses to Wear Mask; Boston Man Due to Arrive with Leary Vaccines," *Los Angeles Times*, Oct. 29, 1918.

4. Howard Markel, *When Germs Travel: Six Major Epidemics That Have Invaded America Since 1900 and the Fears They Have Unleashed* (New York: Pantheon Books, 2004), 54–55.

5. Markel, *When Germs Travel*, 55.

6. Mark Honigsbaum, *The Pandemic Century: One Hundred Years of Panic, Hysteria, and Hubris* (New York: W. W. Norton 2019), 68.

7. Markel, *When Germs Travel*, 51.

8. Honigsbaum, *The Pandemic Century*, 68.

9. Honigsbaum, *The Pandemic Century*, 71.

10. "The Bubonic Plague in San Francisco."

11. "The Bubonic Plague in San Francisco."

12. Gary Kamiya, "S.F. Leaders Denied, Concealed Major Plague Epidemics," *SFGATE*, updated July 18, 2017, https://www.sfgate.com/bayarea/article/S-F-leaders-denied-concealed-major-plague-5768180.php.

13. Merkel, *When Germs Travel*, 65.

14. Quoted in Merkel, *When Germs Travel*, 65.

15. Kamiya, "S.F. Leaders Denied."

16. Kamiya, "S.F. Leaders Denied."

17. For an excellent background, see Erika Lee, *At America's Gates: Chinese Immigration During the Exclusion Era, 1882–1943* (Chapel Hill: University of North Carolina Press, 2003).

18. US Census Bureau, "April 2016—History," last modified Dec. 14, 2020, https://www.census.gov/history/www/homepage_archive/2016/april_2016.html.

19. "Holding the Mob at Bay: United States Troops Ordered to Seattle," *New York Times*, Feb. 10, 1886, 1.

20. J. Thomas Scharf, "The Farce of the Chinese Exclusion Laws," *North American Review* 166, no. 494 (Jan. 1898): 87.

21. See Mary D. Fan, "Post-Racial Proxies: Resurgent State and Local Anti-'Alien' Laws and Unity-Rebuilding Frames for Antidiscrimination Values," *Cardozo Law Review* 32, no. 3 (2011): 914–20.

22. Scharf, "The Farce," 90.

23. The Chinese Exclusion Act of 1882 was repealed in 1943 by the Magnuson Act, 57 Stat. 600. See Mae M. Ngai, *Impossible Subjects: Illegal Aliens and the Making of Modern America* (Princeton, NJ: Princeton University Press, 2004), 169, 204.

24. Jew Ho v. Williamson, 103 F. 10, 26 (C.C.N.D. Cal. 1900).

25. *Jew Ho*, 103 F. at 26.

26. *Jacobson*, 197 U.S. at 38.

27. Merkel, *When Germs Travel*, 66.

28. Honigsbaum, *The Pandemic Century*, 77.

29. "Plague Conference," *Public Health Reports (1896–1970)* 18, no. 6 (1903): 1–41, at 28–29.

30. "Resolutions Concerning the Plague Situation in San Francisco," *Public Health Reports* 18, no. 7 (1903): 199–201.

31. Daniel Sledge, *Health Divided: Public Health and Individual Medicine in the Making of the Modern American State* (Lawrence: University Press of Kansas, 2017), 2–3.

32. Merkel, *When Germs Travel*, 67.

33. David M. Morens and Anthony S. Fauci, "The Forgotten Forefather: Joseph James Kinyoun and the Founding of the National Institutes of Health," *MBio* 3, no. 4 (June 26, 2012), https://doi.org/10.1128/mBio.00139-12.

34. Honigsbaum, *The Pandemic Century*, 76.

35. Kamiya, "S.F. Leaders Denied."

36. Felice Batlan, "Law in the Time of Cholera: Disease, State Power, and Quarantines Past and Future," *Temple Law Review* 80 (2007): 107. According to Batlan, a federal official also delivered an ultimatum to the state: "You are a sovereign state . . . but if you do not take steps to control this vital danger, we will establish a quarantine entirely around you."

37. Transactions of the First Annual Conference of State and Territorial Health Officers (Washington, DC: Government Printing Office, June 3, 1903), 12, http://hdl.handle.net/2027/hvd.hx3ud7.

38. Transactions of the First Annual Conference, 33.

39. Transactions of the First Annual Conference, 24.

40. Transactions of the First Annual Conference, 26.

41. Philip A. Kalisch, "The Black Death in Chinatown: Plague and Politics in San Francisco 1900–1904," *Arizona and the West* 14, no. 2 (1972): 116.

42. Transactions of the First Annual Conference, 26.

43. The Tribune Bureau, "U.S. to Fight Plague: Aid for San Francisco; Government to Assume Cost of Labor and Service on Coast," *New York Tribune*, Nov. 20, 1907.

44. L. T. Gage, "Interstate Quarantine Regulations to Prevent the Spread of Plague in the United States," *Public Health Reports* 15, no. 21 (May 25, 1900): 1261.

45. Alan Kraut, *Silent Travelers: Germs, Genes, and the Immigrant Menace* (Baltimore: Johns Hopkins University Press, 1995), 92.

46. Markel, *When Germs Travel*, 71.

47. Wong Wai v. Williamson, 103 F. 1, 3 (C.C.N.D. Cal. 1900).

48. *Wong Wai*, 103 F. at 3.

49. *Wong Wai*, 103 F. at 7.

50. *Wong Wai*, 103 F. at 9.

51. *Wong Wai*, 103 F. at 7 (quoting telegram from Walter Wyman).

52. *Wong Wai*, 103 F. at 6.

53. Markel, *When Germs Travel*, 71.

54. Markel, *When Germs Travel*, 74.

55. Honigsbaum, *The Pandemic Century*, 71.

56. "The Bubonic Plague in San Francisco," 9.

57. US Census Bureau, "April 2016—History."

58. Honigsbaum, *The Pandemic Century*, 63.

59. Honigsbaum, *The Pandemic Century*, 66.

60. Honigsbaum, *The Pandemic Century*, 67, 80.

61. Honigsbaum, *The Pandemic Century*, 80–81.

62. "Pneumonic Plague Held In," *Boston Daily Globe*, Nov. 3, 1924, 17.

63. "Pneumonic Plague Is Feared After 13 Die in Los Angeles," *Washington Post*, Nov. 2, 1924, 1.

64. "Pneumonic Plague Held In."

65. Honigsbaum, *The Pandemic Century*, 83.

66. Honigsbaum, *The Pandemic Century*, 82.

67. William Francis Deverell, *Whitewashed Adobe, the Rise of Los Angeles, and the Remaking of Its Mexican Past* (Berkeley: University of California Press, 2004), 182.

68. "Plague at Los Angeles," *Austin Statesman*, Nov. 3, 1924, 1.

69. Honigsbaum, *The Pandemic Century*, 86.

70. "Teacher Braves Plague Area to Look After 'Her Children,'" *Baltimore Sun*, Nov. 5, 1924, 7.

71. Honigsbaum, *The Pandemic Century*, 71, 96.

72. "Plague Situation in Los Angeles, Calif.," *Public Health Reports* 39, no. 47 (1924): 2885.

73. Alexandra Stren and Howard Markel, "The Public Health Service and Film Noir: A Look Back at Elia Kazan's 'Panic in the Streets' (1950)," *Public Health Reports* 118, no. 3 (2003): 178–83.

74. CDC, "Ecology and Transmission of Plague," July 31, 2019, https://www.cdc.gov/plague/transmission/index.html.

75. CDC, "Map and Statistics," May 27, 2021, https://cdc.gov/plague/maps/index.html.

76. Markel, *When Germs Travel*, 57.

77. John Frith, "The Three Great Pandemics," *Journal of Military and Veterans' Health* 20, no. 2 (2012), https://jmvh.org/article/the-history-of-plague-part-1-the-three-great-pandemics.

78. "Surgeon-General Rupert Blue," *California State Journal of Medicine* 10, no. 2 (Feb. 1912): 49.

CHAPTER 4: THE 1918 GREAT INFLUENZA

1. William C. Rucker, "Interstate Sanitary Relations," in *Medical Problems of Legislation: Being the Papers and Discussions Presented at the 41st Annual Meeting of the American Academy of Medicine, 1916* (Easton, PA: American Academy of Medicine Press, 1917), 139.

2. Rucker, "Interstate Sanitary Relations," 131–32.

3. "History of Vaccines Timeline," College of Physicians of Philadelphia, https://www.historyofvaccines.org/timeline#EVT_74, accessed June 2, 2021.

4. Institute of Medicine, *A History of the Public Health System, The Future of Public Health* (Washington, DC: National Academies Press, 1988), https://www.ncbi.nlm.nih.gov/books/NBK218224.

5. Academy of Medicine, *Medical Problems of Legislation.*

6. US Public Health Service, *Court Decisions Pertaining to the Public Health Published in the Public Health Reports Before January 1, 1916* (Washington, DC: Government Printing Office, 1916).

7. President's Address, *Proceedings of the Thirty-First Annual Meeting of the Conference of State and Provincial Boards of Health of North America* (Raleigh: Edwards & Broughton, 1916), 8.

8. *Medical Problems of Legislation,* 154.

9. Preface, *Medical Problems of Legislation,* 3.

10. James. A. Tobey, *Public Health Law, A Manual of Law for Sanitarians* (Baltimore: Williams & Wilkins, 1926).

11. John Duffy, *The Sanitarians: A History of American Public Health* (Urbana: University of Illinois Press, 1990).

12. *Proceedings,* 8, 11.

13. Hermann M. Biggs and C. E. A. Winslow, *An Ideal Health Department: Joint Report* (Minneapolis, MN: n.p., 1913).

14. Herman M. Biggs, "The New York State Sanitary Code," in *Medical Problems of Legislation,* 127–28.

15. Rural Sanitation in the Health Service: Hearing on S. 2215 Before the Senate Committee on Public Health and National Quarantine, 64th Cong. 53 (Feb. 14, 1916).

16. "A Momentous Decision," *Journal of the National Medical Association* 8, no. 2 (1916): 105.

17. Seven Cases v. U.S., 239 U.S. 510 (1916).

18. Daniel Sledge, *Health Divided: Public Health and Individual Medicine in the Making of the Modern American State* (Lawrence: University Press of Kansas, 2017), 68.

19. Quoted in Sledge, *Health Divided,* 51–52.

20. Rural Sanitation in the Health Service, 42.

21. Rucker, "Interstate Sanitary Relations," 132–35.

22. Rucker, "Interstate Sanitary Relations," 135–36.

23. Rucker, "Interstate Sanitary Relations," 139.

24. Rucker, "Interstate Sanitary Relations," 136.
25. Nancy K. Bristow, *American Pandemic: The Lost Worlds of the 1918 Influenza Epidemic* (New York: Oxford University Press, 2012), 3–4.
26. John Barry, *The Great Influenza: The Epic Story of the Deadliest Pandemic in History* (New York: Penguin Group, 2004), 302.
27. Suppression of Spanish Influenza: Hearing on H.J. Res. 333 Before the S. Comm. on Appropriations, 65th Cong. (Sept. 28, 1918).
28. "Ask $1,000,000 to Fight Epidemic," *Boston Daily Globe*, Sept. 28, 1918, 2.
29. "United States Public Health Service," *American Journal of Public Health* 10, no. 4 (Apr. 1920): 365–67.
30. "Influenza Deaths in Boston Fewer," *Boston Daily Globe*, Sept. 28, 1918, 1–2.
31. Suppression of Spanish Influenza, 10–11.
32. Suppression of Spanish Influenza, 11.
33. Suppression of Spanish Influenza, 4–5.
34. Suppression of Spanish Influenza, 14.
35. "Takes Steps to Stop Influenza Spread," *New York Times*, Sept. 14, 1918, 13.
36. Annual Report of the Surgeon General of the Public Health Service (Washington, DC: Government Printing Office, 1919), 82.
37. "Health Officers Split on Influenza Scourge," *New York Times*, Dec. 13, 1918, 9.
38. "Health Officers Split," 9.
39. "Health Officers Split," 9.
40. "The 1918 Influenza in Missouri: Centennial Remembrance of the Crisis," *Journal of Missouri State Medical Association* 115, no. 4 (July–Aug. 2018): 319–24, https://www.ncbi.nlm.nih.gov/pmc/articles/PMC6140242.
41. Mira Shetty, "Penn and the 1918 Influenza Epidemic," Penn University Archives and Records Center, 2018, https://archives.upenn.edu/exhibits/penn-history/flu.
42. Richard J. Hatchett et al., "Public Health Interventions and Epidemic Intensity During the 1918 Influenza Pandemic," *Proceedings of the National Academy of Sciences* 104, no. 18 (May 1, 2007): 7582–87.
43. Emma Hurt, "Familiar Echoes: 1918 Atlanta and The Spanish Flu," WABE, Mar. 26, 2020, https://www.wabe.org/familiar-echoes-1918-atlanta-and-the-spanish-flu.
44. Dula v. Board of School Trustees of Lenoir, 177 N.C. 426 (1919).
45. David M. Zimmer, "Before Covid, Spanish Flu of 1918 Gave NJ Leaders a Challenge," NorthJersey.com, Sept. 5, 2020, https://www.northjersey.com/story/news/new-jersey/2020/09/05/before-covid-spanish-flu-1918-gave-nj-leaders-challenge/5683747002.
46. "Newark, New Jersey," *Influenza Encyclopedia*, University of Michigan Library, https://www.influenzaarchive.org/cities/city-newark.html#, accessed Sept. 15, 2021.
47. "Newark, New Jersey," *Influenza Encyclopedia*.
48. "After State Health Head: Mayor Gillen Asks Governor to Remove Dr. Price," *New York Times*, Oct. 26, 1918, 11.
49. "Ex-Mayor Gillen of Newark Dies," *New York Times*, July 1, 1956, 56.

50. "Newark, New Jersey," *Influenza Encyclopedia.*
51. Howard Markel et al., "Nonpharmaceutical Interventions Implemented by US Cities During the 1918–1919 Influenza Pandemic," *Journal of the American Medical Association* 298, no. 6 (2007): 644.
52. David Rosner, "'Spanish Flu, or Whatever It Is . . . ': The Paradox of Public Health in a Time of Crisis," *Public Health Reports* 125, no. S3 (2010): 45.
53. Surgeon General's Report, 22, 58–59.
54. Barry, *The Great Influenza,* 317, 353.
55. Rosner, "Spanish Flu or Whatever It Is," 39.
56. Stanley B. Norvell and William M. Tuttle Jr., "Views of a Negro During 'The Red Summer' of 1919," *Journal of Negro History* 51, no. 3 (1966): 209.
57. Globe School District v. Board of Health, 20 Ariz. 208, 218 (1919); Alden v. State, 20 Ariz. 235 (1919).
58. Barmore v. Robertson, 302 Ill. 422, 432, (1922).
59. Globe School District, 218.
60. "Quarantine Made Effective," *Idaho Recorder,* Nov. 15, 1918, 1.
61. "Court Appeals in Vain for Military Assistance," *Idaho Recorder,* Nov. 22, 1912, 1.
62. "Court Appeals in Vain," 1.
63. "Death Toll Is Still Growing," *Idaho Recorder,* Dec. 27, 1918, 1.
64. "When Doctor Is Haled to Court," *Idaho Recorder,* Jan. 31, 1919.
65. Archbold v. Huntington, 34 Idaho 558 (1921).
66. "Health Officers Split," 9.
67. "Influenza Deaths in Boston Fewer," *Boston Daily Globe,* Sept. 28, 1918, 2.
68. Bradford Luckingham, *Epidemic in the Southwest, 1918–1919* (El Paso: Texas Western Press, 1984), 33.
69. "Refuses to Don Influenza Mask; Shot by Officer," *Bellingham (WA) Herald,* Oct. 28, 1918, 2.
70. Markel et al., "Nonpharmaceutical Interventions," 651–54.
71. Patricia J. Fanning, *Influenza and Inequality: One Town's Tragic Response to the Great Epidemic of 1918* (Amherst: University of Massachusetts Press, 2010), 10.
72. Fanning, *Influenza and Inequality,* 10–11; Edgar Sydenstricker, "The Incidence of Influenza among Persons of Different Economic Status During the Epidemic of 1918," *Public Health Reports* 46, no. 4 (1931): 154–70.
73. Dana Hedgpeth, "Native American Tribes Were Already Being Wiped Out, Then the 1918 Flu Hit," *Washington Post,* Sept. 27, 2020.
74. Benjamin R. Brady and Howard M. Bahr, "The Influenza Epidemic of 1918–1920 among the Navajos: Marginality, Mortality, and the Implications of Some Neglected Eyewitness Accounts," *American Indian Quarterly* 38, no. 4 (2014): 461.
75. Letter from the Secretary of the Treasury, Committee on Appropriations Doc. 221, 66th Congress, 2nd sess., Feb. 13, 1920, 2, 4.
76. John Gomez, "Saints of an Earlier Pandemic," NJ.com, June 18, 2020, https://www.nj.com/galleries/LIFWW45YYNH4PMT5APTJFHWYJU.
77. "Fiesta Spirit Pervades City," *Los Angeles Times,* Dec. 3, 1918, 5.

78. University of Michigan Library, "Rochester, New York," *Influenza Encyclopedia*, https://www.influenzaarchive.org/cities/city-rochester.html, accessed Sept. 15, 2021.

79. Francesco Aimone, "The 1918 Influenza Epidemic in New York City: A Review of the Public Health Response," *Public Health Reports* 125, no. S3 (2010): 75.

80. Hermann Biggs, "The Recent Epidemic of Influenza" *American Review of Reviews* (Jan.–June 1919), *Influenza Encyclopedia*, https://quod.lib.umich.edu/f/flu/2850flu.0016.582/1/—recent-epidemic-of-influenza.

81. Biggs, "The Recent Epidemic," 70–71.

82. Biggs, "The Recent Epidemic," 70–71.

83. Howard Markel, "'Public Health Is Purchasable,'" *Milbank Quarterly* 94, no. 3 (Sept. 2016): 441, 445–46.

84. Herman Biggs, "Public Health Is Purchasable," *Monthly Bulletin of the Department of Health of the City of New York* 1, no. 10 (1911): 225–26.

CHAPTER 5: CONFRONTING TUBERCULOSIS

1. Hermann M. Biggs, "Administrative Control of Tuberculosis," *Public Health Journal* 3, no. 11 (1912): 610.

2. 59 Cong. Rec. 2046–47 (1920) (statements of Sen. Phelan); S.J. Res. 76, 66th Cong. (Oct. 1, 1919).

3. CDC, "Influenza Historic Timeline," last reviewed Jan. 30, 2019, https://www.cdc.gov/flu/pandemic-resources/pandemic-timeline-1930-and-beyond.htm.

4. Wilbur A. Sawyer, "The Health Officer's Interest in Virus Diseases," *Proceedings of the Fifty-Fifth Annual Meeting of the Conference of State and Provincial Health Authorities of North America* (Washington, DC: 1939), 33.

5. Michael E. Teller, *The Tuberculosis Movement: A Public Health Campaign in the Progressive Era* (New York: Greenwood Press, 1988), 17–18.

6. Frank M. Snowden, *Epidemics and Society: From the Black Death to the Present* (New Haven, CT: Yale University Press, 2019), 296.

7. Biggs, "Administrative Control of Tuberculosis," 607; Herman M. Biggs, "Public Health Is Purchasable," *Monthly Bulletin of the Department of Health of the City of New York* 1, no. 10 (1911): 226.

8. "TB in America: 1895–1954," *American Experience*, PBS, https://www.pbs.org/wgbh/americanexperience/features/plague-gallery, accessed Sept. 15, 2021.

9. Nancy Owen Lewis, *Chasing the Cure in New Mexico: Tuberculosis and the Quest for Health* (Santa Fe: Museum of New Mexico Press, 2016), 1.

10. Jeanne E. Abrams, "'Spitting Is Dangerous, Indecent, and Against the Law!' Legislating Health Behavior During the American Tuberculosis Crusade," *Journal of the History of Medicine and Allied Sciences* 68, no. 3 (2013): 416–50.

11. "Spitting and Murdering," *Chicago Daily Tribune*, Oct. 6, 1904, 8.

12. Robert J. Newton, "How the Tuberculosis War Is Spreading Throughout the Union," *New York Times*, June 19, 1910, 15.

13. Newton, "How the Tuberculosis War Is Spreading Throughout the Union," 15.

14. "The American Lung Association," Smithsonian National Postal Museum, https://postalmuseum.si.edu/exhibition/america%E2%80%99s-mailing -industry-industry-segments-nonprofit-organizations/the-american-lung, accessed Sept. 15, 2021.

15. Snowden, *Epidemics in Society*, 302.

16. Snowden, *Epidemics in Society*, 299.

17. Snowden, *Epidemics in Society*, 300.

18. Snowden, *Epidemics in Society*, 300.

19. "To Bar Consumptives: No More Immigrants with Tuberculosis to Be Received," *New York Tribune*, June 5, 1901, 1.

20. Teller, *The Tuberculosis Movement*, 22–23.

21. Biggs, "Administrative Control of Tuberculosis," 610.

22. Teller, *The Tuberculosis Movement*, 65.

23. "Tuberculosis in Mammoth Cave," National Park Service, last updated Apr. 5, 2021, https://www.nps.gov/articles/tuberculosis-mammoth-cave.htm.

24. Lewis, *Chasing the Cure*, 13–21.

25. Ernest A. Sweet, "Interstate Migration of Tuberculosis Persons," *Public Health Reports* 30, no. 15 (1915): 1071.

26. Sweet, "Interstate Migration," 1063, 1074.

27. Sweet, "Interstate Migration," 1073.

28. Sweet, "Interstate Migration," 1075, 1082–84.

29. William B. Grayson, "Some Current Problems in Public Health Administration," *Proceedings of the Fifty-Fifth Annual Meeting of the Conference of State and Provincial Health Authorities of North America* (Washington, DC: 1940), 35.

30. See chapter 1 for a discussion of "poor laws" through the Civil War. Michael B. Katz, *Poverty and Policy in American History* (New York: Academic Press, 1983).

31. "For Buchanan Bill," *Austin Statesman*, Feb. 19, 1911, 2.

32. C. C. Pierce, "Public Health Service Program for Nation-Wide Control of Venereal Diseases," *Public Health Reports* 34, no. 20 (1919) 1056.

33. Scott W. Stern, *The Trials of Nina McCall: Sex, Surveillance, and the Decades-Long Government Plan to Imprison "Promiscuous" Women* (Boston: Beacon Press, 2018).

34. In re Clemente, 215 P. 698 (Cal. Ct. App.) 1923.

35. Nyberg v. Bd. of Comm'rs, 113 Kan. 758, 216 P. 282 (1923).

36. The Associated Press broke the story on July 25, 1972: "AP Was There: Black Men Untreated in Tuskegee Syphilis Study," AP News, May 10, 2017, https://apnews.com/article/race-and-ethnicity-african-americans-medic al-research-syphilis-bill-clinton-e9dd07eaa4e74052878a68132cd3803a.

37. "Remarks by the President in Apology for Study Done in Tuskegee," press release, May 16, 1997, https://clintonwhitehouse4.archives.gov/textonly/New /Remarks/Fri/19970516-898.html.

38. Judith Walzer Leavitt, *Typhoid Mary: Captive to the Public's Health* (Boston: Beacon Press, 1996).

39. Barmore v. Robertson, 302 Ill. 422, 424–25 (Ill. 1922).

40. *Barmore*, 302 Ill. at 433–34.
41. *Barmore*, 302 Ill. at 427.
42. *Barmore*, 302 Ill. at 427.
43. *Barmore*, 302 Ill. at 432.
44. *Barmore*, 302 Ill. at 432 (emphasis added).
45. "Quarantine of Typhoid Carrier Upheld," *Public Health Reports* 37, no. 21 (1922): 1253–59.
46. Teller, *The Tuberculosis Movement*, 91–93.
47. John Fabian Witt, *American Contagions: Epidemics and the Law from Smallpox to COVID-19* (New Haven, CT: Yale University Press, 2020).
48. State v. Snow, 324 S.W.2d 532, 534–36 (Ark. 1959).
49. "TB and COVID-19," Stop TB Partnership, http://www.stoptb.org/covid19.asp, accessed Sept. 15, 2021.
50. CDC, "Tuberculosis: Data & Statistics," https://www.cdc.gov/tb/statistics/default.htm, accessed Oct. 3, 2021.
51. Felicia Tackett, "TB Replacement/Decrease Levy to Appear on Ballot . . . Again," *Courier* (McArthur, OH), Oct. 28, 2013, https://www.vintonjackson courier.com/timesjournal/tb-replacement-decrease-levy-to-appear-on-ballot -again/article_efa87bac-2446-5bb4-bb88-ea4f2a2548cf.html.
52. Marissa Evans, "In Texas, 'A Perception That Tuberculosis No Longer Exists' Raises Alarm for Legislative Attention," *Texas Tribune*, Dec. 18, 2018, https://www.texastribune.org/2018/12/18/texas-tuberculosis-problem-raise s-alarm-legislative-attention.
53. Krista M. Powell et al., "Outbreak of Drug-Resistant *Myobacterium Tuberculosis* among Homeless People in Atlanta, Georgia, 2008–2015," *Public Health Reports* 132, no. 2 (2017): 236, 238.
54. William J. Connors, "Homeless Shelter Context and Tuberculosis Illness Experiences During a Large Outbreak in Atlanta, Georgia," *Public Health Action* 7, no. 3 (2017): 224–30.
55. David P. Holland et al., "Response to Isoniazid-Resistant Tuberculosis in Homeless Shelters, Georgia, USA, 2015–2017," *Emerging Infectious Diseases* 25, no. 3 (2019): 593–95, doi:10.3201/eid2503.181678.
56. Nancy Badertscher, "TB Real Concern at Atlanta Homeless Shelter," *PolitiFact*, Aug. 19, 2015.
57. Vikki Valentine, "A Timeline of Andrew Speaker's Infection," NPR, June 6, 2007, https://legacy.npr.org/news/specials/tb/index.html, accessed Oct. 3, 2021.
58. Valentine, "A Timeline of Andrew Speaker's Infection."
59. David P. Fidler, Lawrence O. Gostin, and Howard Markel, "Through the Quarantine Looking Glass: Drug Resistant Tuberculosis and Public Health Governance, Law, and Ethics," *Journal of Law, Medicine & Ethics* 35, no. 4 (2007): 618, 620–26.
60. Milton Terris, "C.-E. A. Winslow: Scientist, Activist, and Theoretician of the American Public Health Movement throughout the First Half of the Twentieth Century," *Journal of Public Health Policy* 19, no. 2 (1998): 137.
61. Terris, "C.-E. A. Winslow," 137.

CHAPTER 6: THE FIGHT AGAINST POLIO

1. "Pickets Are Gone, But Polio Remains," *Baltimore Afro-American*, May 3, 1958, 9.
2. David M. Oshinsky, *Polio: An American Story* (Oxford: Oxford University Press, 2005), 210.
3. Oshinsky, *Polio*, 210.
4. Emma Goldberg, "Vaccine Memories of Another Time and Place," *New York Times*, Dec. 25, 2020, https://www.nytimes.com/2020/12/25/health/covid-vaccine-polio.html.
5. Frank M. Snowden, *Epidemics and Society: From the Black Death to the Present* (New Haven, CT: Yale University Press, 2019), 386.
6. Oshinsky, *Polio*, 128–29, 188.
7. Earl Ubell, "Anti-Polio Shots Ready for 18 Million by Spring," *New York Herald Tribune*, Oct. 19, 1954, 1.
8. Oshinsky, *Polio*, 211.
9. "Washington Must Act," *New York Herald Tribune*, May 2, 1955, 1.
10. Snowden, *Epidemics and Society*, 396.
11. "Pickets Are Gone, But Polio Remains," 9.
12. "3,248 Children Toted Over Drifts to Get Salk Shots, *Boston Globe*, March 25, 1956, C1.
13. "Curb of Smallpox a 'Miracle,' Says City Health Commissioner," *New York Times*, Apr. 26, 1947, 15.
14. William B. Grayson, "Some Current Problems in Public Health Administration," *Proceedings of the Fifty-Fifth Annual Meeting of the Conference of State and Provincial Health Authorities of North America* (Washington, DC, 1940), 34.
15. "11,267 Receive Salk Vaccine Shots in Day," *Chicago Daily Tribune*, July 24, 1956, 12.
16. "Thousands Storm Chicago Clinic for Polio Vaccine," *New York Herald Tribune*, Aug. 1, 1956, 11.
17. "Confusion over Polio," *New York Times*, May 22, 1955.
18. "Washington Must Act," 1.
19. "Doctors' Probe Calls 9 over Adult Polio Shots," *New York Herald Tribune*, May 3, 1955, 1.
20. "Would Jail Violators of Salk Law," *New York Herald Tribune*, May 3, 1955, 19.
21. "Washington Must Act," 1.
22. Bart Barnes, "Oveta Culp Hobby Dies at 90," *Washington Post*, Aug. 17, 1995, B4.
23. "Administration Details Its Program for Voluntary Controls on the Distribution of Salk Polio Vaccine," *Wall Street Journal*, May 17, 1955, 2.
24. "Confusion over Polio."
25. Oshinsky, *Polio*, 218–19.
26. Public Law 377, 69 Stat. 704 (Aug. 12, 1955).
27. "Parents Sue U.S. Over Polio Death," *Baltimore Sun*, Apr. 19, 1956, 19.
28. Paul Offit, *The Cutter Incident: How America's First Polio Vaccine Led to a Growing Vaccine Crisis* (New Haven, CT: Yale University Press, 2007), 89.

29. Offit, *The Cutter Incident*, xii.
30. Sabin Russell, "When Polio Vaccine Backfired," *San Francisco Chronicle*, Apr. 25, 2005, https://www.sfgate.com/health/article/When-polio-vaccine-backfired-Tainted-batches-2677525.php.
31. Russell, "When Polio Vaccine Backfired."
32. Russell, "When Polio Vaccine Backfired."
33. Offit, *The Cutter Incident*, 166–68.
34. "Polio Fog Lifts," *New York Times*, May 29, 1955, 103.
35. Elizabeth W. Etheridge, *Sentinel for Health: A History of the Centers for Disease Control* (Berkeley: University of California Press, 1992), 69, 73–77.
36. "Extend Delay on Vaccine," *Chicago Daily Tribune*, May 20, 1955, 1.
37. Oshinsky, *Polio*, 272.
38. "Confusion over Polio."
39. "U.S. Aide Explains Polio Shot Scarcity," *New York Times*, Mar. 22, 1957, 28.
40. Alan R. Hinman, "Mass Vaccination Against Polio," *JAMA: Journal of the American Medical Association* 251, no. 22 (June 8, 1984): 2994.
41. CDC, "Polio Elimination in the U.S.," Oct. 25, 2019, https://www.cdc.gov/polio/what-is-polio/polio-us.html.
42. Etheridge, *Sentinel for Health*, 28–29, 69, 79–8 ; Polly J. Price, "Federalization of the Mosquito: Structural Innovation in the New Deal Administrative State," *Emory Law Journal* 60, no. 2 (2010): 325, 327.
43. CDC, "1957–1958 Pandemic (H2N2 Virus)," Jan. 22, 2019, https://www.cdc.gov/flu/pandemic-resources/1957–1958-pandemic.html.
44. Nancy K. Bristow, *American Pandemic: The Lost Worlds of the 1918 Influenza Epidemic* (New York: Oxford University Press, 2012), 3–4.
45. George Dehner, *Influenza: A Century of Science and Public Health Response* (Pittsburgh: University of Pittsburgh Press, 2012), 75–76, 101–2.
46. "The Great Epidemic—The Threat," *Newsweek* 50, no. 9 (Aug. 26, 1957): 65.
47. "The Great Epidemic," 65.
48. "1957–1958 Pandemic."
49. Dehner, *Influenza*, 102.
50. "The Great Epidemic," 68.
51. D. A. Henderson et al., "Public Health and Medical Responses to the 1957–58 Influenza Pandemic," *Biosecurity and Bioterrorism: Biodefense Strategy, Practice, and Science* 7, no. 3 (Sept. 2009): 270.
52. Henderson et al, "Public Health and Medical Responses to the 1957–58 Influenza Pandemic," 270.
53. CDC, "1968 Pandemic (H3N2 Virus)," Jan. 22, 2019, https://www.cdc.gov/flu/pandemic-resources/1968-pandemic.html.
54. Marti Mueller, "Influenza Vaccine: A Long Way from Hong Kong," *Science* 162, no. 3854 (Nov. 8, 1968), 651.
55. Dehner, *Influenza*, 102–3.
56. Dehner, *Influenza*, 2–3, 107.
57. Christopher Klein, "When the US Government Tried to Fast-Track a Flu Vaccine," History.com, https://www.history.com/news/swine-flu-rush-vaccine-election-year-1976, accessed Sept. 2, 2020.
58. Klein, "When the US Government Tried to Fast-Track a Flu Vaccine."

59. CDC, "GBS (Guillain-Barré Syndrome) and Vaccines," Aug. 14, 2020, https://www.cdc.gov/vaccinesafety/concerns/guillain-barre-syndrome.html.

60. Lainie Rutkow et al., "Balancing Consumer and Industry Interests in Public Health: The National Vaccine Injury Compensation Program and Its Influence During the Last Two Decades," *Penn State Law Review* 111 (2007): 682–83.

61. Rutkow et al., "Balancing Consumer and Industry Interests," 683.

62. Daniel O'Brien, "Not If, But When: Pandemic Influenza and the Law of Public Health," *Maryland Bar Journal* 39, no. 12 (2006): 13.

CHAPTER 7: THE AIDS EPIDEMIC

1. "Interview—Jim Curran," *Frontline*, PBS, Feb. 15, 2006, https://www.pbs.org/wgbh/pages/frontline/aids/interviews/curran.html.

2. James W. Curran and Harold W. Jaffe, "AIDS: The Early Years and CDC's Response," *Morbidity and Mortality Weekly Report* 60, no. 4 (2011): 64.

3. John M. Luce, "A Strange New Disease in San Francisco: A Brief History of the City and Its Response to the HIV/AIDS Epidemic," *Annals of the American Thoracic Society* 10, no. 2 (Apr. 2013): 145.

4. "AIDS, the Surgeon General, and the Politics of Public Health," US National Library of Medicine, https://profiles.nlm.nih.gov/spotlight/qq/feature/aids, accessed June 5, 2021.

5. William H. Foege, *Fears of the Rich, The Needs of the Poor: My Years at the CDC* (Baltimore: Johns Hopkins University Press, 2018), 210.

6. Foege, *Fears of the Rich, The Needs of the Poor*, 210–11; Martha McKenzie, "Lessons from 40 Years of HIV/AIDS," Emory News Center, June 1, 2021, https://news.emory.edu/stories/2021/06/er_mmwr_40_hiv_aids/campus.html?utm_source=ebulletin&utm_medium=email&utm_campaign=Emory_Report_EB_010621.

7. Curran and Jaffe, "AIDS: The Early Years," 66.

8. Luce, "A Strange New Disease," 146.

9. Curran and Jaffe, "AIDS: The Early Years," 66.

10. Frank M. Snowden, *Epidemics and Society: From the Black Death to the Present* (New Haven, CT: Yale University Press, 2019), 433.

11. Richard A. McKay, "'Patient Zero': The Absence of a Patient's View of the Early North American AIDS Epidemic," *Bulletin of the History of Medicine* 88, no. 1 (2014): 163–65.

12. "AIDS, the Surgeon General, and the Politics of Public Health."

13. Caitlin Gibson, "A Disturbing New Glimpse at the Reagan Administration's Indifference to AIDS," *Washington Post*, Dec. 1, 2015.

14. "AIDS, the Surgeon General, and the Politics of Public Health."

15. Mike Stobbe, *Surgeon General's Warning: How Politics Crippled America's Doctor* (Oakland: University of California Press, 2014), 184.

16. "AIDS, the Surgeon General, and the Politics of Public Health."

17. "U.S. Will Mail AIDS Advisory to All Households," *New York Times*, May 5, 1988.

18. "Understanding AIDS," Centers for Disease Control, 1988, 3, https://stacks.cdc.gov/view/cdc/6927.

19. "Understanding AIDS," 2.

20. "AIDS, the Surgeon General, and the Politics of Public Health."

21. "U.S. Will Mail AIDS Advisory to All Households."

22. Stobbe, *Surgeon General's Warning*, 170.

23. Snowden, *Epidemics and Society*, 440–41.

24. Elizabeth Fee and Nancy Krieger, "Understanding AIDS: Historical Inter-pretations and the Limits of Biomedical Individualism," *American Journal of Public Health* 83, no. 10 (1993): 1478; Gibson, "A Disturbing New Glimpse"; Snowden, *Epidemics and Society*, 433.

25. Dirk Johnson, "Ryan White Dies of AIDS at 18; His Struggle Helped Pierce Myths," *New York Times*, Apr. 9, 1990.

26. Johnson, "Ryan White Dies."

27. Johnson, "Ryan White Dies."

28. "1,500 Attend Funeral of Courageous AIDS Fighter," *New York Times*, Apr. 12, 1990, B12.

29. Larry Rohter, "11,000 Boycott Start of Classes in AIDS Protest," *New York Times*, Sept. 10, 1985, B1.

30. Robert Steinbrook, "The Times Poll: 42% Would Limit Civil Rights in AIDS Battle," *Los Angeles Times*, July 31, 1987.

31. David C. Colby and David G. Baker, "State Policy Responses to the AIDS Epidemic," *Publius* 18, no. 3 (1987): 116.

32. Wendy Parmet, "AIDS and Quarantine: The Revival of an Archaic Doc-trine," *Hofstra Law Review* 14, no. 1 (1985): 53–54.

33. "Texas Plan for AIDS Quarantine Dropped," *Los Angeles Times*, Jan. 17, 1986.

34. Ariel Hart, "Georgia Lawmaker's Suggestion of HIV 'Quarantine' Sparks Fu-ror," *Atlanta Journal-Constitution*, Oct. 21, 2017, https://www.ajc.com/news /state--regional-govt--politics/georgia-lawmaker-suggestion-hiv-quarantine -sparks-furor/82mQW5GGFgTawz8iesZMEK.

35. Ben Tinker, "Georgia Lawmaker: Can People with HIV Be 'Legally' Quaran-tined?," CNN.com, Oct. 22, 2017.

36. Joseph Allen Garmon, "The Laws of the Past Versus the Medicine of Today: Eradicating the Criminalization of HIV/AIDS," *Howard Law Journal* 57, no. 4 (2014): 669–73; James B. McArthur, "As the Tide Turns: The Changing HIV/AIDS Epidemic and the Criminalization of HIV Exposure," *Cornell Law Review* 94, no. 3 (2009): 716–20.

37. McArthur, "As the Tide Turns," 710.

38. Zach Berg, "Man Accused of Spreading HIV Accepts Plea Deal," *Iowa City Press-Citizen*, Oct. 28, 2016.

39. Garmon, "The Laws of the Past Versus the Medicine of Today," 677–78.

40. Maurice Possley, "Nick Rhoades," National Registry of Exonerations, July 11, 2016, https://www.law.umich.edu/special/exoneration/Pages/casedetail .aspx?caseid=4514.

41. Grant Rodgers, "Iowa Justices Weigh Rhoades HIV Case for Second Time," *Des Moines Register*, Mar. 8, 2016.

42. National Academy of Sciences, "Confronting AIDS: Directions for Public Health, Health Care and Research," *Issues in Science and Technology* 3, no. 2 (1987): 98.

43. David France, "How ACT UP Remade Political Organizing in America," *New York Times*, Apr. 13, 2020, https://www.nytimes.com/interactive/2020 /04/13/t-magazine/act-up-aids.html.

44. Nurith Aizenman, "How to Demand a Medical Breakthrough: Lessons from the AIDS Fight," NPR, Feb. 9, 2019, https://www.npr.org/sections/health -shots/2019/02/09/689924838/how-to-demand-a-medical-breakthrough -lessons-from-the-aids-fight.

45. Aizenman, "How to Demand a Medical Breakthrough."

46. David France, *How to Survive a Plague: The Inside Story of How Citizens and Science Tamed AIDS* (New York: Alfred A. Knopf, 2016).

47. "Interview—Jim Curran," PBS *Frontline*.

48. Foege, *Fears of the Rich*, 216–17.

49. Curran, interview with the author, May 3, 2021.

50. Johnson, "Ryan White Dies."

51. Ryan White Comprehensive AIDS Resources Emergency Act of 1990, Pub. L. No. 101–381, 104 Stat. 576. The measure passed the 101st Congress four months after White's death.

52. Tasleem J. Padamsee, "Fighting an Epidemic in Political Context: Thirty-Five Years of HIV/AIDS Policy Making in the United States," *Social History of Medicine* 33, no. 3 (2020): 1007.

53. Linda Greenhouse, "Justices, 6–3, Bar Veto of Line Items in Bills; See H.I.V. as Disability; Ruling on Bias Law," *New York Times*, June 26, 1998.

54. Bragdon v. Abbott, 524 U.S. 624 (1998).

55. Greenhouse, "H.I.V. as Disability."

56. Ronald Alsop, "These Workers Face Discrimination from Inside, and Out," BBC.com, Mar. 3, 2017, https://www.bbc.com/worklife/article/20170302 -these-workers-face-discrimination-despite-protective-laws.

57. "Houston Nightclub Forced to Pay Nearly $140K for Firing Employee After Unlawful HIV Test Inquiry," KPRC (Houston), Sept. 29, 2016, https://www .click2houston.com/news/2017/01/09/houston-nightclub-forced-to-pay -nearly-140k-for-firing-employee-after-unlawful-hiv-test-inquiry.

58. "Houston Nightclub Forced to Pay Nearly $140K for Firing Employee After Unlawful HIV Test Inquiry."

59. Kaiser Family Foundation, "2012 Survey of Americans on HIV/AIDS," July 2, 2012, https://www.kff.org/hivaids/poll-finding/2012-survey-of-americans -on-hivaids.

60. Bruce D. Walker and Dennis R. Burton, "Toward an AIDS Vaccine," *Science* 320, no. 5877 (2008): 760.

61. Padamsee, "Fighting an Epidemic," 1007.

62. Padamsee, "Fighting an Epidemic," 1019.

63. "2004 Scientist Statement on Restoring Scientific Integrity to Federal Policy Making," Union of Concerned Scientists, Mar. 2004, https://www.ucsusa.org /resources/2004-scientist-statement-scientific-integrity.

64. "Scientific Integrity in Policy Making," July 13, 2008, https://www.ucsusa.org /resources/scientific-integrity-policy-making-0.

65. Padamsee, "Fighting an Epidemic," 1020.

66. Tasleem J. Padamsee, "The Politics of Prevention: Lessons from the Neglected History of US HIV/AIDS Policy," *Journal of Health Politics, Policy and Law* 42, no. 1 (2017): 106.

67. Padamsee, "Fighting an Epidemic," 1023.

68. Mitch Legan, "Indiana Needle Exchange That Helped Contain a Historic HIV Outbreak to Be Shut Down," NPR, June 3, 2021, https://www.npr.org /sections/health-shots/2021/06/01/1001278712/indiana-needle-exchange-that -helped-contain-an-hiv-outbreak-may-be-forced-to-clo.

69. Lena H. Sun, "Trump Budget Calls for 291 Million To Fund HIV Initiative," Washington Post, Mar. 11, 2019; CDC, HIV Surveillance, May 7, 2020, https://www.cdc.gov/hiv/library/reports/hiv-surveillance/vol-31/index.html.

70. James Curran, interview with the author, May 3, 2021.

CHAPTER 8: EBOLA IN DALLAS

1. "Looking Back, Dallas Ebola Crisis Showed Cost of Fear, Value of Leadership," *Dallas Morning News*, Sept. 26, 2015, https://www.dallasnews.com /news/2015/09/27/looking-back-dallas-ebola-crisis-showed-cost-of-fear-value -of-leadership.

2. "Ebola Virus Disease," World Health Organization, updated June 21, 2020, https://www.afro.who.int/health-topics/ebola-virus-disease.

3. The first vaccine for Ebola virus was approved for use in the US by the Food and Drug Administration on Dec. 19, 2019, https://www.cdc.gov/vhf/ebola /clinicians/vaccine/index.html.

4. Eventually, seven Americans who contracted Ebola while volunteering in West Africa were evacuated to the US for treatment; all but one survived. All US patient evacuations were funded privately, not by the federal or a state government.

5. Combatting the Ebola Threat: Hearing Before the Subcommittee on Africa, Global Health, Global Human Rights, and International Organizations of the House Committee on Foreign Affairs, 113th Congress (Aug. 7, 2014), 10–11, https://chrissmith.house.gov/uploadedfiles/2014.08.07_combating_the _ebola_threat.pdf.

6. Bryan Burrough, "Ebola in the U.S.: How Dallas Rallied to Prevent an Epidemic," *Vanity Fair*, Feb. 2015, https://www.vanityfair.com/news/2015/02 /ebola-us-dallas-epidemic#.

7. Clay Jenkins, interview by author, Mar. 21, 2019.

8. Sarah Portlock and Alan Zibel, "U.S. Health Officials Continue to Play Down Ebola Fears," *Wall Street Journal*, Oct. 5, 2014.

9. Portlock and Zibel, "U.S. Health Officials Continue to Play Down Ebola Fears."

10. Jenkins, interview by author.

11. Sherry Jacobson, "Texas Families Isolated by Ebola Struggled for Basics," *Charleston (WV) Sunday Gazette-Mail*, Feb. 15, 2015.

12. Burrough, "Ebola in the U.S." Disposal of the incinerated waste from the apartment was further delayed when the attorney general of Louisiana obtained a court order preventing a waste management company in Lake

Charles, Louisiana, from accepting the ash. Kevin McGill, "Judge Halts Disposal in Louisiana of Texas Ebola-Tainted Ash," *Insurance Journal*, Oct. 15, 2014, https://www.insurancejournal.com/news/southcentral/2014/10/15 /343708.htm.

13. National Public Radio, "Dallas Judge Leads County's Ebola Response," Oct. 16, 2014, https://www.npr.org/2014/10/16/356728028/dallas-judge-leads -countys-ebola-response.

14. Wendy M. Chung et al., "Active Tracing and Monitoring of Contacts Associated with the First Cluster of Ebola in the United States," *Annals of Internal Medicine* 163, no. 3 (Aug. 4, 2015): 168, https://doi.org/10.7326/M15-0968.

15. Quoted in Ana Campoy and Betsy McKay, "Ebola Case in Dallas Points Out Flaws," *Wall Street Journal*, Oct. 5, 2014.

16. Jenkins, interview by author.

17. Chung et al., "Active Tracing and Monitoring of Contacts," 167.

18. Krystina Martinez, "Ebola in Dallas: A Timeline," *KERA News*, Nov. 7, 2014, https://www.keranews.org/health-science-tech/2014-11-07/ebola-in -dallas-a-timeline.

19. Chung et al., "Active Tracing and Monitoring of Contacts," 165.

20. Jenkins, interview by author.

21. Haeyoun Park, "A Cascade of Contacts from One Ebola Case in Dallas," *New York Times*, Oct. 21, 2014, https://www.nytimes.com/interactive/2014 /10/20/us/cascade-of-contacts-from-ebola-case.html.

22. Kevin J. A. Thomas, *Global Epidemics, Local Implications: African Immigrants and the Ebola Crisis in Dallas* (Baltimore: Johns Hopkins University Press, 2019).

23. Roll Call, "Dr. Anthony Fauci Delivers Remarks on Ebola at the National Press Club," Nov. 21, 2014.

24. Emanuella Grinberg, "Nurse Who Got Ebola Settles Hospital Lawsuit," CNN, Oct. 24, 2016, https://www.cnn.com/2016/10/24/health/nina-pham -ebola-hospital-lawsuit-settled/index.html.

25. Matt Katz, "Governors Defend Decisions on Ebola Quarantines," NPR, Oct. 26, 2014, https://www.npr.org/2014/10/26/359120784/governors-defend -decisions-on-ebola-quarantines.

26. Jess Bidgood and Kate Zernike, "From Governors, a Mix of Hard-Line Acts and Conciliation Over Ebola," *New York Times*, Oct. 30, 2014, https://www .nytimes.com/2014/10/31/us/kaci-hickox-nurse-under-ebola-quarantine-takes -bike-ride-defying-maine-officials.html?_r=0.

27. CDC, "Notes on the Interim U.S. Guidance for Monitoring and Movement of Persons with Potential Ebola Virus Exposure," last reviewed Dec. 27, 2017, https://www.cdc.gov/vhf/ebola/exposure/monitoring-and-movement -of-persons-with-exposure.html.

28. Helen Ouyang, "Today, the New York Doctor Who Contracted Ebola Is Feeling Fine," *New York Magazine*, June 7, 2015, http://nymag.com/daily /intelligencer/2015/06/craig-spencer-after-ebola.html.

29. Kaci Hickox, "Caught between Civil Liberties and Public Safety Fears: Personal Reflections from a Healthcare Provider Treating Ebola," *Journal of Health & Biomedical Law* 11, no. 1 (2015): 11.

30. Mayhew v. Hickox, No. CV-201 4–36 (Me. Dist. Ct. Oct. 31, 2014).
31. Sheri Fink, "Connecticut Faces Lawsuit over Ebola Quarantine Policies," *New York Times*, Feb. 7, 2016, http://www.nytimes.com/2016/02/08/ny region/connecticut-faces-lawsuit-over-ebola-quarantine-policies.html.
32. American Civil Liberties Union and Yale Global Health Justice Partnership, *Fear, Politics, and Ebola: How Quarantines Hurt the Fight Against Ebola and Violate the Constitution* (2015), https://www.aclu.org/report/fear-politics -and-ebola.
33. Associated Press, "Judge Dismisses Lawsuit Against Malloy, State over Ebola Quarantines," *Hartford Courant*, Apr. 3, 2017, http://www.courant.com /news/connecticut/hc-malloy-ebola-quarantine-20170403-story.html.
34. Marc Santora, "New Jersey Accepts Rights for People in Quarantine to End Ebola Suit," *New York Times*, Dec. 22, 2017, https://www.nytimes.com/2017 /07/27/nyregion/new-jersey-accepts-rights-for-people-in-quarantine-to-end -ebola-suit.html.
35. Hickox, "Caught between Civil Liberties," 23.
36. Lisa Chedekel, "Recalling the Public Panic in Famous Ebola Court Case," *BU Today*, Mar. 21, 2017, http://www.bu.edu/today/2017/kaci-hickox-ebola-nurse.
37. The State of Texas for the Best Interest and Protection of M.W.L., DC-14– 11773 (134th Judicial District, Dallas County, Oct. 2014).
38. Burrough, "Ebola in the U.S."
39. Burrough, "Ebola in the U.S."
40. Under Texas law, a peace officer may take a person into custody without a warrant or court order if the officer "has reason to believe the person is a person with mental illness, and because of that mental illness there is a sub-stantial risk of serious harm to the person or to others unless the person is immediately restrained." The officer must also believe that "there is not suffi-cient time to obtain a warrant before taking the person into custody." Texas Mental Health & Safety Code §573.0001.
41. Tex. Health & Safety Code §§ 81.152; 81.161.
42. Tex. Health & Safety Code § 81.162.
43. *Application for the Management of a Person with a Communicable Disease for M.W.L.*, DC-14–11773 (134th Judicial District, Dallas County, Oct. 6, 2014).
44. Abbott would later become the governor of Texas and lead the state's re-sponse to COVID—this time defending individual liberties against state-mandated measures, like mask wearing, that would safeguard public health. Julián Aguilar, "Appeals Court Again Halts El Paso County's Shutdown of Nonessential Businesses," *Texas Tribune*, Nov. 14, 2020, https://www.texas tribune.org/2020/11/13/el-paso-county-shutdown-halted.
45. University of Houston Health Law & Policy Institute, "Control Measures and Public Health Emergencies: A Texas Bench Book" (2010), 23.
46. Burrough, "Ebola in the U.S."
47. Manny Fernandez and Kevin Sack, "Dozens Declared Free of Ebola Risk in Texas," *New York Times*, Oct. 19, 2014.
48. Fernandez and Sack, "Dozens Declared Free of Ebola Risk in Texas."
49. Park, "A Cascade of Contacts."

50. CNN, interview with Rep. Pete Sessions, Oct. 6, 2014, http://www.cnn.com /TRANSCRIPTS/1410/06/nday.04.html.

51. Todd J. Gillman, "At Ebola Hearing, Frieden and Fauci Face Tough Questions," *Dallas Morning News*, Oct. 16, 2014, https://www.dallasnews.com /news/politics/2014/10/16/at-ebola-hearing-frieden-and-fauci-face-tough -questions.

52. Rob Savillo and Matt Gertz, "Report: Ebola Coverage on TV News Plummeted after Midterms," Nov. 18, 2014, https://www.mediamatters.org /msnbc/report-ebola-coverage-tv-news-plummeted-after-midterms.

53. Jonathan Fielding et al., *Report of the Independent Panel on the U.S. Department of Health and Human Services (HHS) Ebola Response* (2016), iv, https://asprtracie.hhs.gov/technical-resources/resource/3544/report-of-the -independent-panel-on-the-us-department-of-health-and-human-services -hhs-ebola-response.

54. Reeve Hamilton, "Report Concludes How Texas Could Have Handled Ebola Better," *Governing*, Dec. 8, 2014, https://www.governing.com/archive /tt-ebola-texas.html.

55. Senate Committee Report, S.B. 538, An Act Relating to the Control of Infectious Diseases, Mar. 2, 2015, https://capitol.texas.gov/billlookup/text.aspx ?LegSess=84R&Bill=SB538.

56. Jim Malewitz, "Senate Moves to Bolster Infectious Disease Response," *Texas Tribune*, Apr. 1, 2015.

57. Jay Root and Shannon Najmabadi, "In 2015, Texas Lawmakers Rejected Effort to Upgrade State's Disease Response," *Texas Tribune*, Mar. 13, 2020, https://infoweb.newsbank.com/apps/news/document-view?p=WORLDNEWS &docref=news/179B303F5BA75880.

58. "Editorial: Hits and Misses," *Dallas Morning News*, Apr. 4, 2015.

59. Malewitz, "Senate Moves to Bolster Infectious Disease Response."

60. "Looking Back, Dallas Ebola Crisis Showed Cost of Fear, Value of Leadership."

61. "The Atlantic Health Forum," Mar. 18, 2015, https://www.theatlantic.com /live/events/atlantic-health-forum/2015.

CHAPTER 9: A CORONAVIRUS PANDEMIC

1. Eric Schmidt and Antonio Guterres, "Episode 1: How to Build Back Together," *Reimagine* (podcast), Sept. 1, 2020, https://www.reimaginepod.org /episode/ep-1-how-to-build-back-together.

2. Lauren Egan, "'70,000-Ton Message of Hope': Trump Sees off Navy Hospital Ship as It Heads for NYC," *NBC News*, Mar. 28, 2020, https://www .nbcnews.com/politics/white-house/70-000-ton-message-hope-trump-sees -navy-hospital-ship-n1171256.

3. Ashley Collman, "A Timeline of USNS Comfort's Short and Dramatic Stay in New York City," *Business Insider*, Apr. 26, 2020, https://www.business insider.com/usns-comfort-nyc-coronavirus-timeline-2020-4.

4. David Vergun, "USNS Mercy Arrives in Los Angeles to Aid COVID-19 Response," US Department of Defense, Mar. 27, 2020, https://www.defense .gov/Explore/News/Article/Article/2129077/usns-mercy-arrives-in-los-angeles -to-aid-covid-19-response.

5. Terri Moon Cronk, "USNS Mercy, USNS Comfort Receiving Patients in LA, New York City," US Department of Defense, Apr. 2, 2020, https://www.defense.gov/Explore/News/Article/Article/2134688/usns-mercy-usns-comfort-receiving-patients-in-la-new-york-city.

6. Mary Van Beusekom, "COVID-19 Spread Freely Aboard USS Theodore Roosevelt, Report Shows," Center for Infectious Disease Research and Policy, Oct. 1, 2020, https://www.cidrap.umn.edu/news-perspective/2020/10/covid-19-spread-freely-aboard-uss-theodore-roosevelt-report-shows.

7. Eric. D. Hargan, "Setting Expectations for the Federal Role in Public Health Emergencies," *Journal of Law, Medicine & Ethics* 36, no. S1 (2008): 9.

8. "GHS Index Map," The Global Health Security Index, https://www.ghsindex.org.

9. Mark Johnson, "The U.S. Was the World's Best Prepared Nation to Confront a Pandemic. How Did It Spiral to 'Almost Inconceivable' Failure?," *Milwaukee Journal Sentinel*, Oct. 14, 2020, updated Jan. 21, 2021.

10. Timothy P. Alben Sr., interview with the author, June 8, 2021.

11. John M. Barry, *The Great Influenza: The Epic Story of the Deadliest Plague in History* (New York: Viking, 2004).

12. Alben, interview with the author.

13. Michael Lewis, *The Premonition: A Pandemic Story* (New York: W. W. Norton, 2021). As Lewis relates, Bush came to this realization after reading John Barry's *The Great Influenza* (the same book that influenced Tim Alben).

14. Pandemic and All-Hazards Preparedness Act, PL 109–417, Dec. 19, 2006, 120 Stat 2831.

15. Timothy P. Alben, "Compliance with Community Mitigation and Interventions in Pandemic Influenza: A Community Policing Strategy" (master's thesis, Naval Postgraduate School, 2007), v, https://calhoun.nps.edu/handle/10945/3344.

16. Quoted from remarks at Health Law Professors Conference, Atlanta, June 10, 2017; James F. Childress and Ruth Gaare Bernheim, "Beyond the Liberal and Communitarian Impasse: A Framework and Vision for Public Health," *Florida Law Review* 55, no. 5 (Dec. 2003): 1191–219.

17. "Community Policing Defined," US Department of Justice, last modified 2014, https://cops.usdoj.gov/RIC/Publications/cops-p157-pub.pdf.

18. J. David Goodman, "As Hospitalizations Soar, El Paso Brings in New Mobile Morgues," *New York Times*, Nov. 11, 2020.

19. Arelis R. Hernández and Alexandra Hinojosa, "El Paso Was Still Grieving When the Coronavirus Arrived. Now, Death Has Overwhelmed It," *Washington Post*, Nov. 27, 2020.

20. Mark Price, "Growing Number of North Carolina Sheriffs Say They Won't Enforce Statewide Mask Order," *Raleigh News & Observer*, June 25, 2020.

21. Rachel Weiner and Ariana Eunjung Cha, "Amid Threats and Political Pushback, Public Health Officials Are Leaving Their Posts," *Washington Post*, June 22, 2020.

22. Ben Collins and Brandy Zadrozny, "In Trump's 'LIBERATE' Tweets, Extremists See a Call to Arms," *NBC News*, Apr. 17, 2020, https://www.nbcnews.com/tech/security/trump-s-liberate-tweets-extremists-see-call-arms-n1186561.

23. Daniel A. Farber et al., *Disaster Law and Policy* (New York: Wolters Kluwer, 2015), 185–86.
24. Lindsay F. Wiley, "Democratizing the Law of Social Distancing," *Yale Journal of Health Policy, Law, and Ethics* 19, no. 3 (2020): 61.
25. "State Executive Orders—COVID-19 Resources for State Leaders," Council of State Governments, https://web.csg.org/covid19/executive-orders.
26. Alan Judd, "Georgia Governor Ignored Experts as the Pandemic Raged," *Atlanta Journal-Constitution*, Mar. 26, 2021.
27. Maya T. Prabhu, "Georgia Law Bars Limiting of Gun Sales During Pandemic," *Atlanta Journal-Constitution*, Apr. 3, 2020.
28. Prabhu, "Georgia Law Bars Limiting of Gun Sales During Pandemic."
29. Lauren Weber and Anna Maria Barry-Jester, "Over Half of States Have Rolled Back Public Health Powers in a Pandemic," *Kaiser Health News*, Sept. 15, 2021, https://khn.org/news/article/over-half-of-states-have-rolled-back-public-health-powers-in-pandemic.
30. Andrew DeMillo, "Arkansas Governor, Top Lawmakers to Meet on Mask Mandate Ban," Associated Press, July 26, 2021, https://apnews.com/article/business-science-health-arkansas-coronavirus-pandemic-db3b9d141319c5a828d79a44196fe891.
31. "Over Half of States."
32. Emma Platoff and Juan Pablo Garnham, "Dallas Rescinds Plan That Prioritized Vaccines for Communities of Color," *Texas Tribune*, Jan. 20, 2021.
33. Antonia Noori Farzan, "'Stupid and Crazy': Local Officials Protest Gov. Kemp's Decision to Reopen Beaches in Hard-Hit Georgia," *Washington Post*, Apr. 6, 2020.
34. Henry Gass and Patrik Jonsson, "'It Can't Happen Here.' Coronavirus Hits Rural America," *Christian Science Monitor*, Apr. 13, 2020.
35. Fabick v. Evers 956 N.W.2d 856, 859 (Wis. 2021).
36. Collin Dwyer and Allison Aubrey, "CDC Now Recommends Americans Consider Wearing Cloth Face Coverings in Public," NPR, Apr. 3, 2020, https://www.npr.org/sections/coronavirus-live-updates/2020/04/03/826219824/president-trump-says-cdc-now-recommends-americans-wear-cloth-masks-in-public.
37. Leah Asmelash, "The Surgeon General Wants Americans to Stop Buying Face Masks," CNN, Mar. 2, 2020, https://www.cnn.com/2020/02/29/health/face-masks-coronavirus-surgeon-general-trnd/index.html.
38. Tressi L. Cordaro and Cressinda D. Schlag, "Navigating Employer Obligations to Provide Employees with Masks, Face Coverings," *National Law Review* 10, no. 118 (2020): Apr. 27, 2020, https://www.natlawreview.com/article/navigating-employer-obligations-to-provide-employees-masks-face-coverings.
39. Vanessa Romo, "Target, CVS Shoppers Will Be Required to Wear Masks," NPR, July 16, 2020, https://www.npr.org/sections/coronavirus-live-updates/2020/07/16/892146238/target-cvs-shoppers-will-be-required-to-wear-masks.
40. Katie Shepherd, "An Idaho Official Left a Meeting in Tears as Anti-Maskers Swarmed Her Home," *Washington Post*, Dec. 9, 2020.

41. "Valley County Face Covering Order," Central District Health, Aug. 11, 2020, https://www.cdhd.idaho.gov/dac-coronavirus-valleyorder.php.

42. Derek Hawkins, "Idaho Lieutenant Governor Banned Mask Mandates While the Governor Was Out of Town. It Didn't Last," *Washington Post*, May 28, 2021.

43. Eduardo Medina and Michael Levenson, "Idaho's Governor and Lieutenant Governor Duel Over Vaccine Mandates," *New York Times*, Oct. 6, 2021, https://www.nytimes.com/2021/10/07/us/idaho-vaccine-mandate.html.

44. Derek Hawkins, "Idaho Morgues Are Running Out of Space for Bodies as Covid-19 Deaths Mount," *Washington Post*, Sept. 25, 2021, https://www.washingtonpost.com/health/2021/09/25/idaho-funeral-homes-coronavirus.

45. CDC, "Guidance for COVID-19 Prevention in K-12 Schools," updated Aug. 5, 2021, https://www.cdc.gov/coronavirus/2019-ncov/community/schools-childcare/k-12-guidance.html.

46. American Academy of Pediatrics," American Academy of Pediatrics Updates Recommendations for Opening Schools in Fall 2021," July 19, 2021, https://www.aap.org/en/news-room/news-releases/aap/2021/american-academy-of-pediatrics-updates-recommendations-for-opening-schools-in-fall-2021.

47. Cathryn Stout and Julia Baker, "Two Lawsuits Supporting Face Masks in Schools Challenge Tennessee Gov. Bill Lee's Opt-Out Order," *Chalkbeat Tennessee*, Aug. 27, 2021, https://tn.chalkbeat.org/2021/8/27/22644870/masks-optional-shelby-county-lawsuit-gov-bill-lee-tennessee.

48. *Jacobson*, 197 U.S. at 26.

49. South Bay United Pentecostal Church v. Newsom, 140 S. Ct. 1613, 1613–14 (2020).

50. *South Bay*, 140 S. Ct. at 1614 (quoting from earlier US Supreme Court decisions).

51. Emily Anthes and Alexandra E. Petri, "C.D.C. Director Warns of a 'Pandemic of the Unvaccinated,'" *New York Times*, July 22, 2021, https://www.nytimes.com/2021/07/16/health/covid-delta-cdc-walensky.html.

52. Patricia Mazzei et al., "Florida's Governor Bans Agencies and Businesses from Requiring 'Vaccine Passports,'" *New York Times*, Apr. 2, 2021.

53. Alex Seitz-Wald, "Cruise Lines and Florida Gov. DeSantis Square Off over Vaccine Passports," *NBC News*, May 31, 2021, https://www.nbcnews.com/politics/2020-election/cruise-lines-florida-gov-desantis-square-over-vaccine-passports-n1269029.

54. Hannah Sampson, "'Political Buffoonery': Cruise Lines Head for Showdown with DeSantis over Vaccine Requirement Ban," *Washington Post*, May 28, 2021.

55. Hannah Sampson, "Judge Says Norwegian Cruise Can Require Vaccination Proof, Despite DeSantis Ban," *Washington Post*, Aug. 9, 2021, https://www.washingtonpost.com/travel/2021/08/09/desantis-passport-ban-norwegian-cruise.

56. Lisa J. Huriash, "Governor Opposes Letting Ship with 189 Sick People Dock in South Florida," *South Florida Sun Sentinel*, Mar. 30, 2020, https://www.sun-sentinel.com/coronavirus/fl-ne-sick-ship-approval-fort-lauderdale-20200329-pymhibz6bvduxbwfgk2mil23ku-story.html; Minyvonne Burke

and Kerry Sanders, "Cruise Ship with Sick Passengers and Sister Ship Dock in Florida," *NBC News*, Apr. 2, 2020, https://www.nbcnews.com/news/us -news/cruise-ship-sick-passengers-sister-ship-will-be-allowed-dock-n1174796.

57. Lawrence O. Gostin et al., "Mandating COVID-19 Vaccines," *JAMA* 325, no. 6 (2021): 532.

58. Adam Liptak, "The Supreme Court Won't Block Indiana University's Vaccine Mandate," *New York Times*, Aug. 12, 2021, https://www.nytimes.com/2021 /08/12/us/supreme-court-indiana-university-covid-vaccine-mandate.html.

59. Corky Siemaszko, "250,000 COVID-19 Infections from Sturgis? 'Made up' Numbers, S.D. Governor Says," *NBC News*, Sept. 9, 2020, https://www .nbcnews.com/news/us-news/250-000-covid-19-infections-sturgis-made -numbers-s-d-n1239657.

60. Melanie J. Firestone et al., "COVID-19 Outbreak Associated with a 10-Day Motorcycle Rally in a Neighboring State—Minnesota, August–September 2020," *Morbidity and Mortality Weekly Report* 69, no. 47 (2020): 1171.

61. Mark Walker and Jack Healy, "A Motorcycle Rally in a Pandemic? 'We Kind of Knew What Was Going to Happen'—The New York Times," *New York Times*, Nov. 6, 2020.

62. Bryan Walsh and Alison Snyder, "Scientists Caught Between Pandemic and Protests," *Axios*, June 10, 2020, https://www.axios.com/black-lives-matter -protests-coronavirus-science-15acc619-633d-47c2-9c76-df91f826a73c.html.

63. Todd J. Gillman, "Trump Claims 'Total' Authority During Pandemic but Even States Don't Have That," *Dallas News*, Apr. 15, 2020.

64. Governor Abbott Issues Executive Order Relating to Expanding Travel With- out Restrictions," Office of the Texas Governor, Apr. 28, 2020, https://gov .texas.gov/news/post/governor-abbott-issues-executive-order-relating-to -expanding-travel-without-restrictions.

65. "Quarantine Restrictions on Travelers Arriving in New York," New York State Governor, June 24, 2020, https://www.governor.ny.gov/news/no-205 -quarantine-restrictions-travelers-arriving-new-york.

66. Brian Mann, "Some States to Out-of-Towners: If You Come Visit, Plan to Quarantine for 2 Weeks," NPR, July 2, 2020, https://www.npr.org/2020/07 /02/886596560/some-states-to-out-of-towners-if-you-come-visit-plan-to -quarantine-for-two-weeks.

67. Polly J. Price, "Do State Lines Make Public Health Emergencies Worse? Federal Versus State Control of Quarantine," *Emory Law Journal* 67, no. 3 (2018): 526–29.

68. Bracey Harris and Adiel Kaplan, "The Eviction Moratorium Is About to End, Yet Federal Relief Funds Largely Remain Unspent," *NBC News*, July 28, 2021, https://www.nbcnews.com/news/us-news/eviction-moratorium-about -end-yet-federal-relief-funds-largely-remain-n1275297.

69. Abby Goodnough, "Trump Program to Cover Uninsured Covid-19 Patients Falls Short of Promise," *New York Times*, Aug. 29, 2020, https://www.ny times.com/2020/08/29/health/Covid-obamacare-uninsured.html.

70. Egan Kemp, "Unprepared for COVID-19: How the Pandemic Makes the Case for Medicare for All," *Public Citizen*, Mar. 16, 2021, https://www .citizen.org/article/unprepared-covid-report.

71. Goodnough, "Trump Program to Cover Uninsured."
72. Alben, interview with the author.
73. Dhruv Khullar, "Do You Trust the Medical Profession?," *New York Times*, Jan. 23, 2018, https://www.nytimes.com/2018/01/23/upshot/do-you-trust -the-medical-profession.html.

EPILOGUE: LAW FOR THE NEXT PANDEMIC

1. Quoted in Institute of Medicine, *Ethical and Legal Considerations in Mitigating Pandemic Disease* (Washington, DC: National Academies Press, 2007), 18.
2. Dennis Thompson, "1 in 500 Americans Has Died from COVID-19," *U.S. News & World Report*, Sept. 15, 2021, https://www.usnews.com/news/health -news/articles/2021-09-15/1-in-500-americans-has-died-from-covid-19.
3. "Live Webcast and a Message from Dean Mary Bobinski," Emory University School of Law, remarks by Gregory L. Fenves, at minute 21, https://vgrad2 .z19.web.core.windows.net/emory/285/viii/index.html, accessed Oct. 23, 2021.
4. "Live Webcast," remarks of Dr. Anthony Fauci, at minute 23.
5. "Live Webcast," remarks by Dr. Anthony Fauci, at minute 23.
6. "Live Webcast," remarks of Dr. Anthony Fauci, at minute 24.
7. Cassandra Maddox, "A Career of Service, from Doctor to Social Justice Lawyer," *Emory Report*, May 7, 2021, https://news.emory.edu/stories/2021/05 /er_commencement_profile_law_malempati/campus.htm.
8. "Live Webcast," remarks of Suman Malempati, at minute 31.
9. "Live Webcast," remarks of Suman Malempati, at minute 35.
10. "Live Webcast," remarks of Suman Malempati, at minute 39.
11. Andrea Salcedo, "A Georgia Vaccine Site Had to Close After Protesters Bullied Health-Care Workers," *Washington Post*, Sept. 1, 2021, https://www .washingtonpost.com/nation/2021/09/01/georgia-vaccination-site-shuts-down.
12. Anna King, "Embattled Public Health Workers Leaving at 'Steady and Alarming' Rate," NPR, Nov. 25, 2020, https://www.npr.org/2020/11/25 /938873547/embattled-public-health-workers-leaving-at-steady-and-alarming -rate.
13. 42 U.S. Code §264(a).
14. Mark Sherman, "Supreme Court Allows Evictions to Resume During Pandemic," Associated Press, Aug. 26, 2021, https://apnews.com/article/health -courts-pandemics-coronavirus-pandemic-daa34fb48a04dc9f3ddad94fb6 b4cbb2.
15. Sandro Galea et al., "Eight Operational Suggestions for a Renewed CDC," *Milbank Quarterly Opinion*, Jan. 5, 2021, https://doi.org/10.1599/mqop .2021.0105; Garrett Jones, "COVID-19 Failures Show Why the CDC and FDA Should Be More Independent," Discourse, Apr. 16, 2020, https://www .discoursemagazine.com/politics/2020/04/16/covid-19-failures-show-why -the-cdc-and-fda-should-be-more-independent.
16. Polly J. Price, "Immigration Policy and Public Health," *Indiana Health Law Review* 16, no. 2 (2019): 245–47.
17. Wendy M. Chung et al., "The 2012 West Nile Encephalitis Epidemic in Dallas, Texas," *JAMA* 310, no. 3 (July 17, 2013): 297, https://doi.org/10.1001 /jama.2013.8267.

18. Alan R. Hinman, "Vaccine-Preventable Diseases, Immunizations, and MMWR, 1961–2011," *Morbidity and Mortality Weekly Report* 60 Supplement (Oct. 7, 2011): 95.

19. Pandemic and All-Hazards Preparedness Act, PL 109–417, Dec. 19, 2006, 120 Stat 2831.

20. "President Signs Off on PAHPA Reauthorization," *CIDRAP*, June 25, 2019, https://www.cidrap.umn.edu/news-perspective/2019/06/news-scan-jun-25-2019.

21. Kim Riley, "Several Pandemic Preparedness Bills Under Consideration in U.S. Congress," Homeland Preparedness News, Aug. 12, 2021, https://homeland prepnews.com/stories/72353-several-pandemic-preparedness-bills-under -consideration-in-u-s-congress.

22. Department of Health and Human Services, Office of Infectious Disease and HIV/AIDS Policy, "Viral Hepatitis in the United States: Data and Trends," https://www.hhs.gov/hepatitis/learn-about-viral-hepatitis/data-and-trends /index.html.

23. CDC, "*Legionella* (Legionnaires' Disease and Pontiac Fever)," last reviewed Mar. 25, 2021, https://www.cdc.gov/legionella/index.html.

24. CDC, "Legionnaires' Disease History, Burden, and Trends," last reviewed Mar. 25, 2021, https://www.cdc.gov/legionella/about/history.html.

25. CDC, "Antibiotic-Resistant Germs: New Threats," Mar. 2, 2021, https:// www.cdc.gov/drugresistance/biggest-threats.html.

26. Laura Ungar, "Hepatitis A Races Across the Country," *Kaiser Health News*, Aug. 13, 2019, https://khn.org/news/hepatitis-a-spreads-across-country.

27. CDC, "Viral Hepatitis A Surveillance Report 2019," last reviewed May 17, 2021, https://www.cdc.gov/hepatitis/statistics/2019surveillance/HepA.htm.

28. CDC, "Widespread Person-to-Person Outbreaks of Hepatitis A Across the United States," last reviewed Sept. 13, 2021, https://www.cdc.gov/hepatitis /outbreaks/2017March-HepatitisA.htm.

29. Ungar, "Hepatitis A Races Across the Country."

30. Brennan Weiss, "California Is Fighting the Deadliest Hepatitis A Outbreak in Decades," *Business Insider*, Oct. 17, 2017, https://www.businessinsider.com /hepatitis-a-outbreak-california-hep-2017-10.

31. South Bay United Pentecostal Church v. Newsom, 140 S. Ct. 1613, 1613–14 (2020).

IMAGE CREDITS

Preface, page viii: Courtesy of the National Library of Medicine.

Chapter 1, page xvi: Courtesy of the National Library of Medicine.

Chapter 2, page 20: Courtesy of the National Library of Medicine.

Chapter 3, page 40: Courtesy of the National Library of Medicine.

Chapter 4, page 58: Courtesy of the Library of Congress, LC-USZ62-13459.

Chapter 5, page 84: Courtesy of Claude Moore Health Sciences Library, University of Virginia.

Chapter 6, page 106: Bettman/Getty Images via Getty Images.

Chapter 7: page 126: AP Photo/J. Scott Applewhite.

Chapter 8, page 146: Mark Wilson/Getty Images News via Getty Images.

Chapter 9, page 166: Reuters/Mike Segar.

Epilogue, page 192: Photo by Allison Bailey/NurPhoto via AP.

Acknowledgments, page 204: Photo by author.

INDEX

Page numbers for images are italicized.

Abbott, Greg, 159, 163, 180, 229n44
Abbott, Sidney, 140
Acquired Immunity Deficiency Syndrome. *See* HIV/AIDS epidemic
An Act to Encourage Vaccination (1813), 15
ACT UP (AIDS Coalition to Unleash Power), *126*, 137–38
Ada County, ID: anti-mask protests, 178
Adams, Jerome, 177
Adams, John, inoculation of, 12
Aedes aegypti mosquito, 24
African Americans. *See* Black Americans; immigrants, blaming for disease outbreaks/epidemics
Aikman, W. H., 28
Aizenman, Nurith, 138
Alabama: flu-related restrictions, 1918, 68; refusal to accept COVID evacuees in, 172; restriction on smallpox reporting, 6; and smallpox vaccination, 16; the Tuskegee syphilis study, 96; *Wilson v. Alabama* (MS, 1900), 4; yellow fever quarantines, 27, 31
Alaska, 1918 flu in, 79
Alben, Timothy, 168–72, 189
Alden v. State, 20 Ariz., 235 (1919), 73
almshouses, 9–12. *See also* pesthouses
American Academy of Medicine, "Medical Problems of Legislation" (1916), 59–60
American Academy of Pediatrics, mask recommendation for children in school, 180

American Medical Association (AMA), 32, 61, 62, 120
American Public Health Association, 68, 104
Americans with Disabilities Act (ADA), 140
Ann Arbor, MI: announcement of the efficacy of the Salk vaccine, 107, 109, 114
antibiotics: bacterial resistance to, 201; and the end to harsh quarantines, 99; for plague, 55; for tuberculosis, 87, 94; for typhoid, 99; for viral diseases/flus, 119, 150
anti-Chinese racism, 42–45, 49, 51. *See also* bubonic plague, San Francisco, 1900–1904; Chinese Exclusion Act 1882
anti-vaccinationism/anti-vaccinationists: Massachusetts Anti-Compulsory Vaccination Society, 17; *Morris v. City of Columbus* (1898), 16–17; resistance to COVID-19 vaccine mandates, 175, 183; resistance to smallpox inoculation, 12–14. See also *Jacobson v. Massachusetts* (1905); *Massachusetts v. Jacobson* (1903)
Archbold v. Huntington (ID, 1921), 76–77
Arizona: *Alden v. State*, 20 Ariz., 235 (1919), 73; Arizona Supreme Court rulings, 73–74; flu deaths among Native Americans, 78; *Globe School District v. Board of Health* (1919), 73; objections to business